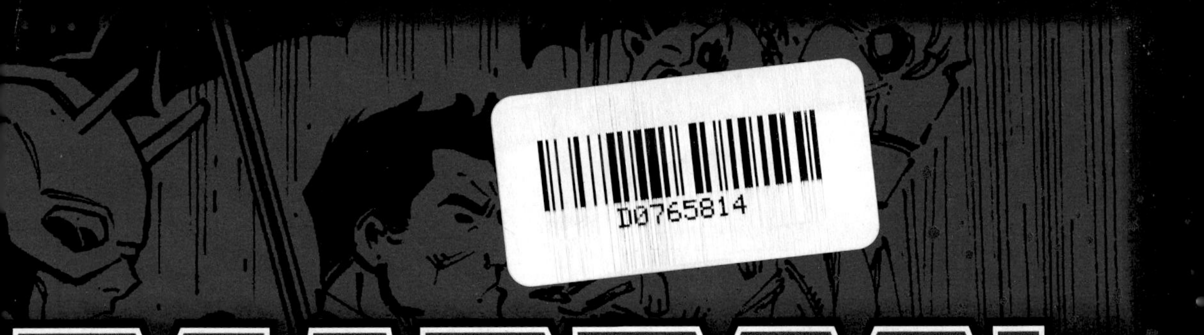
D0765814

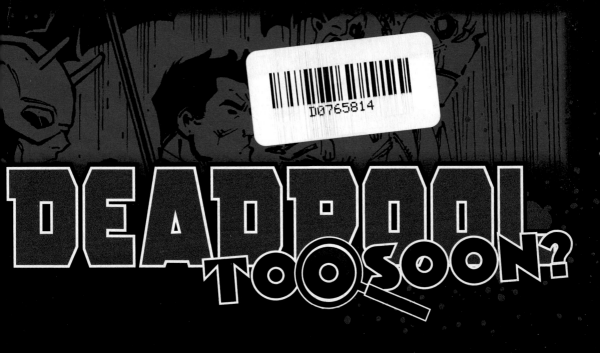

DEADPOOL TOO SOON?

JOSHUA CORIN
WRITER

TODD NAUCK
ARTIST

JIM CHARALAMPIDIS (#1-2) &
ANDY TROY (#3-4)
COLORISTS

REILLY BROWN (#1-2) &
TODD NAUCK (#3-4)
LAYOUT ARTISTS

VC's JOE SABINO
LETTERER

ANNIE CHENG
PRODUCTION

TIM SMITH 3
PRODUCTION MANGER

GWENPOOL HOLIDAY SPECIAL: MERRY MIX-UP #1

"DEADPOOLOWEEN"

CHYNNA CLUGSTON FLORES
WRITER/ARTIST

GUY MAJOR
COLORIST

VC's CLAYTON COWLES
LETTERER

SPECIAL THANKS TO
RICHARD NEAL &
IAN SHAUGHNESSY

COLLECTION EDITOR **JENNIFER GRÜNWALD**
ASSISTANT EDITOR **CAITLIN O'CONNELL**
ASSOCIATE MANAGING EDITOR **KATERI WOODY**
EDITOR, SPECIAL PROJECTS **MARK D. BEAZLEY**

VP PRODUCTION & SPECIAL PROJECTS **JEFF YOUNGQUIST**
SVP PRINT, SALES & MARKETING **DAVID GABRIEL**
BOOK DESIGNER **ADAM DEL RE**

EDITOR IN CHIEF **AXEL ALONSO**
CHIEF CREATIVE OFFICER **JOE QUESADA**
PUBLISHER **DAN BUCKLEY**
EXECUTIVE PRODUCER **ALAN FINE**

DEADPOOL: TOO SOON? Contains material originally published in magazine form as DEADPOOL: TOO SOON? #1-4 and GWENPOOL HOLIDAY SPECIAL: MERRY MIX-UP #1. First printing 2017. ISBN# 978-1-302-90298-8. Published by MARVEL WORLDWIDE, INC., a subsidiary of MARVEL ENTERTAINMENT, LLC. OFFICE OF PUBLICATION: 135 West 50th Street, New York, NY 10020. **Printed in the U.S.A.** ALAN FINE, President, Marvel Entertainment; DAN BUCKLEY, President, TV, Publishing & Brand Management; JOE QUESADA, Chief Creative Officer; TOM BREVOORT, SVP of Publishing; DAVID BOGART, SVP of Business Affairs & Operations, Publishing & Partnership; C.B. CEBULSKI, VP of Brand Management & Development, Asia; DAVID GABRIEL, SVP of Sales & Marketing, Publishing; JEFF YOUNGQUIST, VP of Production & Special Projects; DAN CARR, Executive Director of Publishing Technology; ALEX MORALES, Director of Publishing Operations; SUSAN CRESPI, Production Manager; STAN LEE, Chairman Emeritus. For information regarding advertising in Marvel Comics or on Marvel.com, please contact Vit DeBellis, Integrated Sales Manager, at vdebellis@marvel.com. For Marvel subscription inquiries, please call 888-511-5480. **Manufactured between 1/27/2017 and 2/28/2017 by QUAD/GRAPHICS WASECA, WASECA, MN, USA.**

10 9 8 7 6 5 4 3 2 1

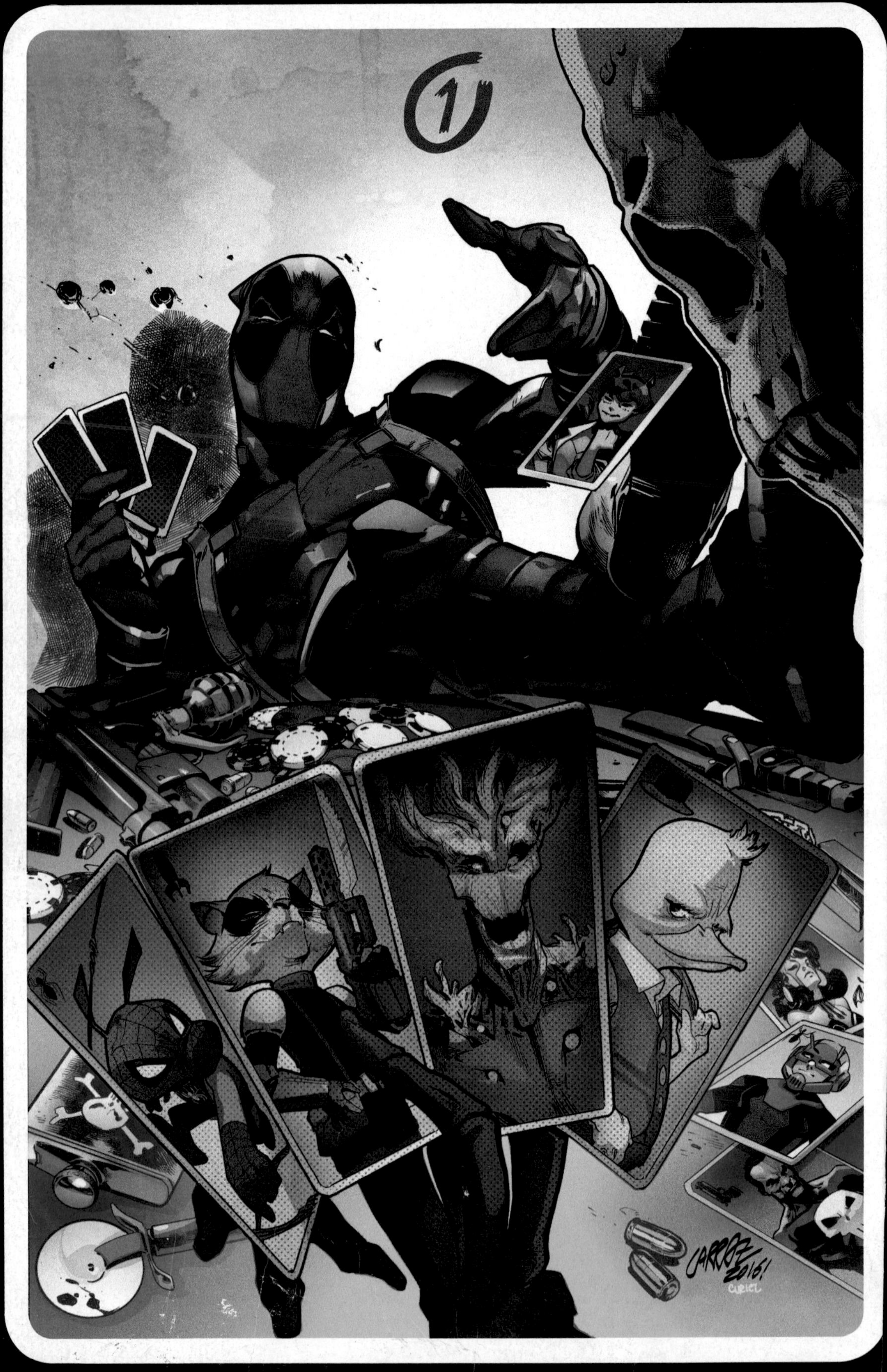
1

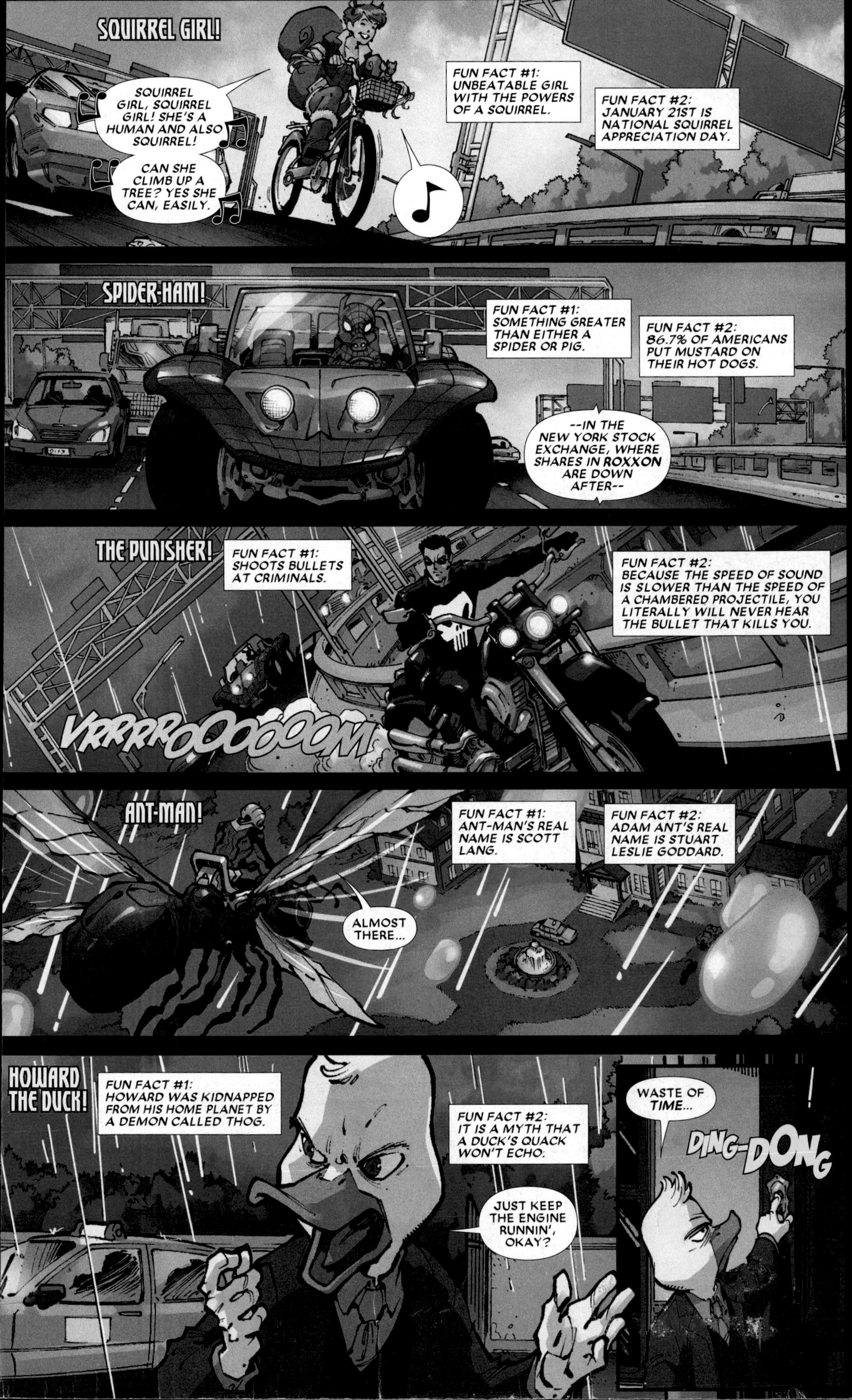
SQUIRREL GIRL!
SQUIRREL GIRL, SQUIRREL GIRL! SHE'S A HUMAN AND ALSO SQUIRREL!
CAN SHE CLIMB UP A TREE? YES SHE CAN, EASILY.
FUN FACT #1: UNBEATABLE GIRL WITH THE POWERS OF A SQUIRREL.
FUN FACT #2: JANUARY 21ST IS NATIONAL SQUIRREL APPRECIATION DAY.
SPIDER-HAM!
FUN FACT #1: SOMETHING GREATER THAN EITHER A SPIDER OR PIG.
FUN FACT #2: 86.7% OF AMERICANS PUT MUSTARD ON THEIR HOT DOGS.
--IN THE NEW YORK STOCK EXCHANGE, WHERE SHARES IN ROXXON ARE DOWN AFTER--
THE PUNISHER!
FUN FACT #1: SHOOTS BULLETS AT CRIMINALS.
FUN FACT #2: BECAUSE THE SPEED OF SOUND IS SLOWER THAN THE SPEED OF A CHAMBERED PROJECTILE, YOU LITERALLY WILL NEVER HEAR THE BULLET THAT KILLS YOU.
VRRRROOOOOOOM
ANT-MAN!
FUN FACT #1: ANT-MAN'S REAL NAME IS SCOTT LANG.
FUN FACT #2: ADAM ANT'S REAL NAME IS STUART LESLIE GODDARD.
ALMOST THERE...
HOWARD THE DUCK!
FUN FACT #1: HOWARD WAS KIDNAPPED FROM HIS HOME PLANET BY A DEMON CALLED THOG.
FUN FACT #2: IT IS A MYTH THAT A DUCK'S QUACK WON'T ECHO.
JUST KEEP THE ENGINE RUNNIN', OKAY?
WASTE OF TIME...
DING-DONG

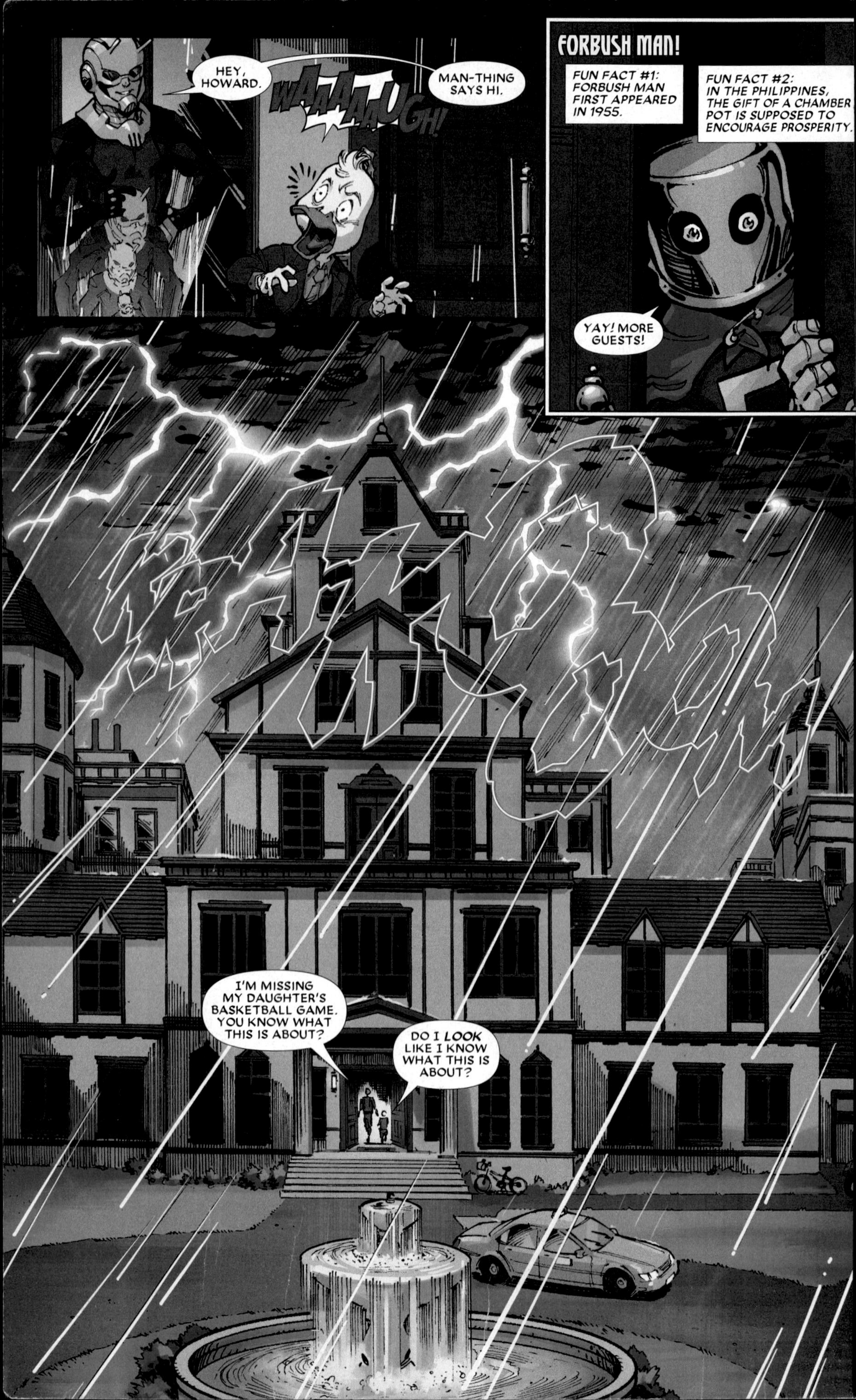
HEY, HOWARD.
MAN-THING SAYS HI.
FORBUSH MAN!
FUN FACT #1: FORBUSH MAN FIRST APPEARED IN 1955.
FUN FACT #2: IN THE PHILIPPINES, THE GIFT OF A CHAMBER POT IS SUPPOSED TO ENCOURAGE PROSPERITY.
YAY! MORE GUESTS!
I'M MISSING MY DAUGHTER'S BASKETBALL GAME. YOU KNOW WHAT THIS IS ABOUT?
DO I LOOK LIKE I KNOW WHAT THIS IS ABOUT?

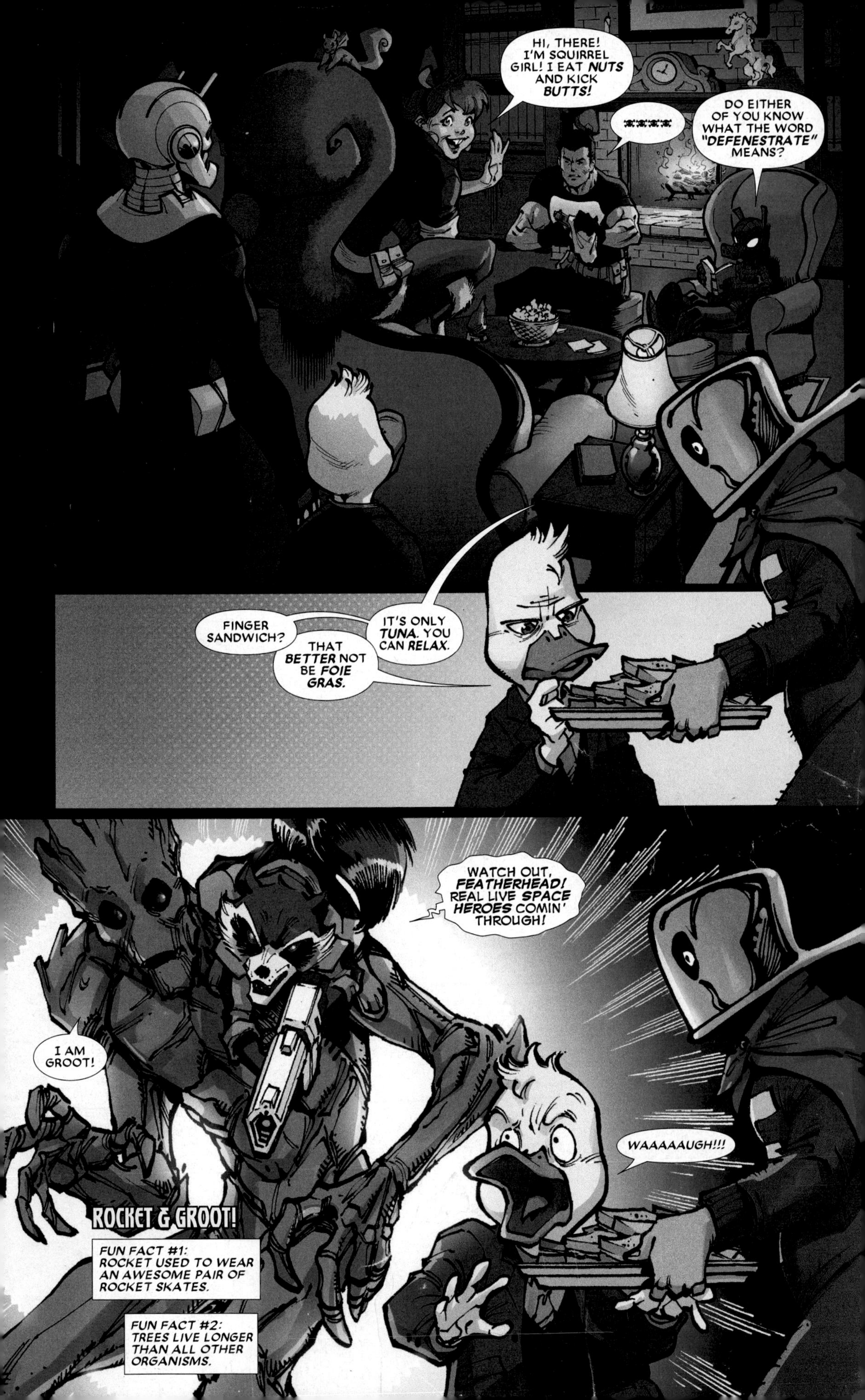
HI, THERE! I'M SQUIRREL GIRL! I EAT NUTS AND KICK BUTTS!
DO EITHER OF YOU KNOW WHAT THE WORD "DEFENESTRATE" MEANS?
FINGER SANDWICH?
THAT BETTER NOT BE FOIE GRAS.
IT'S ONLY TUNA. YOU CAN RELAX.
WATCH OUT, FEATHERHEAD! REAL LIVE SPACE HEROES COMIN' THROUGH!
I AM GROOT!
WAAAAAUGH!!!
ROCKET & GROOT!
FUN FACT #1: ROCKET USED TO WEAR AN AWESOME PAIR OF ROCKET SKATES.
FUN FACT #2: TREES LIVE LONGER THAN ALL OTHER ORGANISMS.

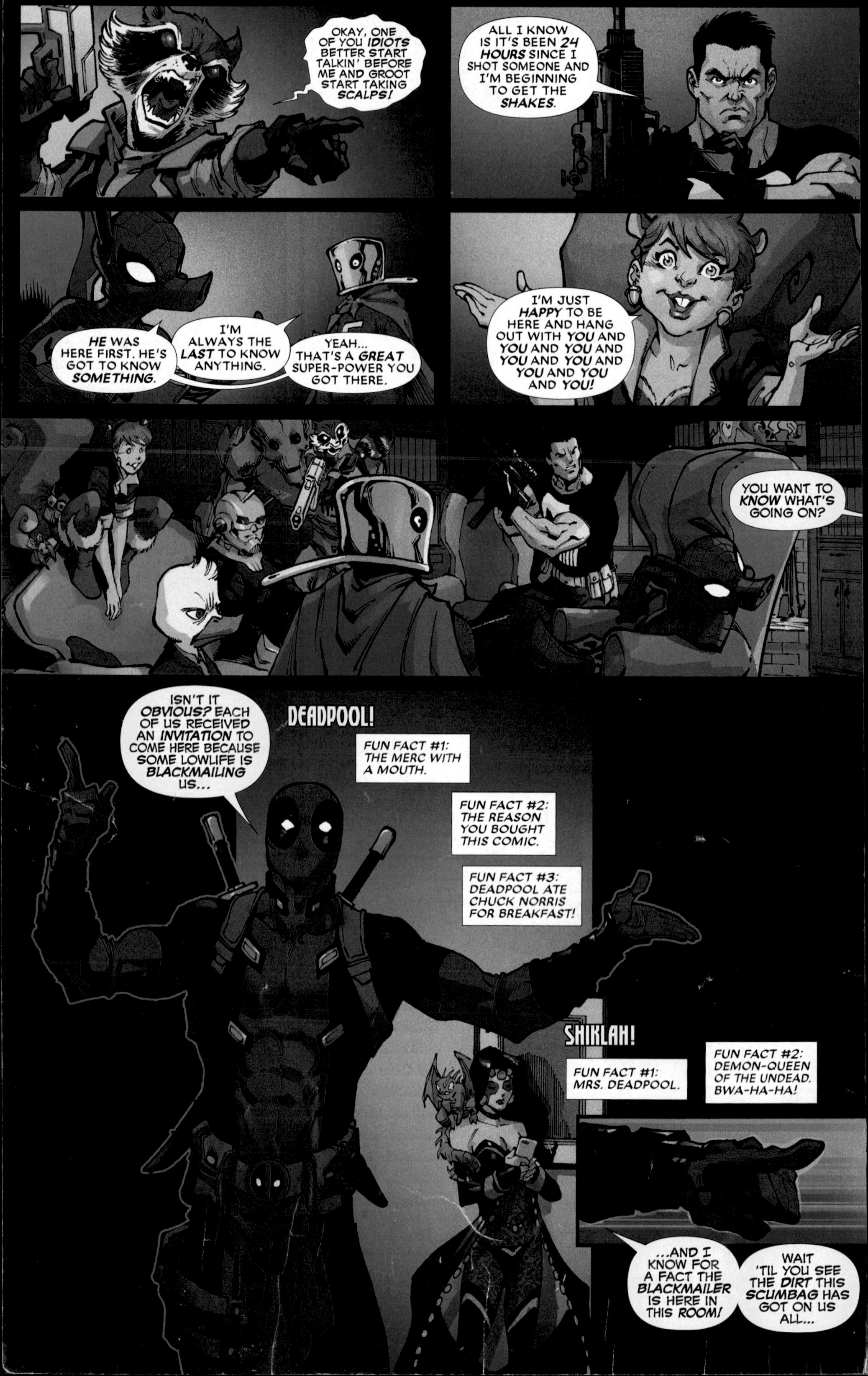

OKAY, ONE OF YOU IDIOTS BETTER START TALKIN' BEFORE ME AND GROOT START TAKING SCALPS!
ALL I KNOW IS IT'S BEEN 24 HOURS SINCE I SHOT SOMEONE AND I'M BEGINNING TO GET THE SHAKES.
HE WAS HERE FIRST. HE'S GOT TO KNOW SOMETHING.
I'M ALWAYS THE LAST TO KNOW ANYTHING.
YEAH... THAT'S A GREAT SUPER-POWER YOU GOT THERE.
I'M JUST HAPPY TO BE HERE AND HANG OUT WITH YOU AND YOU AND YOU AND YOU AND YOU AND YOU AND YOU AND YOU!
YOU WANT TO KNOW WHAT'S GOING ON?
ISN'T IT OBVIOUS? EACH OF US RECEIVED AN INVITATION TO COME HERE BECAUSE SOME LOWLIFE IS BLACKMAILING US...
DEADPOOL!
FUN FACT #1: THE MERC WITH A MOUTH.
FUN FACT #2: THE REASON YOU BOUGHT THIS COMIC.
FUN FACT #3: DEADPOOL ATE CHUCK NORRIS FOR BREAKFAST!
SHIKLAH!
FUN FACT #1: MRS. DEADPOOL.
FUN FACT #2: DEMON-QUEEN OF THE UNDEAD. BWA-HA-HA!
...AND I KNOW FOR A FACT THE BLACKMAILER IS HERE IN THIS ROOM!
WAIT 'TIL YOU SEE THE DIRT THIS SCUMBAG HAS GOT ON US ALL...

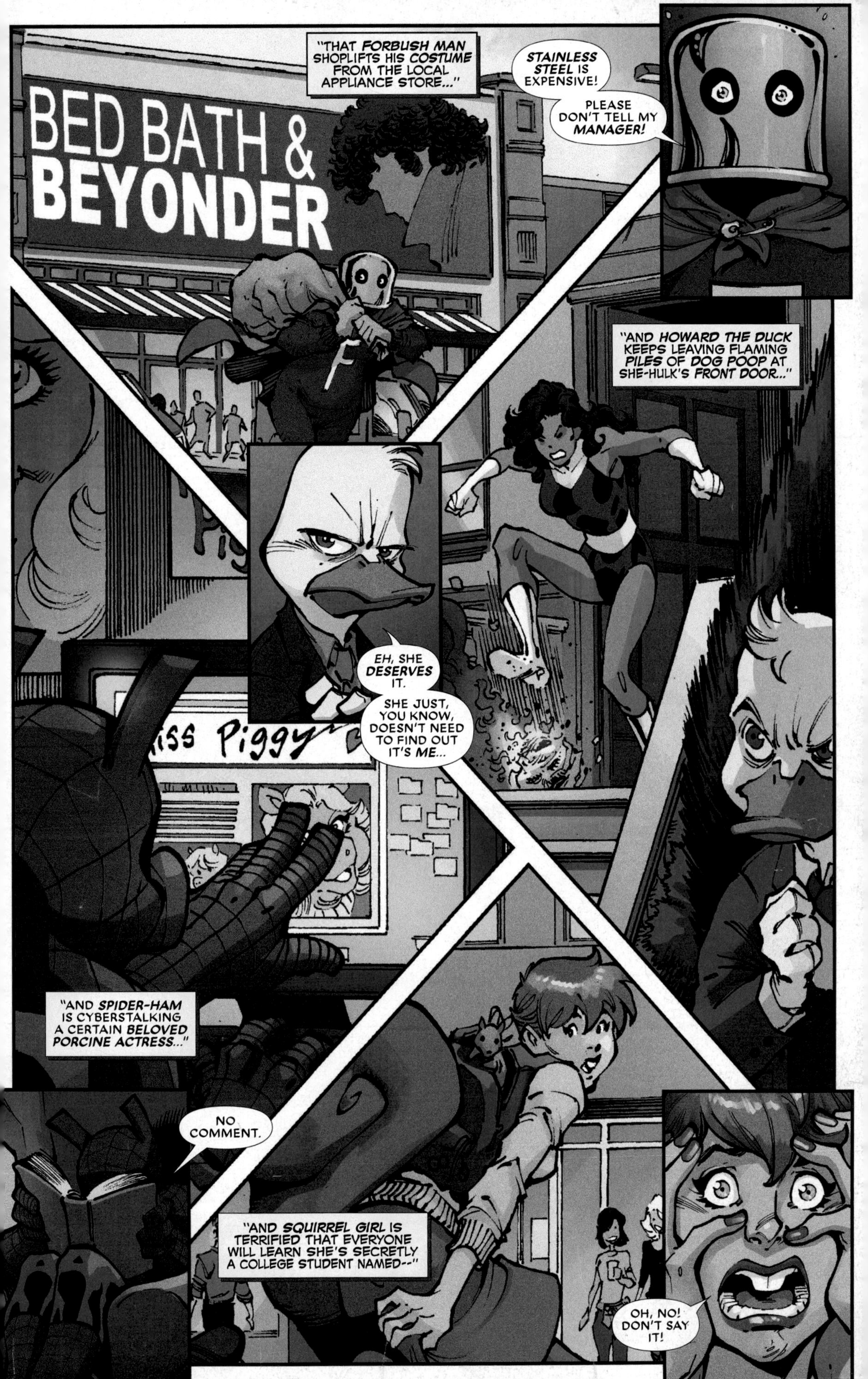
BED BATH &
BEYONDER
"THAT FORBUSH MAN SHOPLIFTS HIS COSTUME FROM THE LOCAL APPLIANCE STORE..."
STAINLESS STEEL IS EXPENSIVE!
PLEASE DON'T TELL MY MANAGER!
"AND HOWARD THE DUCK KEEPS LEAVING FLAMING PILES OF DOG POOP AT SHE-HULK'S FRONT DOOR..."
EH, SHE DESERVES IT.
SHE JUST, YOU KNOW, DOESN'T NEED TO FIND OUT IT'S ME...
"AND SPIDER-HAM IS CYBERSTALKING A CERTAIN BELOVED PORCINE ACTRESS..."
NO COMMENT.
"AND SQUIRREL GIRL IS TERRIFIED THAT EVERYONE WILL LEARN SHE'S SECRETLY A COLLEGE STUDENT NAMED--"
OH, NO! DON'T SAY IT!

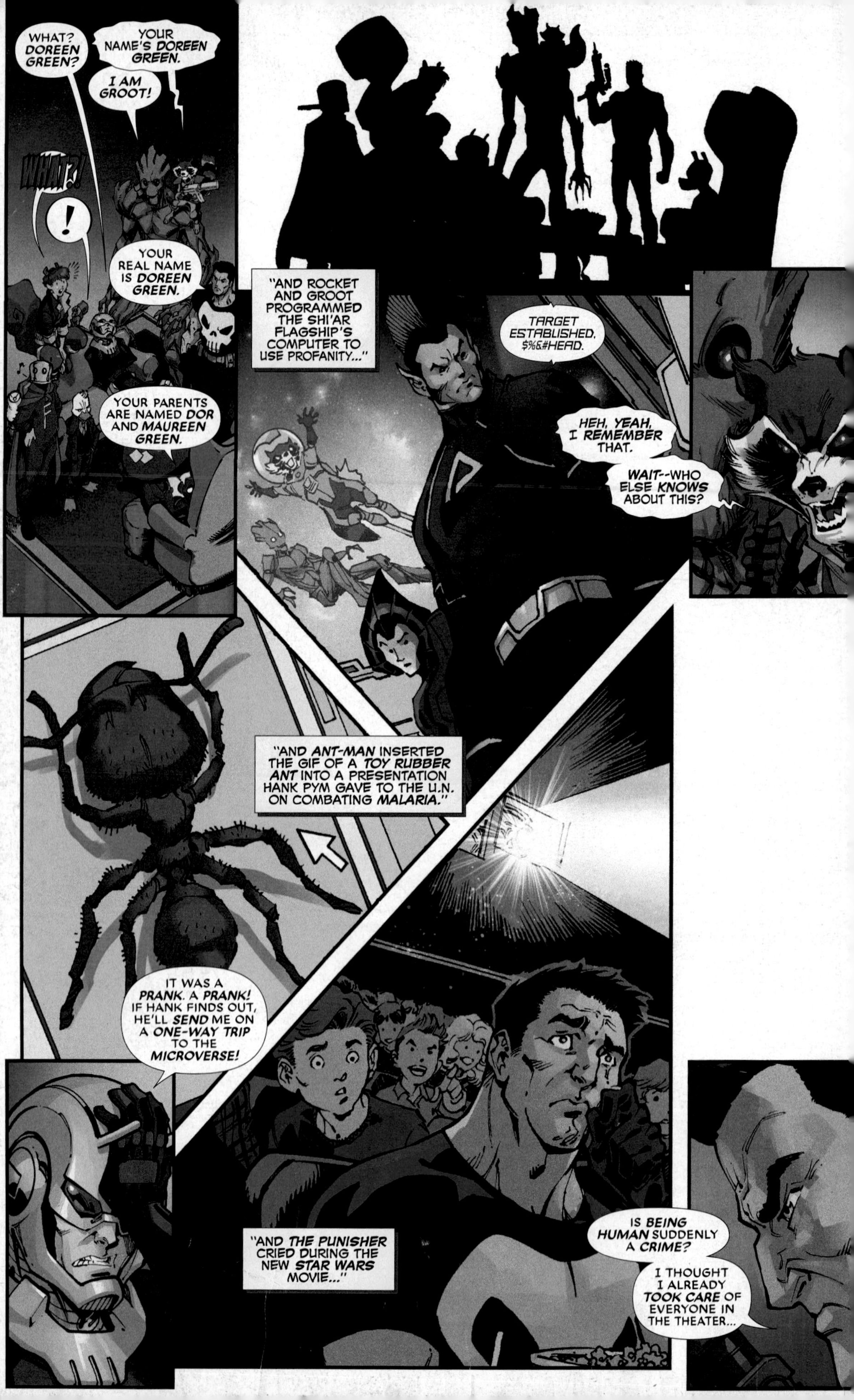
WHAT? DOREEN GREEN?
YOUR NAME'S DOREEN GREEN.
I AM GROOT!
WHAT?!
!
YOUR REAL NAME IS DOREEN GREEN.
YOUR PARENTS ARE NAMED DOR AND MAUREEN GREEN.
"AND ROCKET AND GROOT PROGRAMMED THE SHI'AR FLAGSHIP'S COMPUTER TO USE PROFANITY..."
TARGET ESTABLISHED, $%&#HEAD.
HEH, YEAH, I REMEMBER THAT.
WAIT--WHO ELSE KNOWS ABOUT THIS?
"AND ANT-MAN INSERTED THE GIF OF A TOY RUBBER ANT INTO A PRESENTATION HANK PYM GAVE TO THE U.N. ON COMBATING MALARIA."
IT WAS A PRANK. A PRANK! IF HANK FINDS OUT, HE'LL SEND ME ON A ONE-WAY TRIP TO THE MICROVERSE!
"AND THE PUNISHER CRIED DURING THE NEW STAR WARS MOVIE..."
IS BEING HUMAN SUDDENLY A CRIME?
I THOUGHT I ALREADY TOOK CARE OF EVERYONE IN THE THEATER...

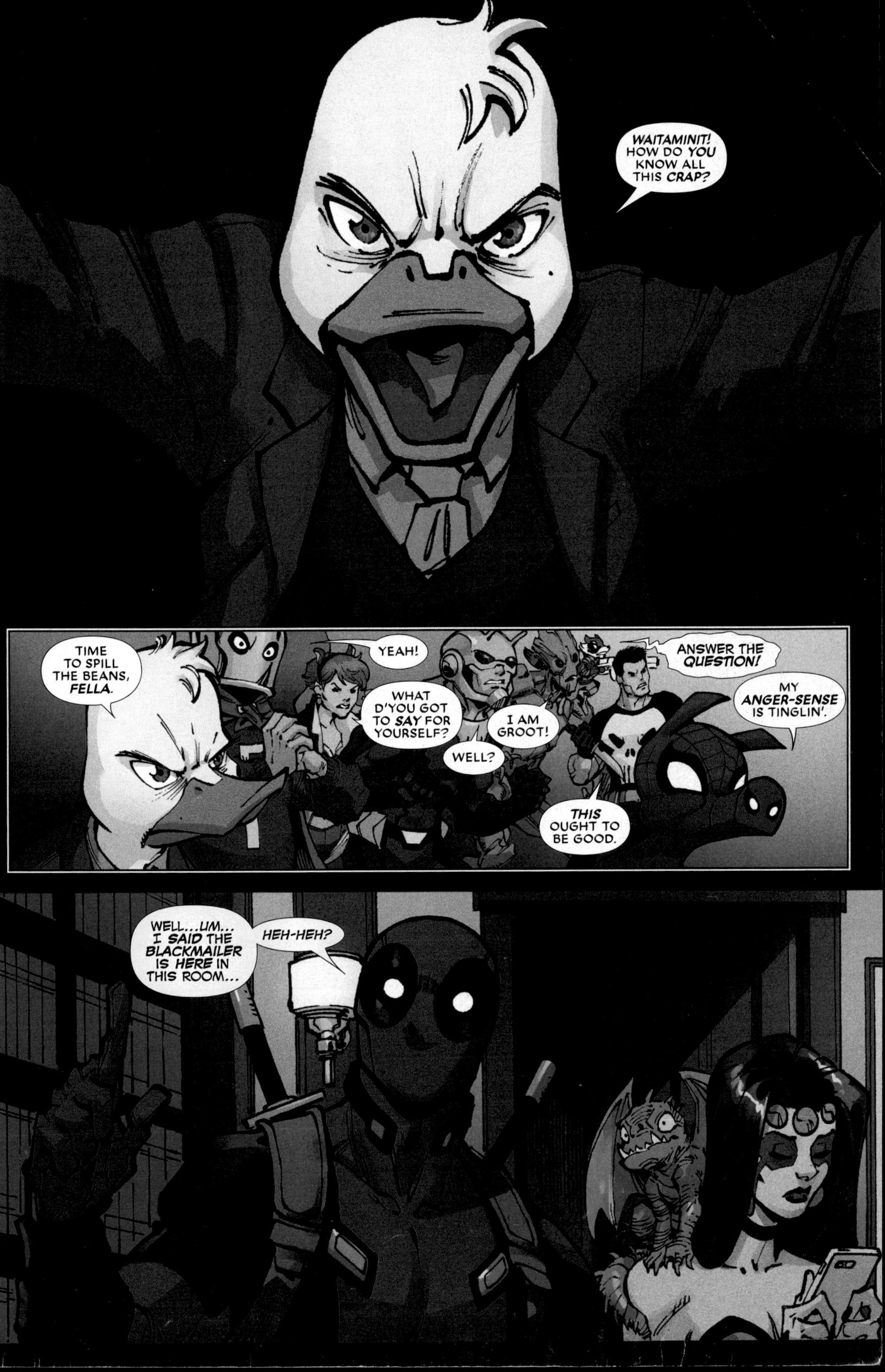

WAITAMINIT! HOW DO YOU KNOW ALL THIS CRAP?
TIME TO SPILL THE BEANS, FELLA.
YEAH!
WHAT D'YOU GOT TO SAY FOR YOURSELF?
WELL?
I AM GROOT!
ANSWER THE QUESTION!
MY ANGER-SENSE IS TINGLIN'.
THIS OUGHT TO BE GOOD.
WELL...UM... I SAID THE BLACKMAILER IS HERE IN THIS ROOM...
HEH-HEH?

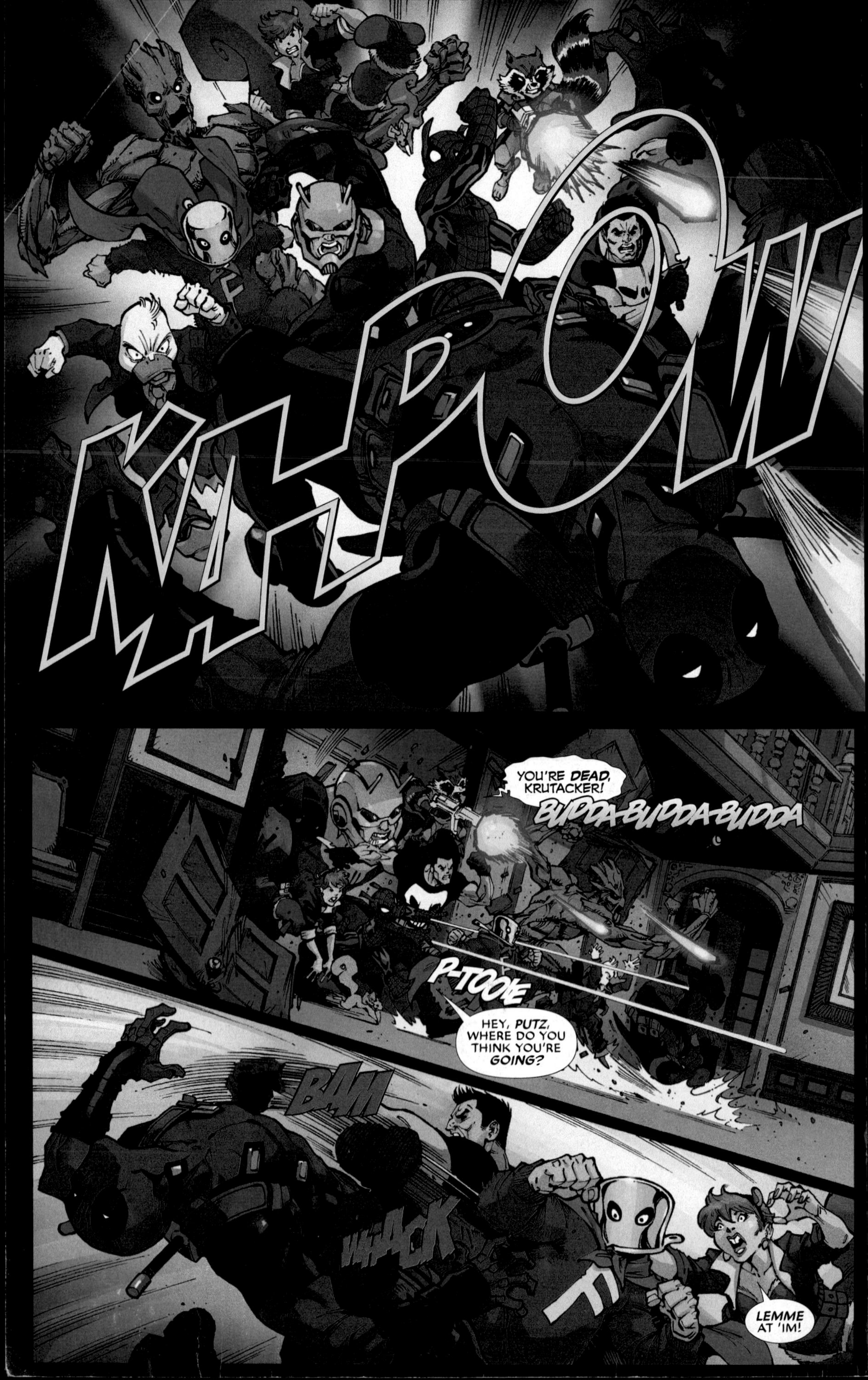

KRAPOW
YOU'RE DEAD, KRUTACKER!
BUDDA-BUDDA-BUDDA
P-TOOIE
HEY, PUTZ, WHERE DO YOU THINK YOU'RE GOING?
BAM
WHACK
LEMME AT 'IM!

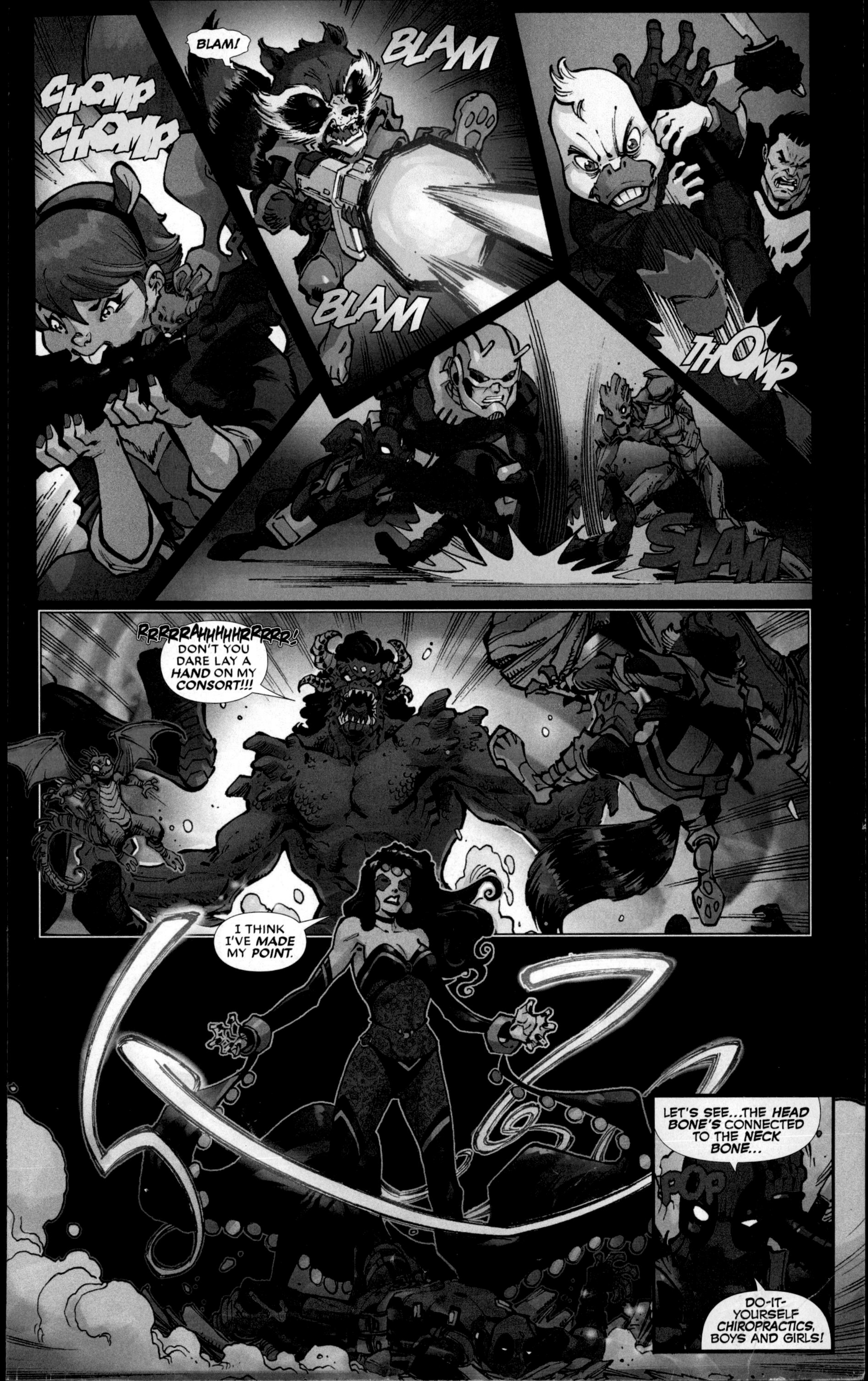
CHOMP
CHOMP
BLAM!
BLAM
BLAM
THOMP
SLAM
RRRRRAHHHHHRRRRR!
DON'T YOU DARE LAY A HAND ON MY CONSORT!!!
I THINK I'VE MADE MY POINT.
LET'S SEE...THE HEAD BONE'S CONNECTED TO THE NECK BONE...
POP
DO-IT-YOURSELF CHIROPRACTICS, BOYS AND GIRLS!

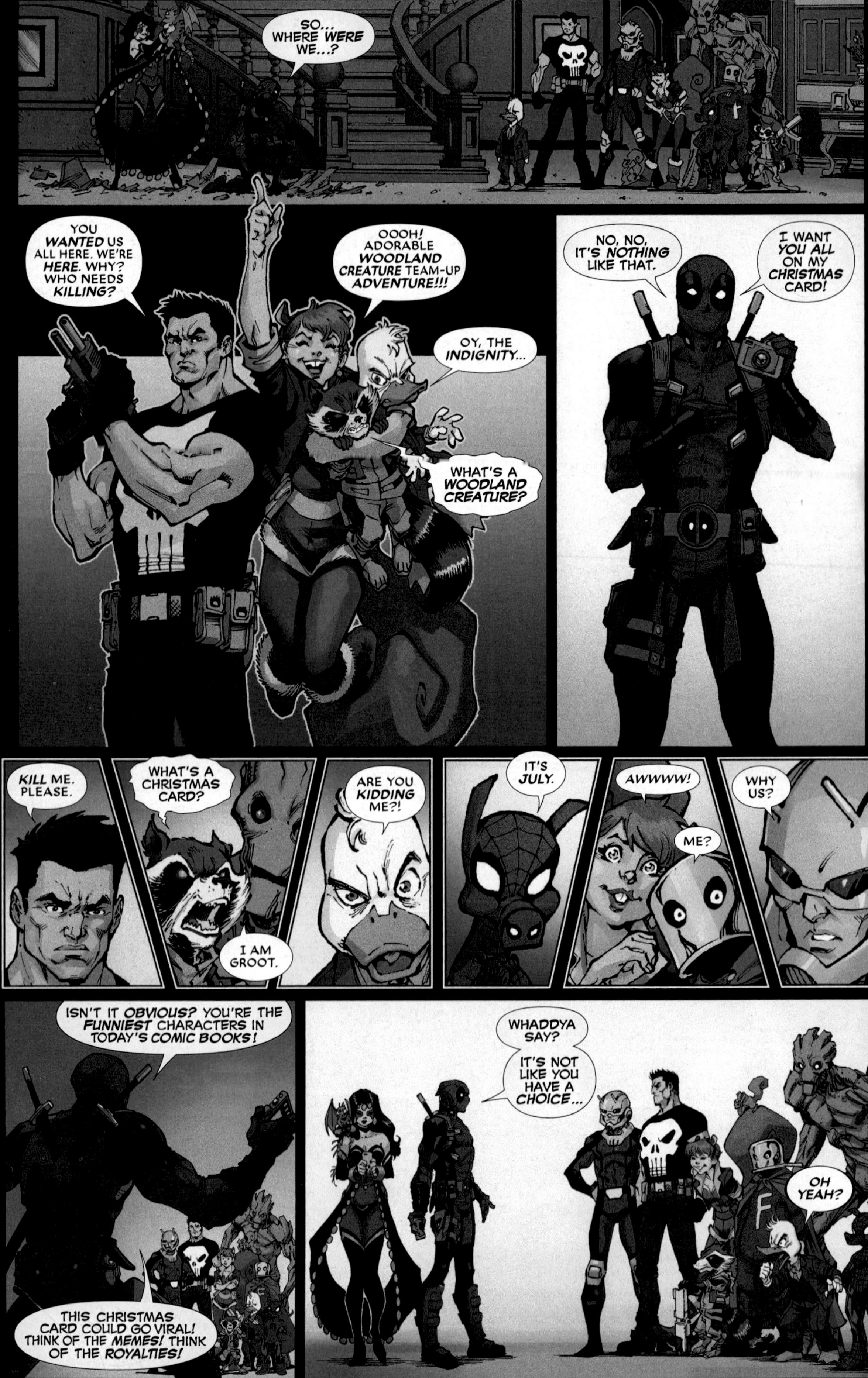
SO... WHERE WERE WE...?
YOU WANTED US ALL HERE. WE'RE HERE. WHY? WHO NEEDS KILLING?
OOOH! ADORABLE WOODLAND CREATURE TEAM-UP ADVENTURE!!!
OY, THE INDIGNITY...
WHAT'S A WOODLAND CREATURE?
NO, NO, IT'S NOTHING LIKE THAT.
I WANT YOU ALL ON MY CHRISTMAS CARD!
KILL ME. PLEASE.
WHAT'S A CHRISTMAS CARD?
I AM GROOT.
ARE YOU KIDDING ME?!
IT'S JULY.
AWWWW!
ME?
WHY US?
ISN'T IT OBVIOUS? YOU'RE THE FUNNIEST CHARACTERS IN TODAY'S COMIC BOOKS!
THIS CHRISTMAS CARD COULD GO VIRAL! THINK OF THE MEMES! THINK OF THE ROYALTIES!
WHADDYA SAY?
IT'S NOT LIKE YOU HAVE A CHOICE...
OH YEAH?

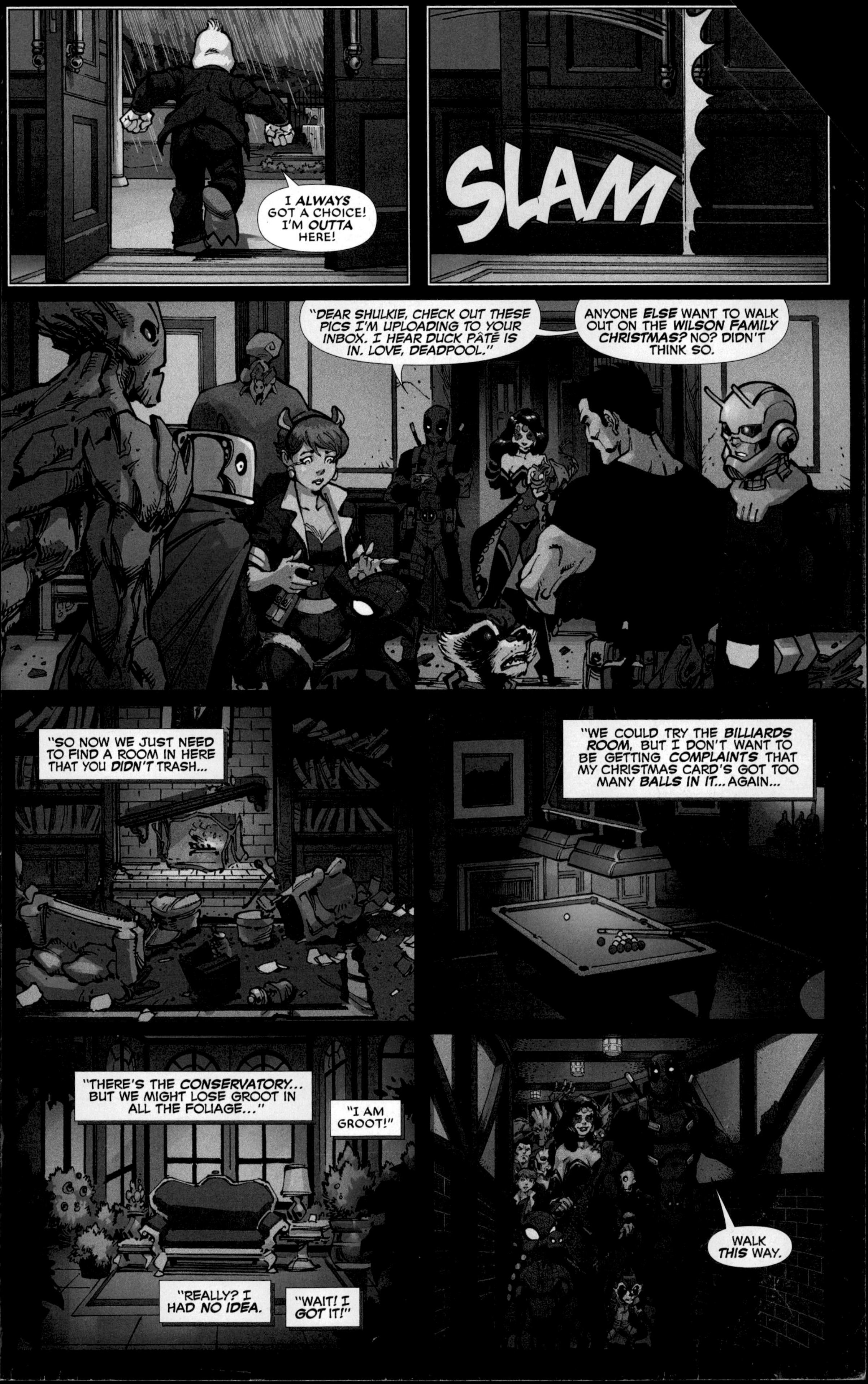
I ALWAYS GOT A CHOICE! I'M OUTTA HERE!
SLAM
"DEAR SHULKIE, CHECK OUT THESE PICS I'M UPLOADING TO YOUR INBOX. I HEAR DUCK PÂTÉ IS IN. LOVE, DEADPOOL."
ANYONE ELSE WANT TO WALK OUT ON THE WILSON FAMILY CHRISTMAS? NO? DIDN'T THINK SO.
"SO NOW WE JUST NEED TO FIND A ROOM IN HERE THAT YOU DIDN'T TRASH...
"WE COULD TRY THE BILLIARDS ROOM, BUT I DON'T WANT TO BE GETTING COMPLAINTS THAT MY CHRISTMAS CARD'S GOT TOO MANY BALLS IN IT... AGAIN...
"THERE'S THE CONSERVATORY... BUT WE MIGHT LOSE GROOT IN ALL THE FOLIAGE..."
"I AM GROOT!"
"REALLY? I HAD NO IDEA.
"WAIT! I GOT IT!"
WALK THIS WAY.

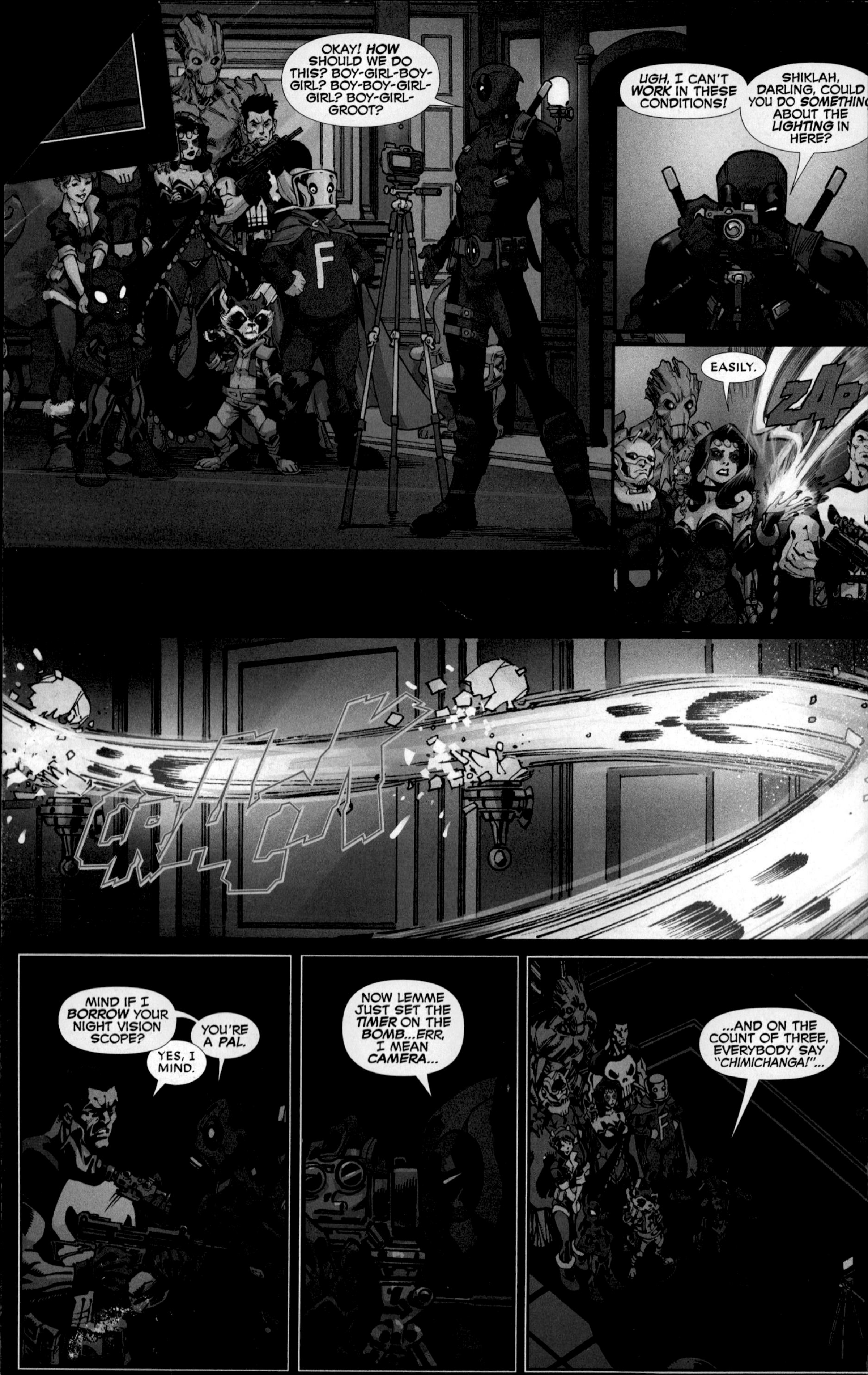
OKAY! HOW SHOULD WE DO THIS? BOY-GIRL-BOY-GIRL? BOY-BOY-GIRL-GIRL? BOY-GIRL-GROOT?
UGH, I CAN'T WORK IN THESE CONDITIONS!
SHIKLAH, DARLING, COULD YOU DO SOMETHING ABOUT THE LIGHTING IN HERE?
EASILY.
ZAP
MIND IF I BORROW YOUR NIGHT VISION SCOPE?
YES, I MIND.
YOU'RE A PAL.
NOW LEMME JUST SET THE TIMER ON THE BOMB...ERR, I MEAN CAMERA...
...AND ON THE COUNT OF THREE, EVERYBODY SAY "CHIMICHANGA!"...

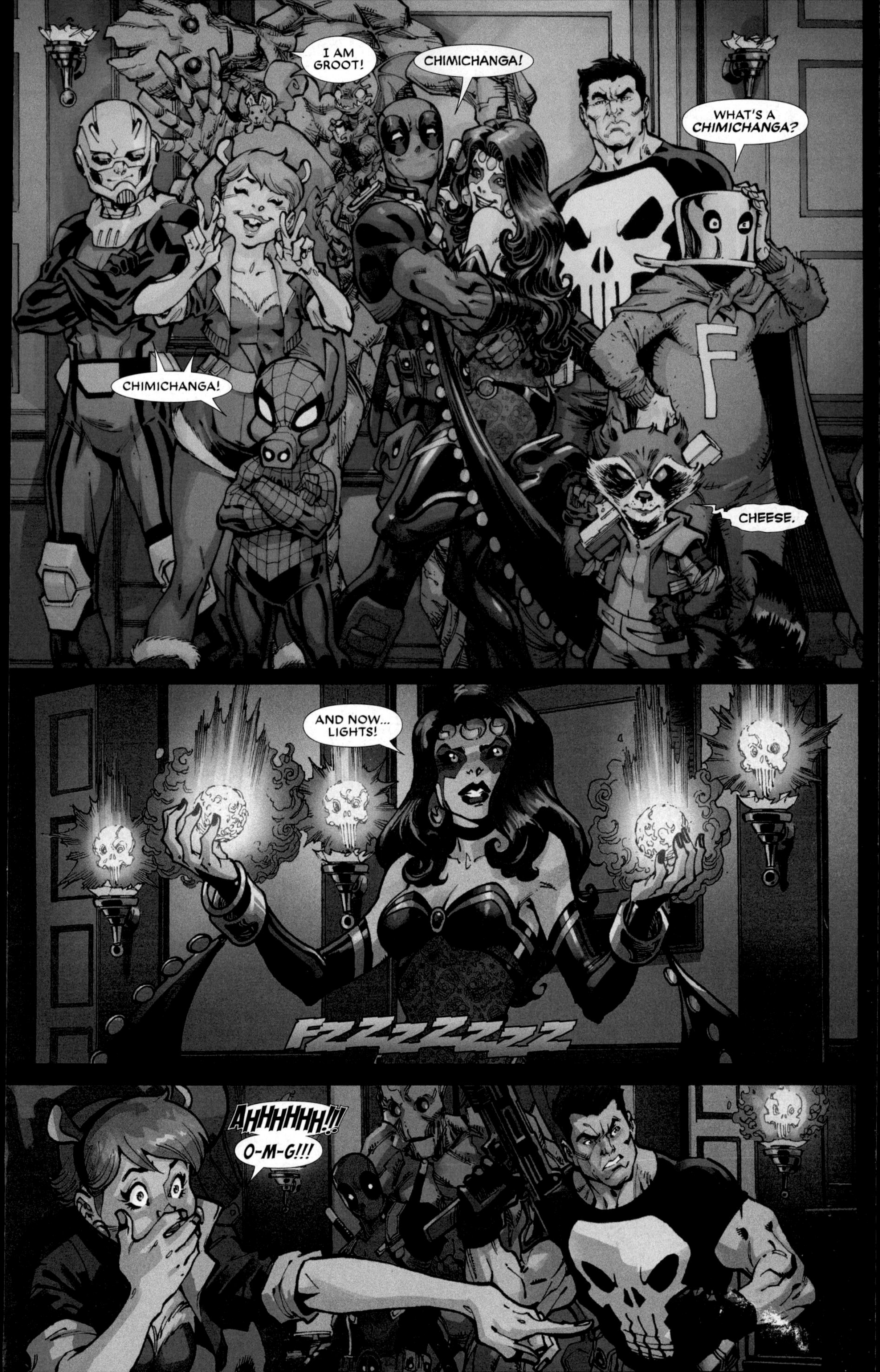
I AM GROOT!
CHIMICHANGA!
WHAT'S A CHIMICHANGA?
CHIMICHANGA!
CHEESE.
AND NOW... LIGHTS!
FZZZZZZZZ
AHHHHHH!!!
O-M-G!!!

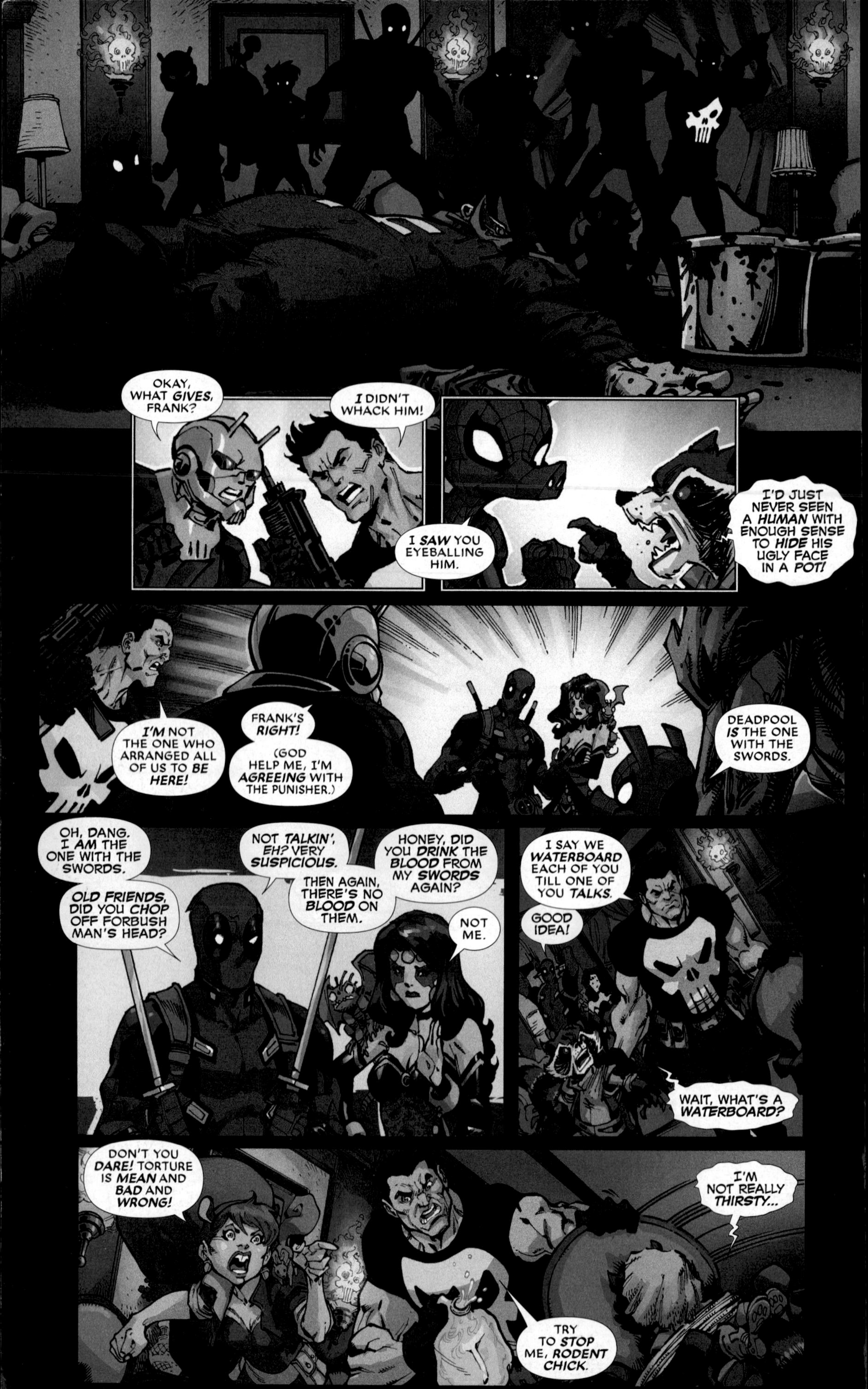

OKAY, WHAT *GIVES*, FRANK?
I DIDN'T WHACK HIM!
I *SAW* YOU EYEBALLING HIM.
I'D JUST NEVER SEEN A *HUMAN* WITH ENOUGH SENSE TO *HIDE* HIS UGLY FACE IN A *POT!*
I'M NOT THE ONE WHO ARRANGED ALL OF US TO *BE HERE!*
FRANK'S *RIGHT!*
(GOD HELP ME, I'M *AGREEING* WITH THE PUNISHER.)
DEADPOOL *IS* THE ONE WITH THE SWORDS.
OH, DANG. I *AM* THE ONE WITH THE SWORDS.
OLD FRIENDS, DID YOU *CHOP* OFF FORBUSH MAN'S HEAD?
NOT *TALKIN'*, EH? VERY *SUSPICIOUS*.
THEN AGAIN, THERE'S NO *BLOOD* ON THEM.
HONEY, *DID* YOU *DRINK* THE *BLOOD* FROM MY *SWORDS* AGAIN?
NOT ME.
I SAY WE *WATERBOARD* EACH OF YOU TILL ONE OF YOU *TALKS*.
GOOD IDEA!
WAIT, WHAT'S A *WATERBOARD?*
DON'T YOU *DARE!* TORTURE IS *MEAN* AND *BAD* AND *WRONG!*
I'M NOT REALLY *THIRSTY...*
TRY TO *STOP* ME, *RODENT CHICK*.

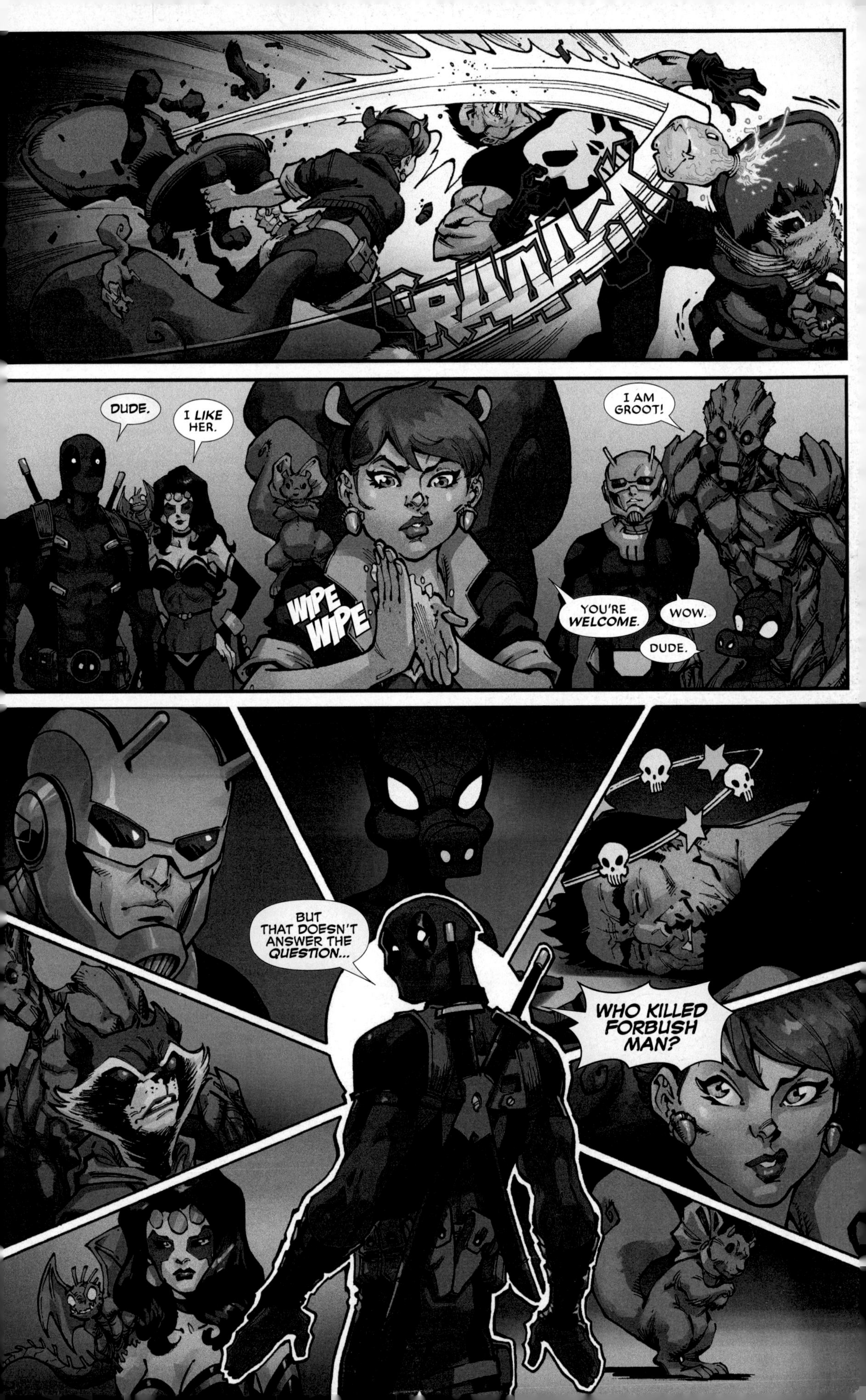
KRAAAKK
DUDE.
I LIKE HER.
I AM GROOT!
WIPE WIPE
YOU'RE WELCOME.
WOW.
DUDE.
BUT THAT DOESN'T ANSWER THE QUESTION...
WHO KILLED FORBUSH MAN?

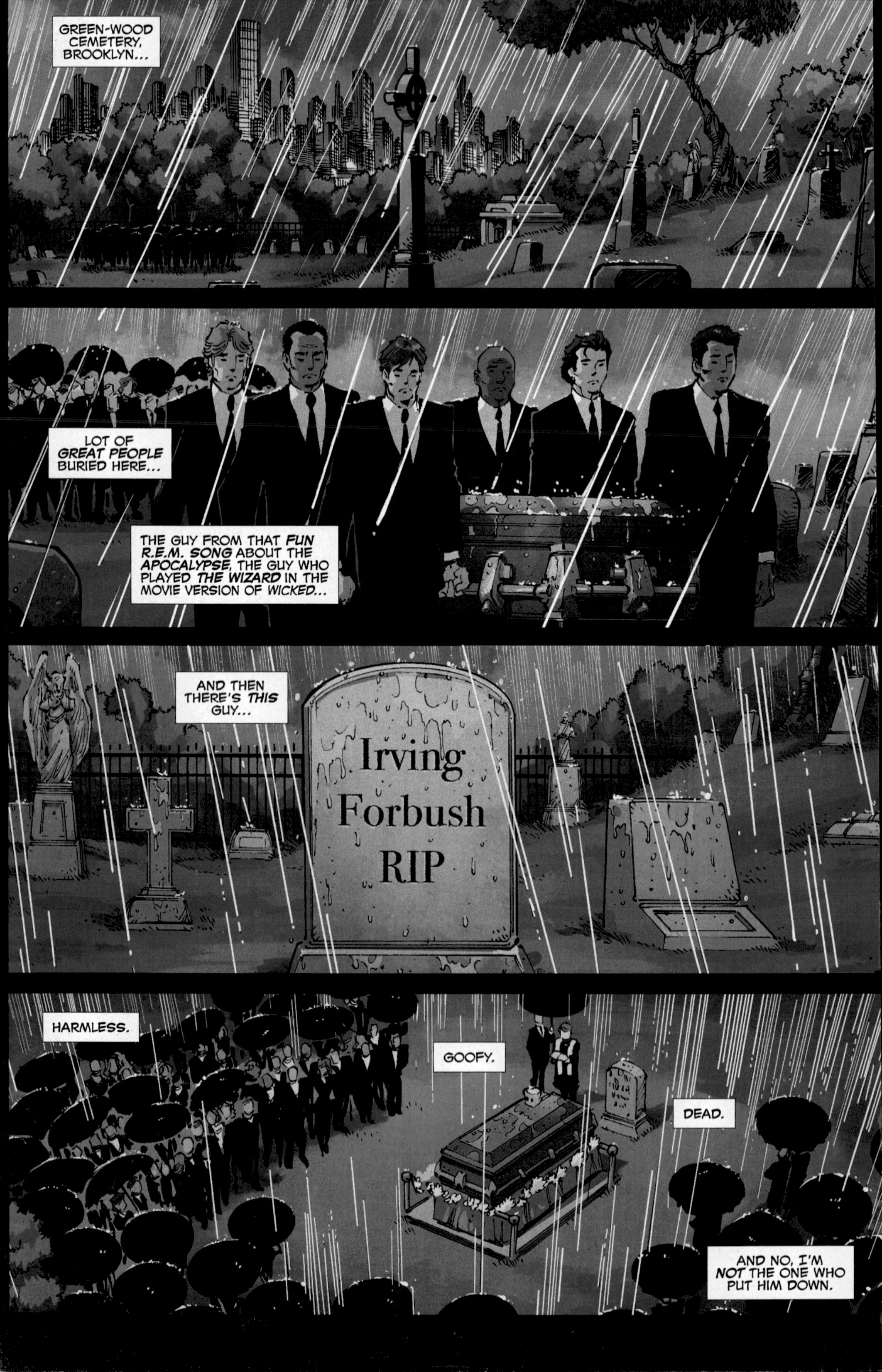
GREEN-WOOD CEMETERY, BROOKLYN...
LOT OF GREAT PEOPLE BURIED HERE...
THE GUY FROM THAT FUN R.E.M. SONG ABOUT THE APOCALYPSE, THE GUY WHO PLAYED THE WIZARD IN THE MOVIE VERSION OF WICKED...
AND THEN THERE'S THIS GUY...
Irving Forbush RIP
HARMLESS.
GOOFY.
DEAD.
AND NO, I'M NOT THE ONE WHO PUT HIM DOWN.

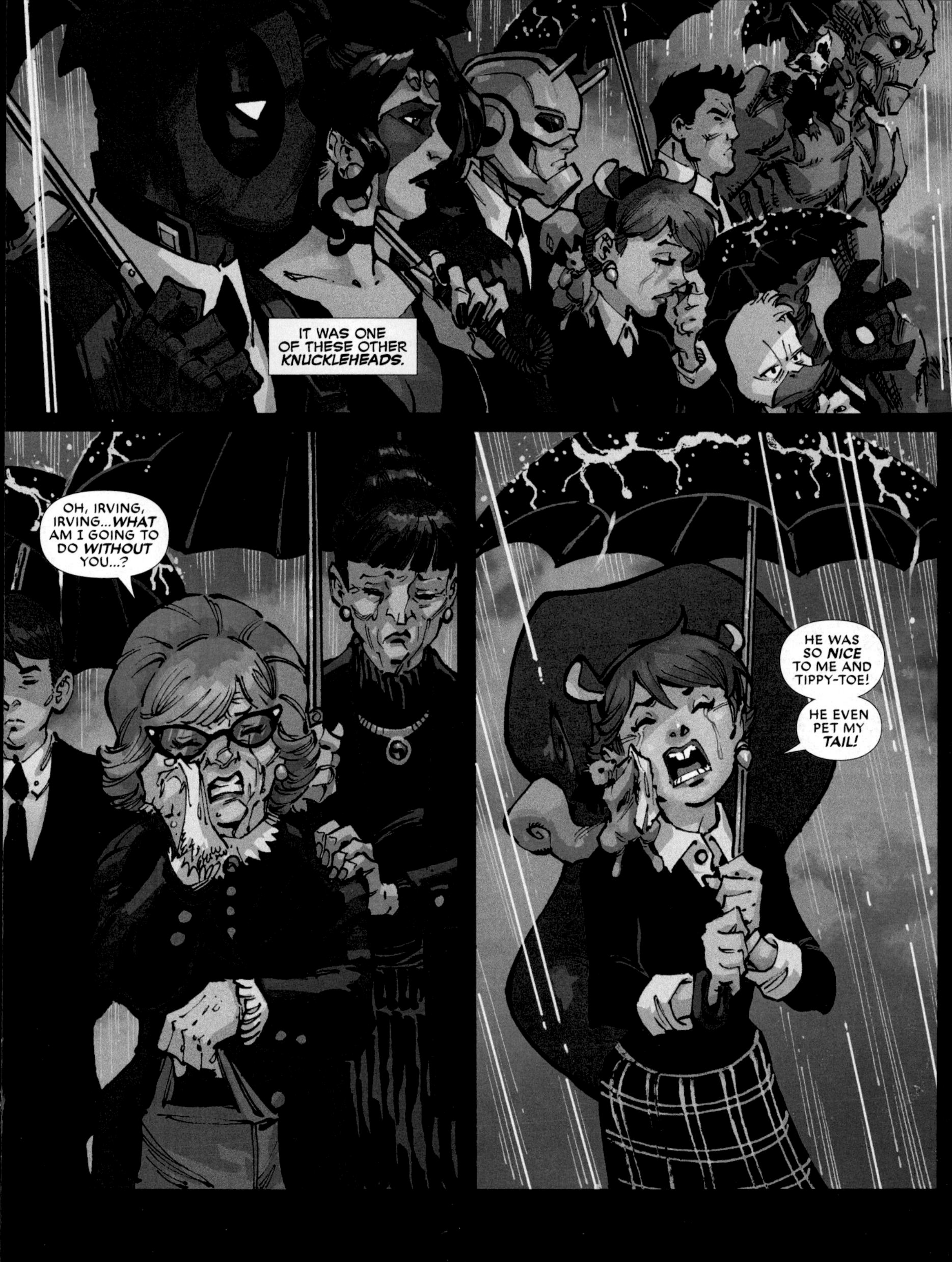
IT WAS ONE OF THESE OTHER KNUCKLEHEADS.
OH, IRVING, IRVING...WHAT AM I GOING TO DO WITHOUT YOU...?
HE WAS SO NICE TO ME AND TIPPY-TOE!
HE EVEN PET MY TAIL!

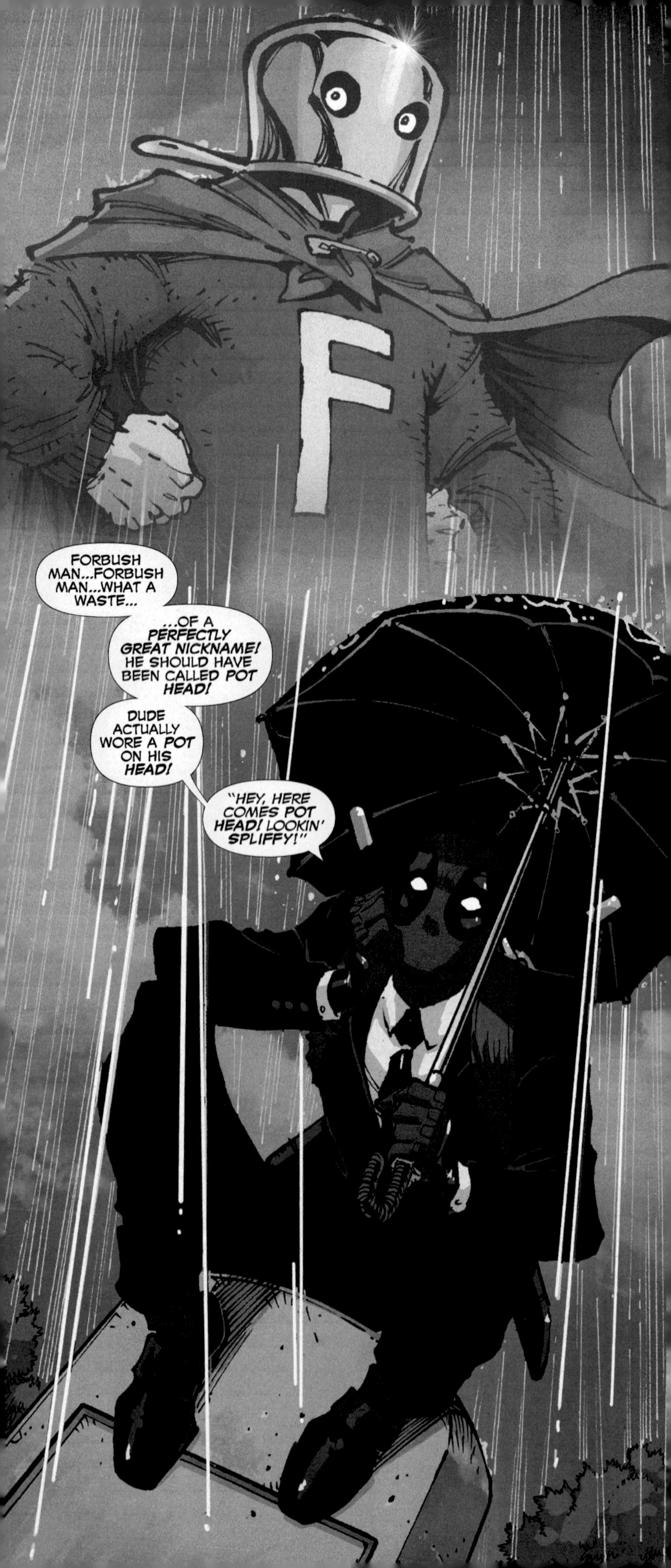

FORBUSH MAN...FORBUSH MAN...WHAT A WASTE...
...OF A PERFECTLY GREAT NICKNAME! HE SHOULD HAVE BEEN CALLED POT HEAD!
DUDE ACTUALLY WORE A POT ON HIS HEAD!
"HEY, HERE COMES POT HEAD! LOOKIN' SPLIFFY!"

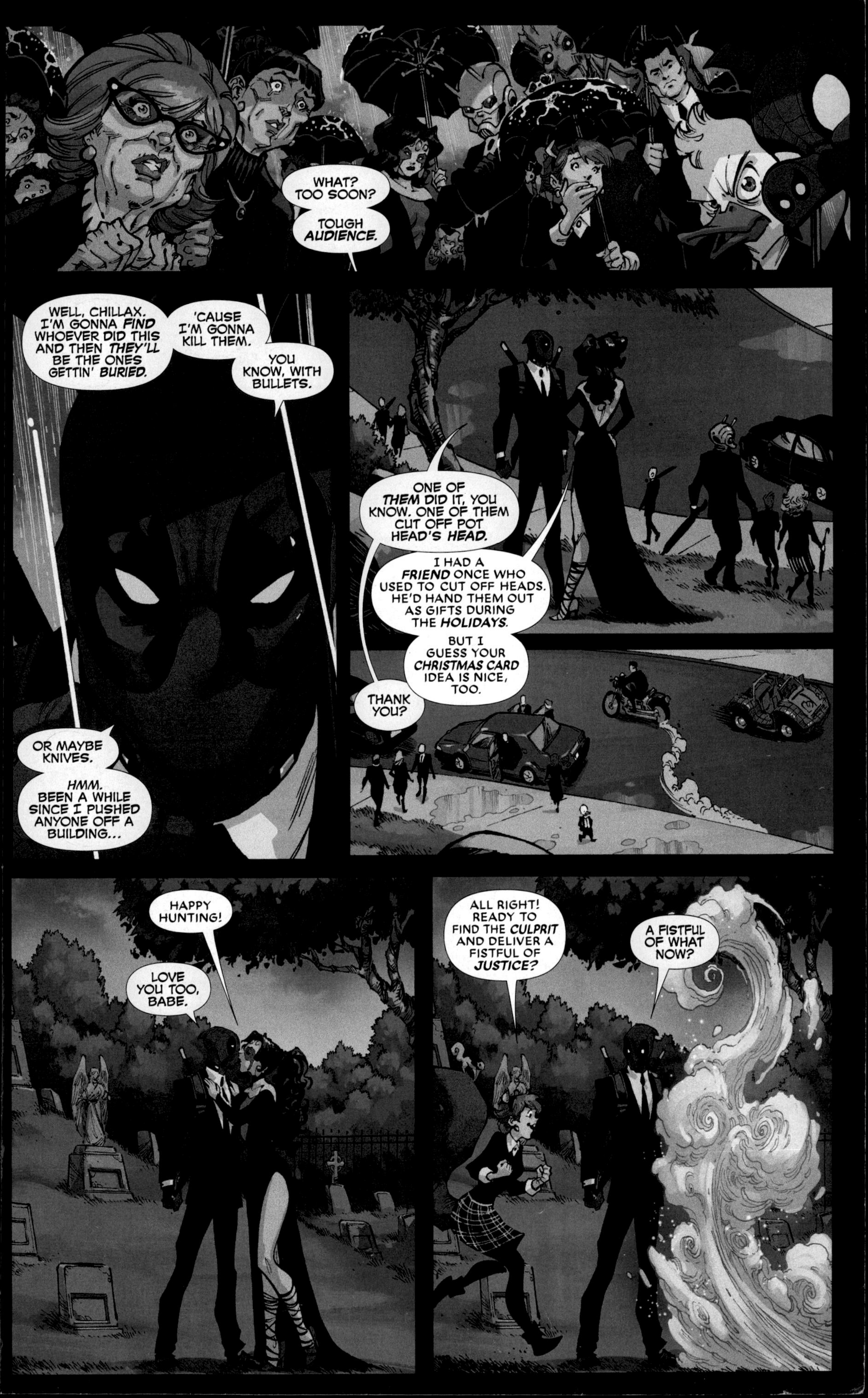
WHAT? TOO SOON?
TOUGH AUDIENCE.
WELL, CHILLAX. I'M GONNA FIND WHOEVER DID THIS AND THEN THEY'LL BE THE ONES GETTIN' BURIED.
'CAUSE I'M GONNA KILL THEM.
YOU KNOW, WITH BULLETS.
OR MAYBE KNIVES.
HMM. BEEN A WHILE SINCE I PUSHED ANYONE OFF A BUILDING...
ONE OF THEM DID IT, YOU KNOW. ONE OF THEM CUT OFF POT HEAD'S HEAD.
I HAD A FRIEND ONCE WHO USED TO CUT OFF HEADS. HE'D HAND THEM OUT AS GIFTS DURING THE HOLIDAYS.
BUT I GUESS YOUR CHRISTMAS CARD IDEA IS NICE, TOO.
THANK YOU?
HAPPY HUNTING!
LOVE YOU TOO, BABE.
ALL RIGHT! READY TO FIND THE CULPRIT AND DELIVER A FISTFUL OF JUSTICE?
A FISTFUL OF WHAT NOW?

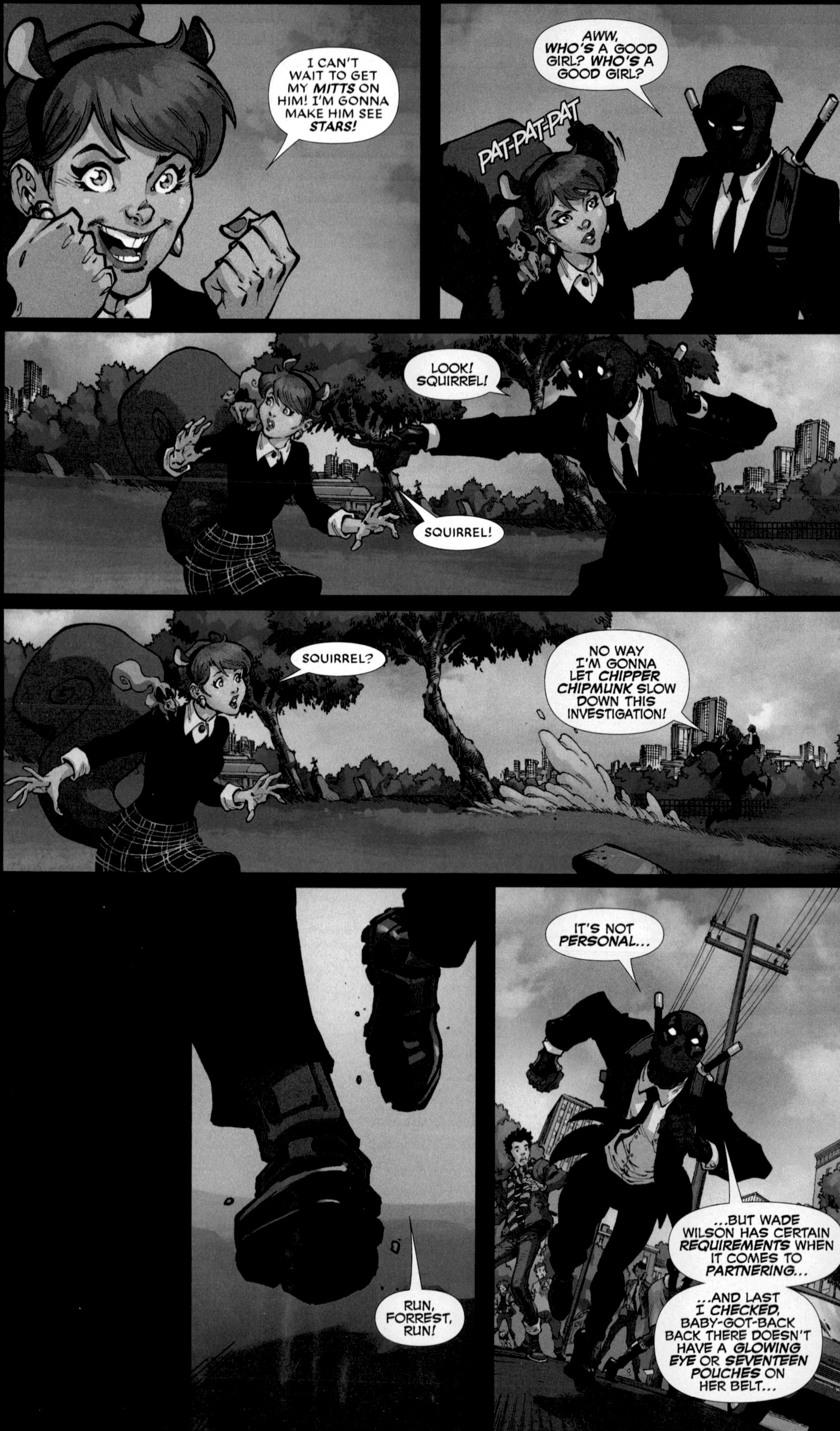
I CAN'T WAIT TO GET MY MITTS ON HIM! I'M GONNA MAKE HIM SEE STARS!
AWW, WHO'S A GOOD GIRL? WHO'S A GOOD GIRL?
PAT-PAT-PAT
LOOK! SQUIRREL!
SQUIRREL!
SQUIRREL?
NO WAY I'M GONNA LET CHIPPER CHIPMUNK SLOW DOWN THIS INVESTIGATION!
RUN, FORREST, RUN!
IT'S NOT PERSONAL...
...BUT WADE WILSON HAS CERTAIN REQUIREMENTS WHEN IT COMES TO PARTNERING...
...AND LAST I CHECKED, BABY-GOT-BACK BACK THERE DOESN'T HAVE A GLOWING EYE OR SEVENTEEN POUCHES ON HER BELT...

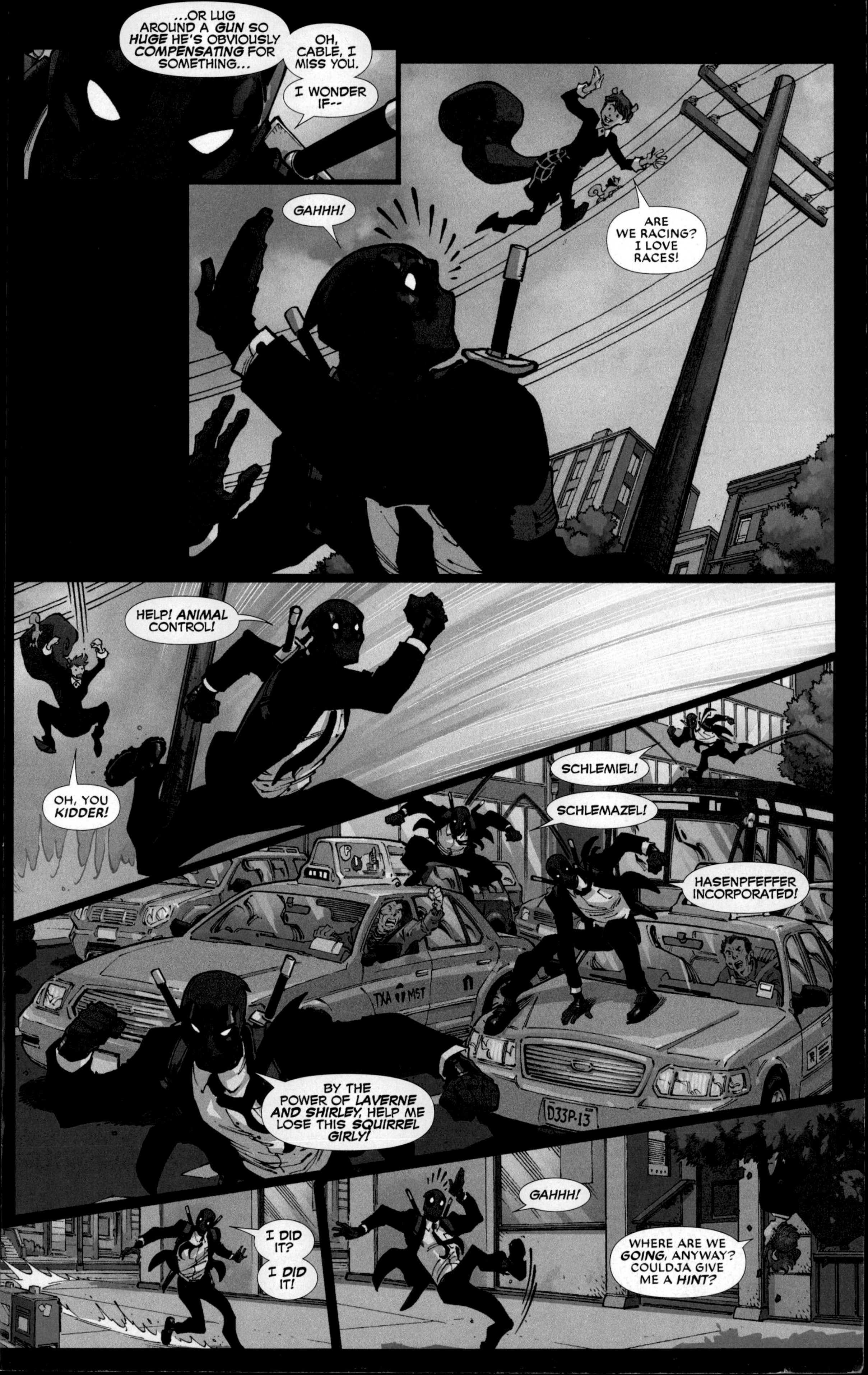

...OR LUG AROUND A GUN SO HUGE HE'S OBVIOUSLY COMPENSATING FOR SOMETHING...
OH, CABLE, I MISS YOU.
I WONDER IF--
GAHHH!
ARE WE RACING? I LOVE RACES!
HELP! ANIMAL CONTROL!
OH, YOU KIDDER!
SCHLEMIEL!
SCHLEMAZEL!
HASENPFEFFER INCORPORATED!
BY THE POWER OF LAVERNE AND SHIRLEY, HELP ME LOSE THIS SQUIRREL GIRL!
D33P-13
GAHHH!
I DID IT?
I DID IT!
WHERE ARE WE GOING, ANYWAY? COULDJA GIVE ME A HINT?

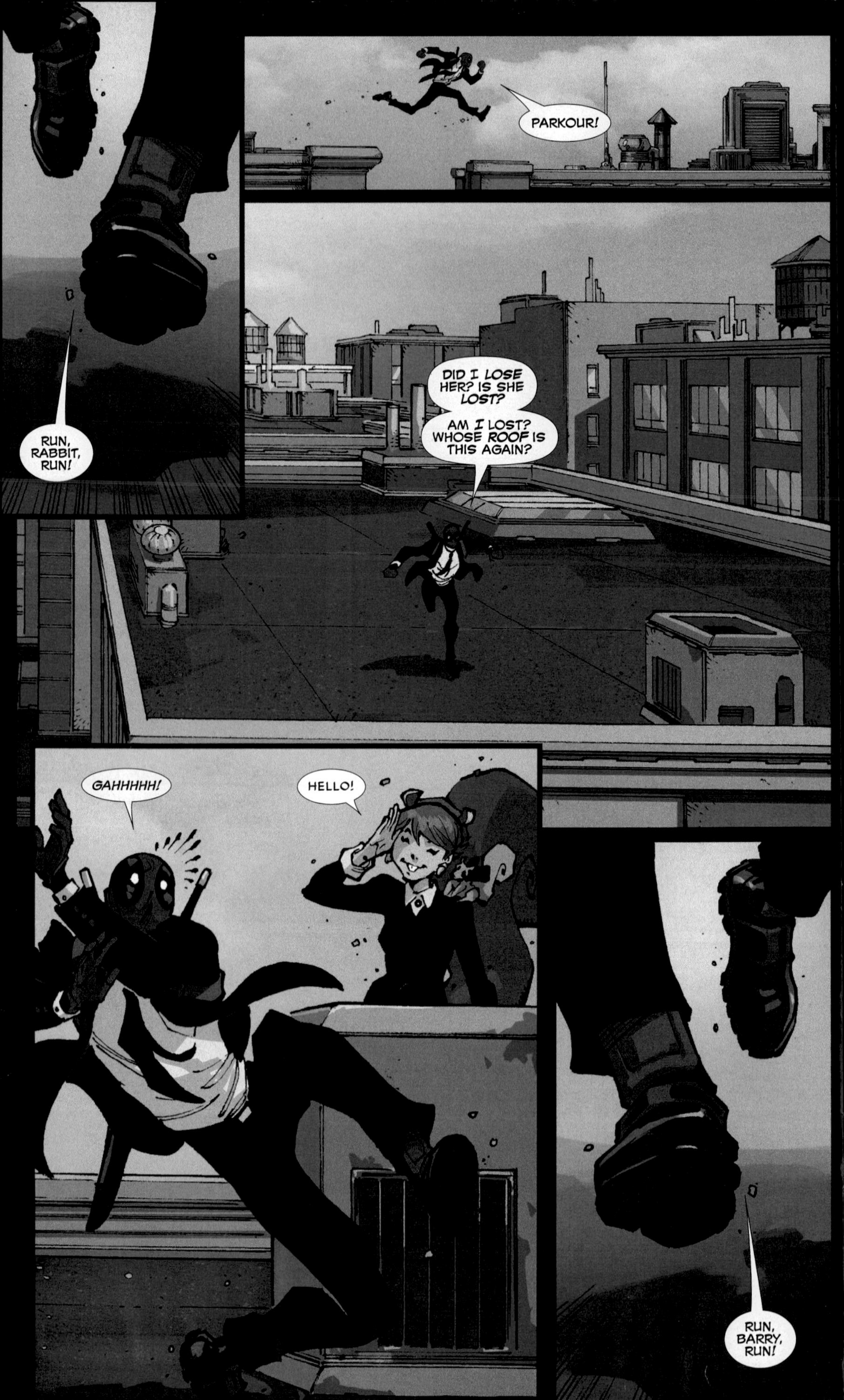

RUN, RABBIT, RUN!
PARKOUR!
DID I LOSE HER? IS SHE LOST?
AM I LOST? WHOSE ROOF IS THIS AGAIN?
GAHHHHH!
HELLO!
RUN, BARRY, RUN!

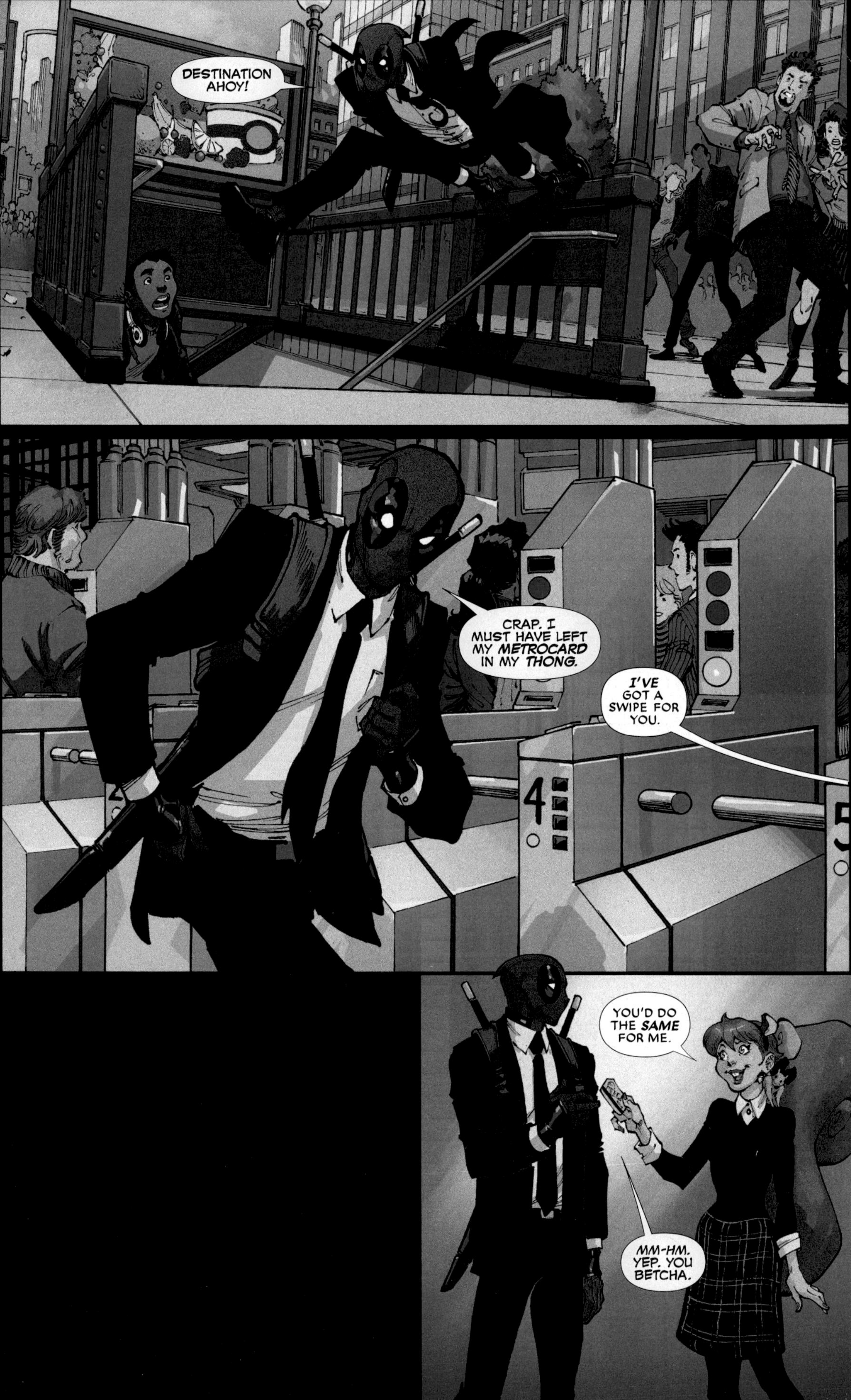
DESTINATION AHOY!
CRAP. I MUST HAVE LEFT MY *METROCARD* IN MY *THONG.*
I'VE GOT A SWIPE FOR YOU.
YOU'D DO THE *SAME* FOR ME.
MM-HM. YEP. YOU BETCHA.

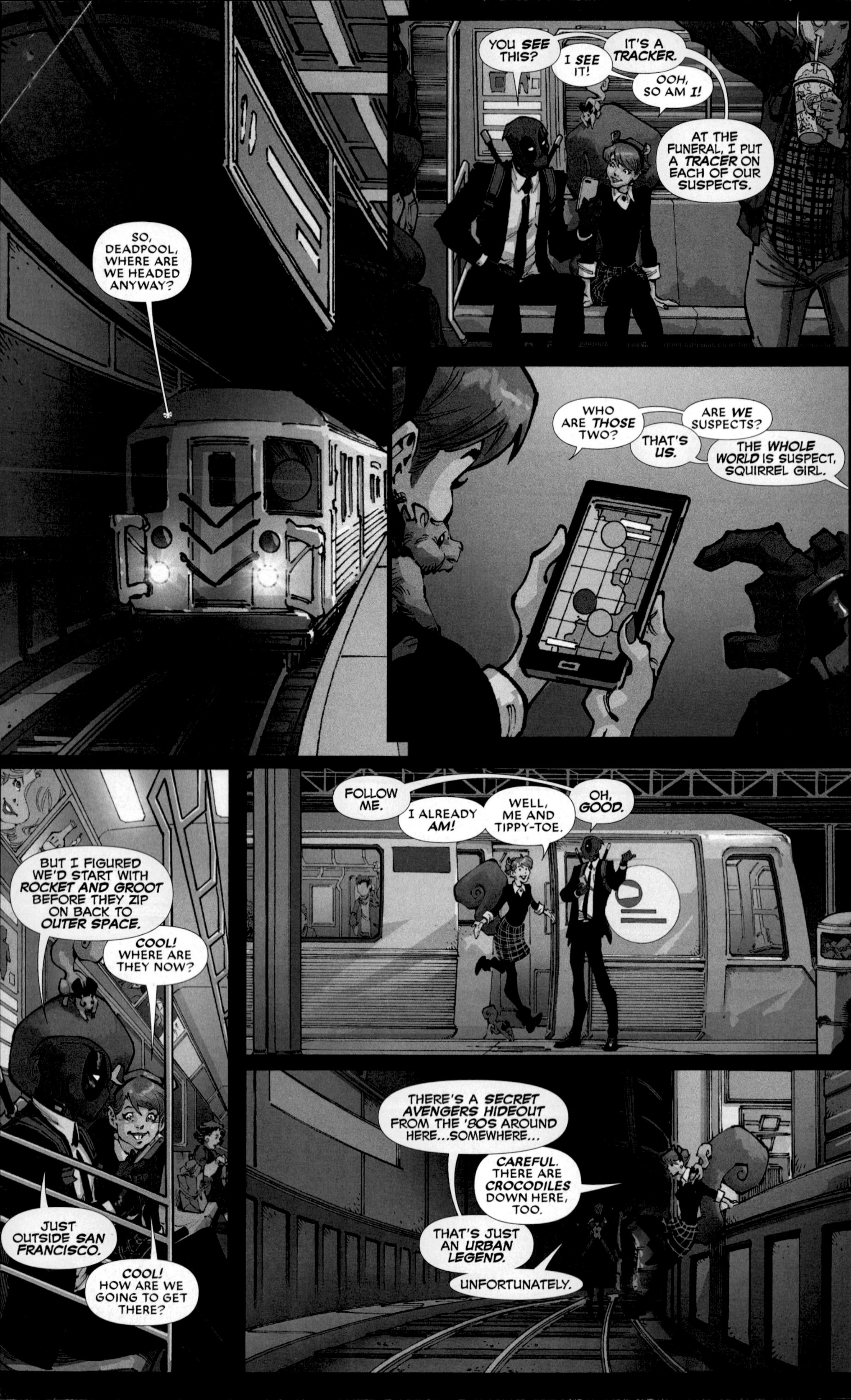
SO, DEADPOOL, WHERE ARE WE HEADED ANYWAY?
YOU SEE THIS?
I SEE IT!
IT'S A TRACKER.
OOH, SO AM I!
AT THE FUNERAL, I PUT A TRACER ON EACH OF OUR SUSPECTS.
WHO ARE THOSE TWO?
ARE WE SUSPECTS?
THAT'S US.
THE WHOLE WORLD IS SUSPECT, SQUIRREL GIRL.
BUT I FIGURED WE'D START WITH ROCKET AND GROOT BEFORE THEY ZIP ON BACK TO OUTER SPACE.
COOL! WHERE ARE THEY NOW?
JUST OUTSIDE SAN FRANCISCO.
COOL! HOW ARE WE GOING TO GET THERE?
FOLLOW ME.
I ALREADY AM!
WELL, ME AND TIPPY-TOE.
OH, GOOD.
THERE'S A SECRET AVENGERS HIDEOUT FROM THE '80S AROUND HERE...SOMEWHERE...
CAREFUL. THERE ARE CROCODILES DOWN HERE, TOO.
THAT'S JUST AN URBAN LEGEND.
UNFORTUNATELY.

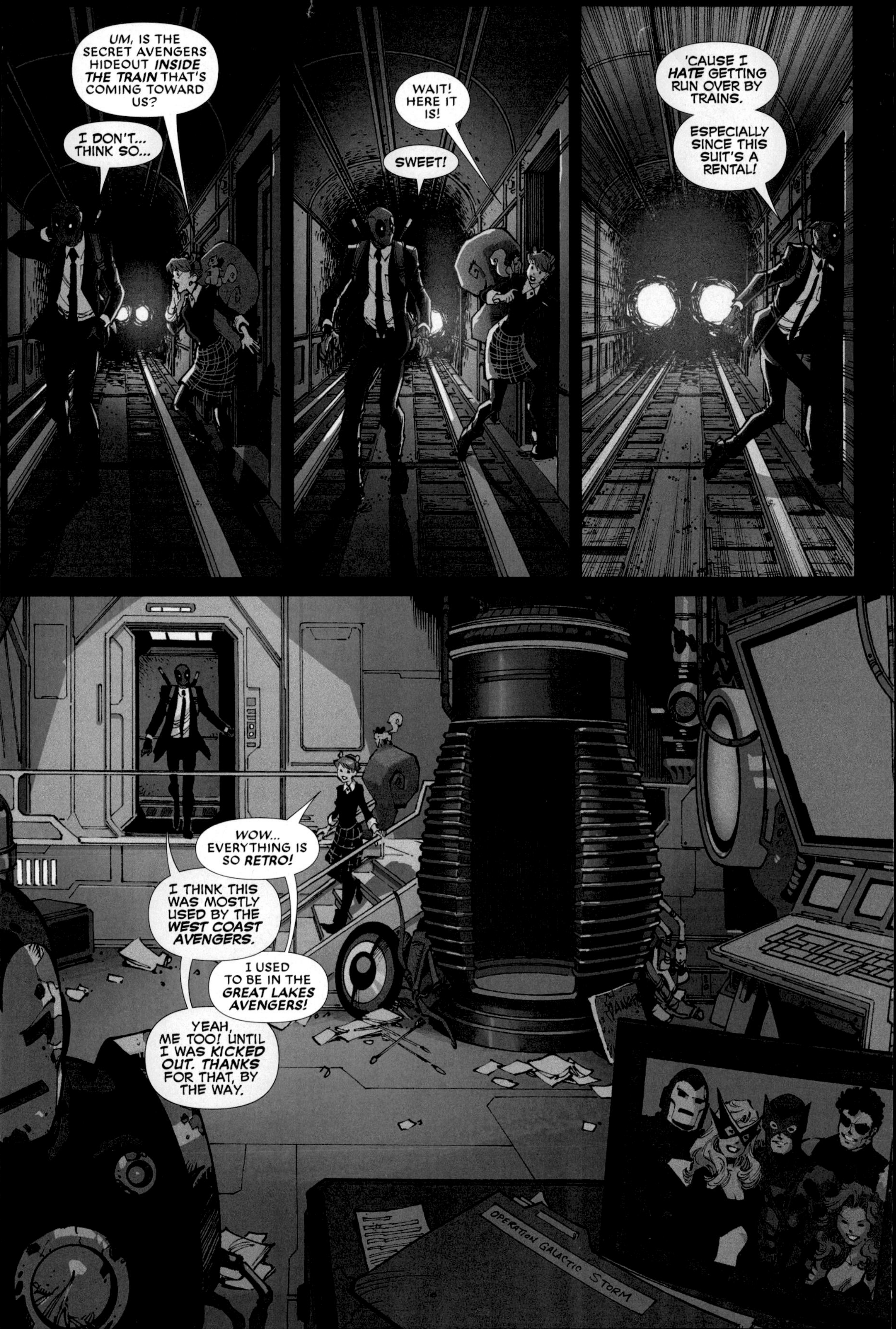
UM, IS THE SECRET AVENGERS HIDEOUT INSIDE THE TRAIN THAT'S COMING TOWARD US?
I DON'T... THINK SO...
WAIT! HERE IT IS!
SWEET!
'CAUSE I HATE GETTING RUN OVER BY TRAINS.
ESPECIALLY SINCE THIS SUIT'S A RENTAL!
WOW... EVERYTHING IS SO RETRO!
I THINK THIS WAS MOSTLY USED BY THE WEST COAST AVENGERS.
I USED TO BE IN THE GREAT LAKES AVENGERS!
YEAH, ME TOO! UNTIL I WAS KICKED OUT. THANKS FOR THAT, BY THE WAY.
OPERATION GALACTIC STORM

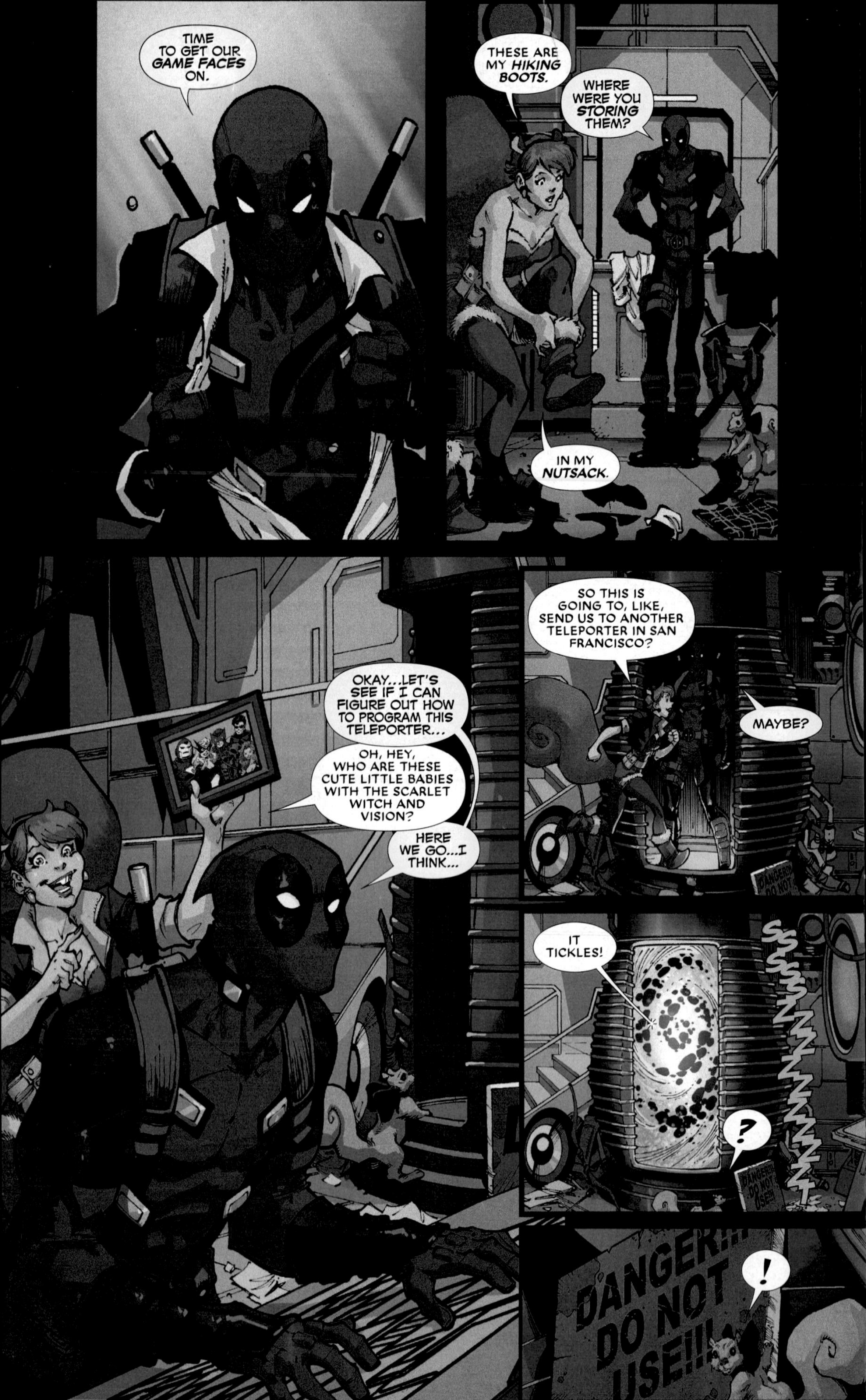
TIME TO GET OUR GAME FACES ON.
THESE ARE MY HIKING BOOTS.
WHERE WERE YOU STORING THEM?
IN MY NUTSACK.
OKAY...LET'S SEE IF I CAN FIGURE OUT HOW TO PROGRAM THIS TELEPORTER...
OH, HEY, WHO ARE THESE CUTE LITTLE BABIES WITH THE SCARLET WITCH AND VISION?
HERE WE GO...I THINK...
SO THIS IS GOING TO, LIKE, SEND US TO ANOTHER TELEPORTER IN SAN FRANCISCO?
MAYBE?
IT TICKLES!
SSSSZZZZZZZZ
?
DANGER!!! DO NOT USE!!!
!

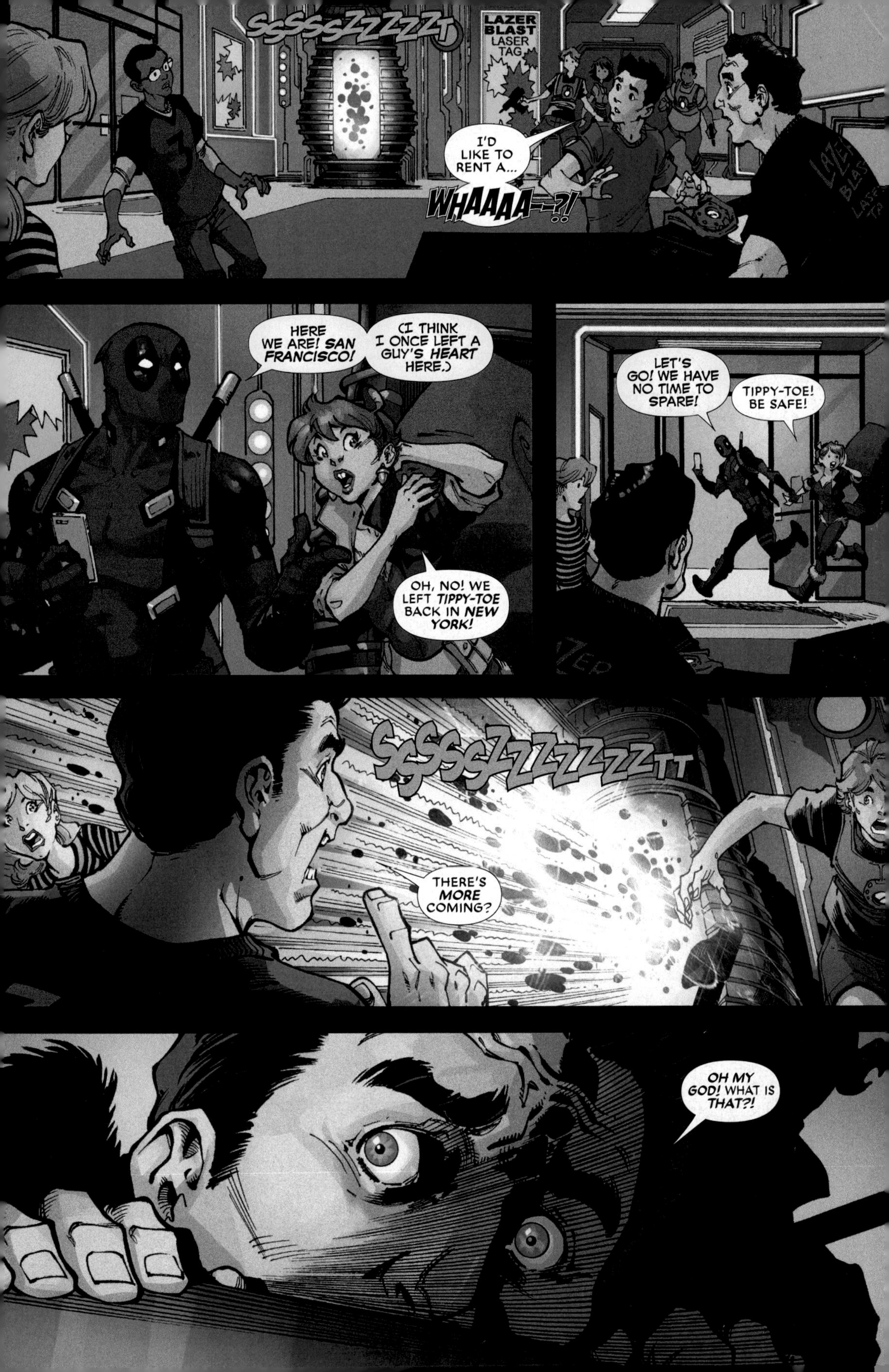
SGSSSSZZZZZT
LAZER BLAST LASER TAG
I'D LIKE TO RENT A...
WHAAAA--?!
HERE WE ARE! SAN FRANCISCO!
(I THINK I ONCE LEFT A GUY'S HEART HERE.)
OH, NO! WE LEFT TIPPY-TOE BACK IN NEW YORK!
LET'S GO! WE HAVE NO TIME TO SPARE!
TIPPY-TOE! BE SAFE!
SGSSSSZZZZZZZZTT
THERE'S MORE COMING?
OH MY GOD! WHAT IS THAT?!

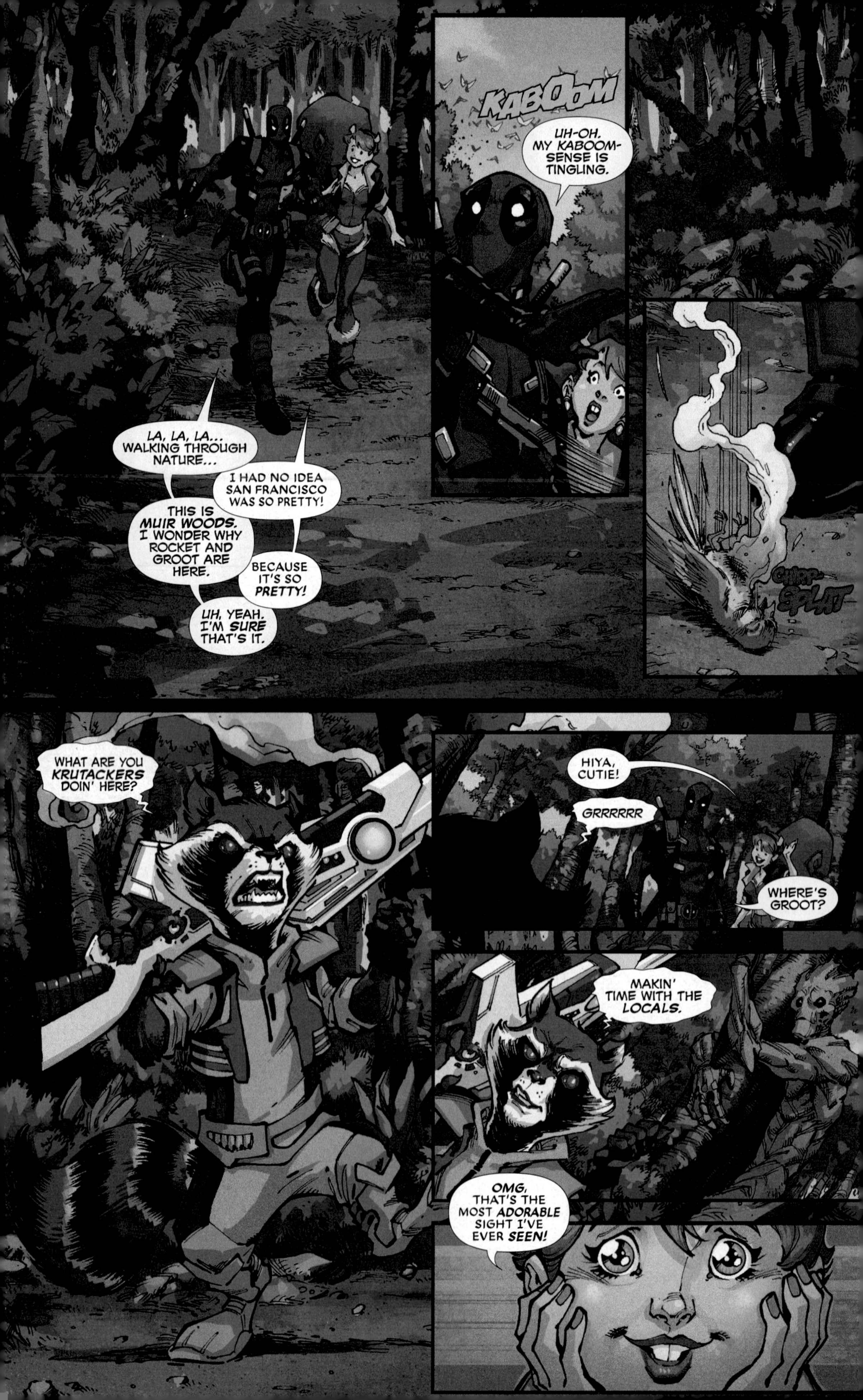
LA, LA, LA... WALKING THROUGH NATURE...
I HAD NO IDEA SAN FRANCISCO WAS SO PRETTY!
THIS IS MUIR WOODS. I WONDER WHY ROCKET AND GROOT ARE HERE.
BECAUSE IT'S SO PRETTY!
UH, YEAH. I'M SURE THAT'S IT.
KABOOM
UH-OH. MY KABOOM-SENSE IS TINGLING.
CHIRP-
SPLAT
WHAT ARE YOU KRUTACKERS DOIN' HERE?
HIYA, CUTIE!
GRRRRRR
WHERE'S GROOT?
MAKIN' TIME WITH THE LOCALS.
OMG, THAT'S THE MOST ADORABLE SIGHT I'VE EVER SEEN!

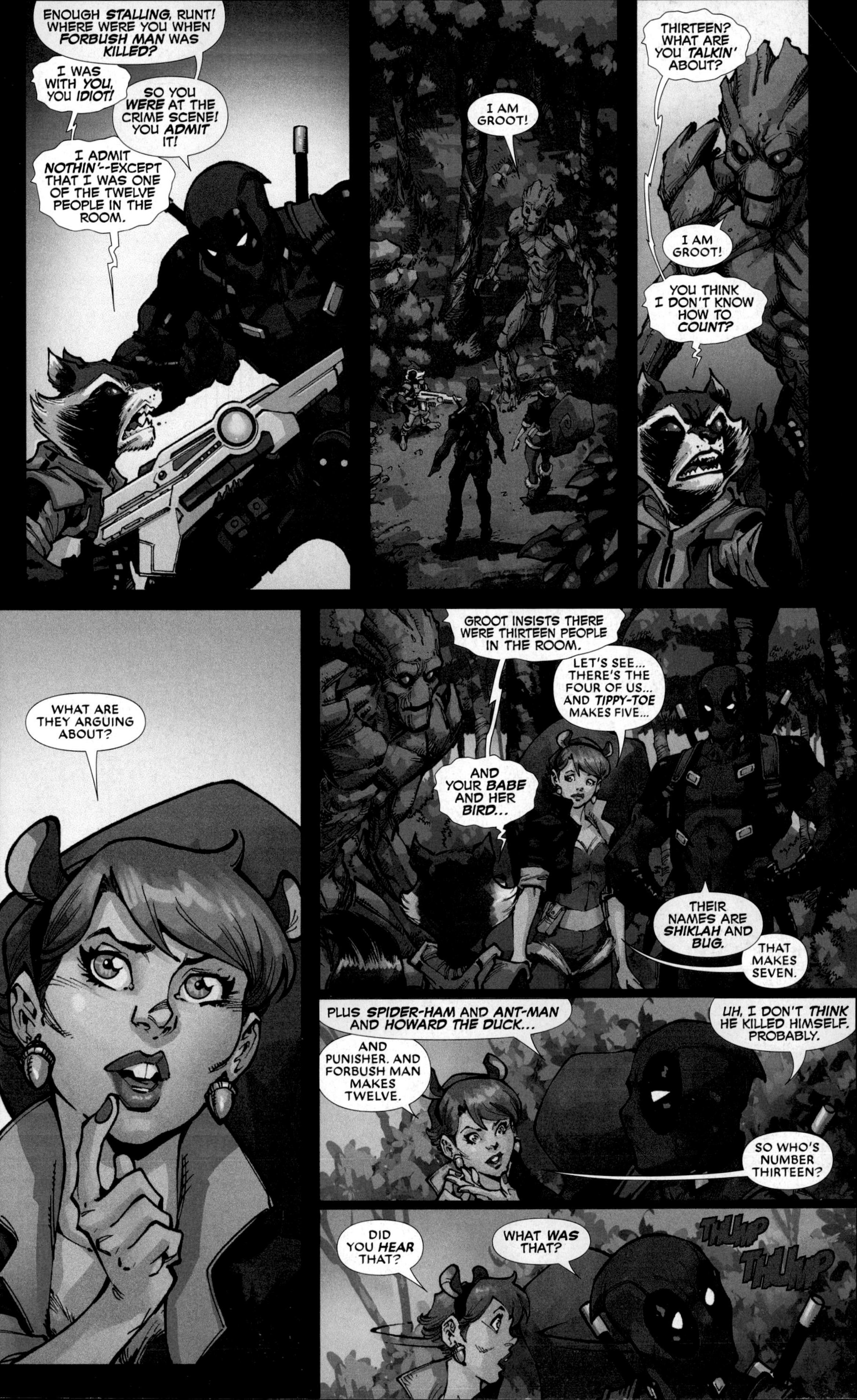
ENOUGH STALLING, RUNT! WHERE WERE YOU WHEN FORBUSH MAN WAS KILLED?
I WAS WITH YOU, YOU IDIOT!
SO YOU WERE AT THE CRIME SCENE! YOU ADMIT IT!
I ADMIT NOTHIN'--EXCEPT THAT I WAS ONE OF THE TWELVE PEOPLE IN THE ROOM.
I AM GROOT!
THIRTEEN? WHAT ARE YOU TALKIN' ABOUT?
I AM GROOT!
YOU THINK I DON'T KNOW HOW TO COUNT?
WHAT ARE THEY ARGUING ABOUT?
GROOT INSISTS THERE WERE THIRTEEN PEOPLE IN THE ROOM.
LET'S SEE... THERE'S THE FOUR OF US... AND TIPPY-TOE MAKES FIVE...
AND YOUR BABE AND HER BIRD...
THEIR NAMES ARE SHIKLAH AND BUG.
THAT MAKES SEVEN.
PLUS SPIDER-HAM AND ANT-MAN AND HOWARD THE DUCK...
AND PUNISHER. AND FORBUSH MAN MAKES TWELVE.
UH, I DON'T THINK HE KILLED HIMSELF. PROBABLY.
SO WHO'S NUMBER THIRTEEN?
DID YOU HEAR THAT?
WHAT WAS THAT?
THUMP
THUMP

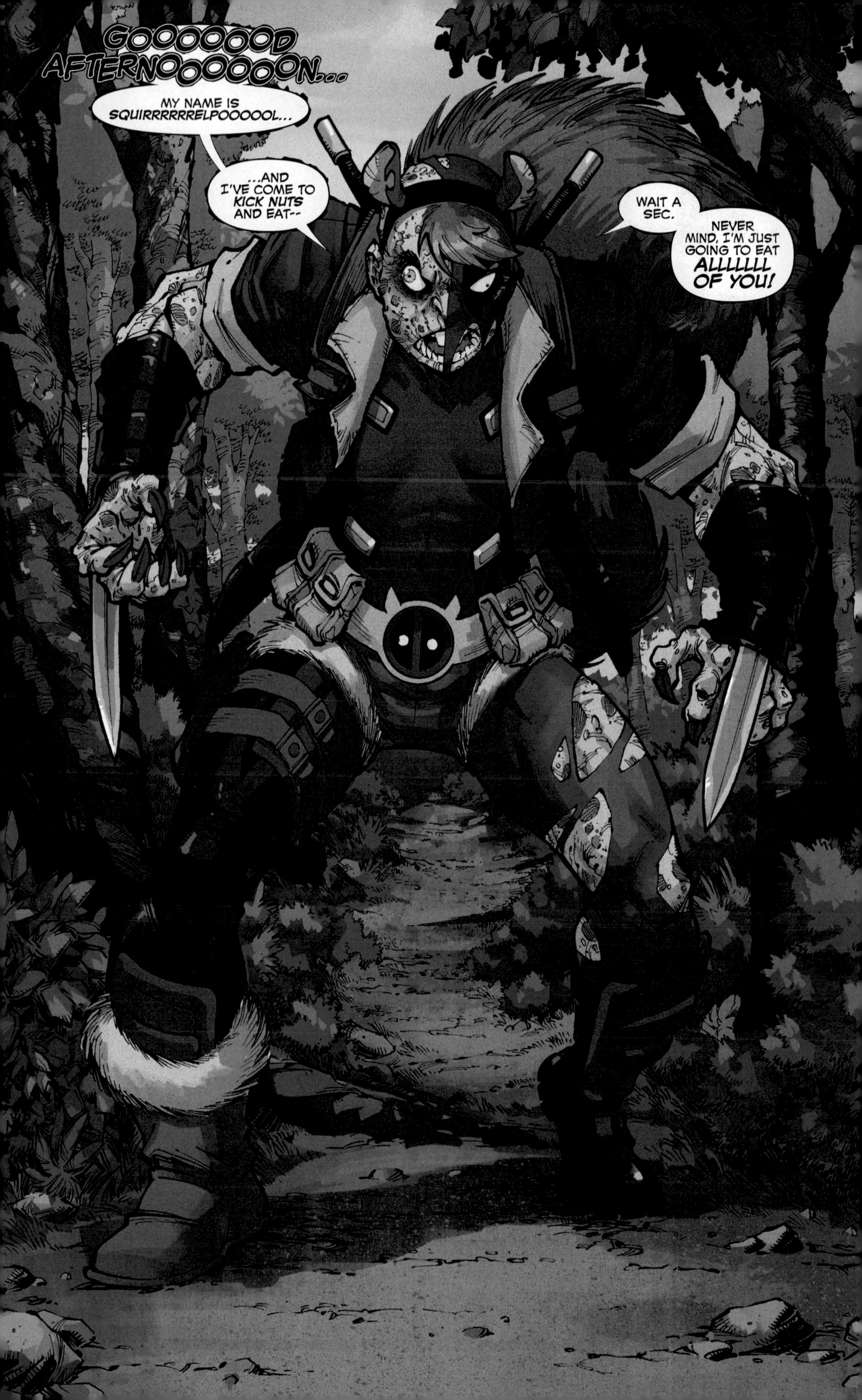
GOOOOOOOD AFTERNOOOOOOOON...
MY NAME IS SQUIRRRRRRELPOOOOOL...
...AND I'VE COME TO KICK NUTS AND EAT--
WAIT A SEC.
NEVER MIND, I'M JUST GOING TO EAT ALLLLLLL OF YOU!

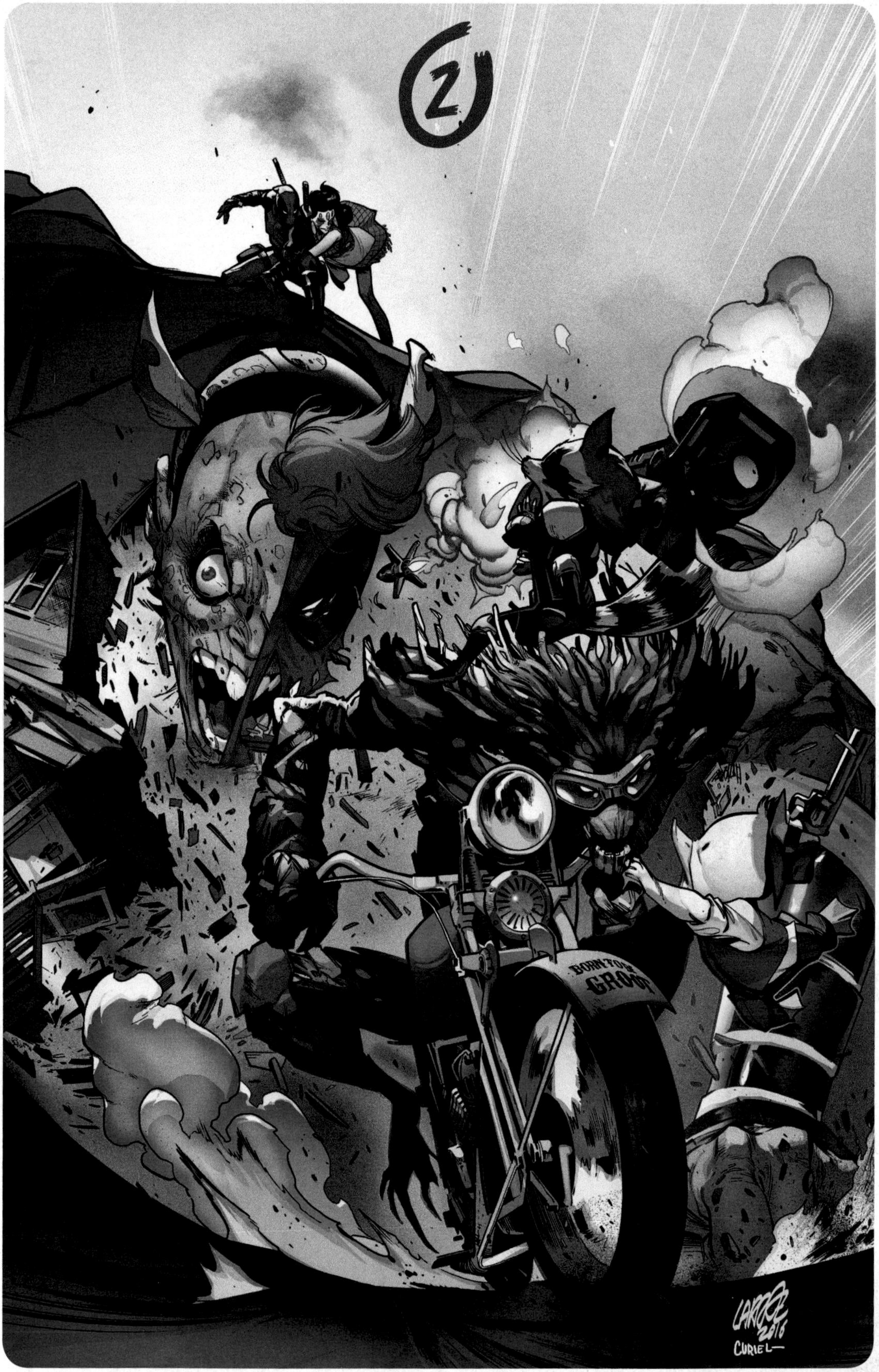
2
2016
CURIEL

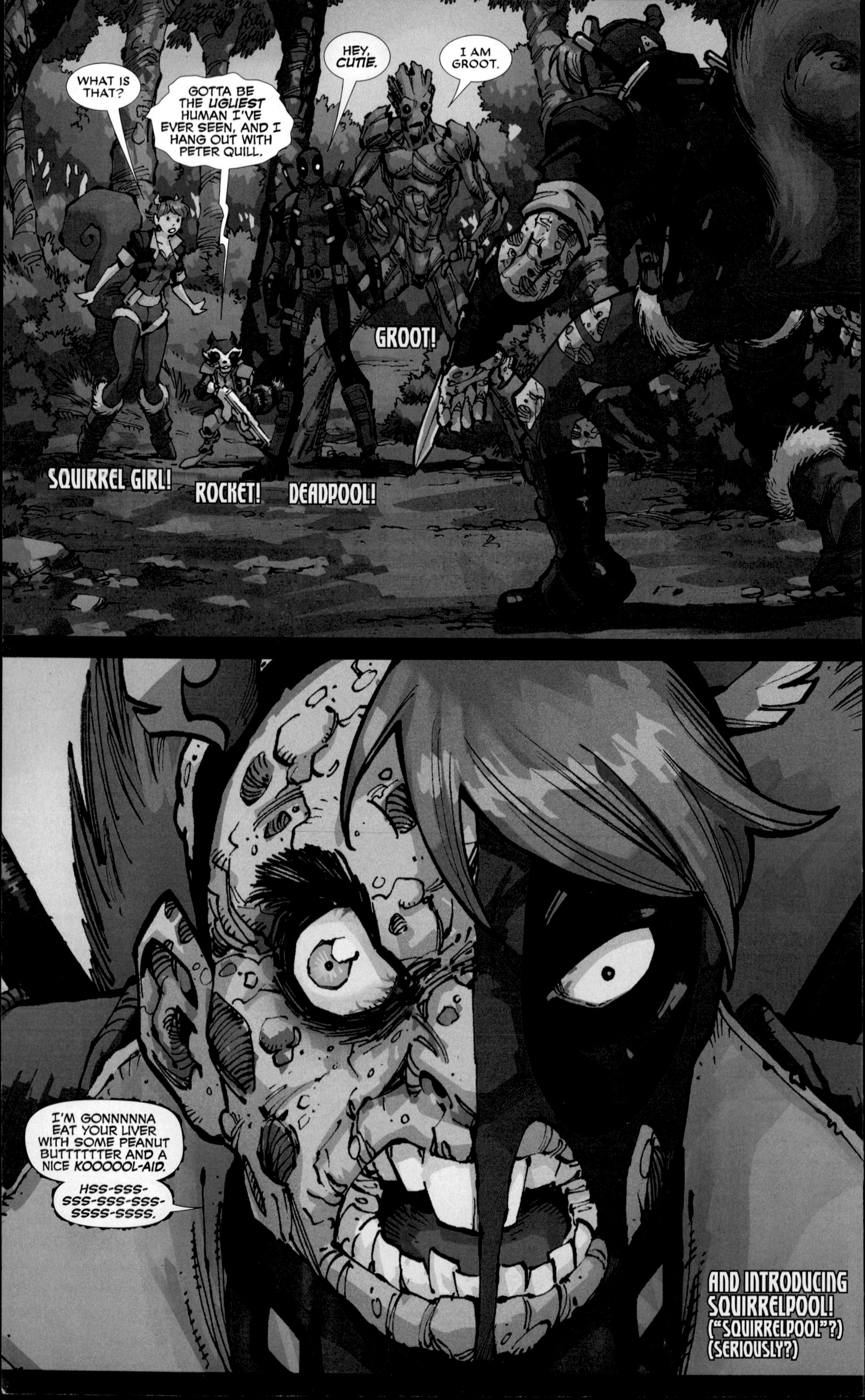

WHAT IS THAT?
GOTTA BE THE UGLIEST HUMAN I'VE EVER SEEN, AND I HANG OUT WITH PETER QUILL.
HEY, CUTIE.
I AM GROOT.
SQUIRREL GIRL!
ROCKET!
DEADPOOL!
GROOT!
I'M GONNNNNA EAT YOUR LIVER WITH SOME PEANUT BUTTTTTTER AND A NICE KOOOOOL-AID.
HSS-SSS-SSS-SSS-SSS-SSSS-SSSS.
AND INTRODUCING SQUIRRELPOOL!
("SQUIRRELPOOL"?)
(SERIOUSLY?)

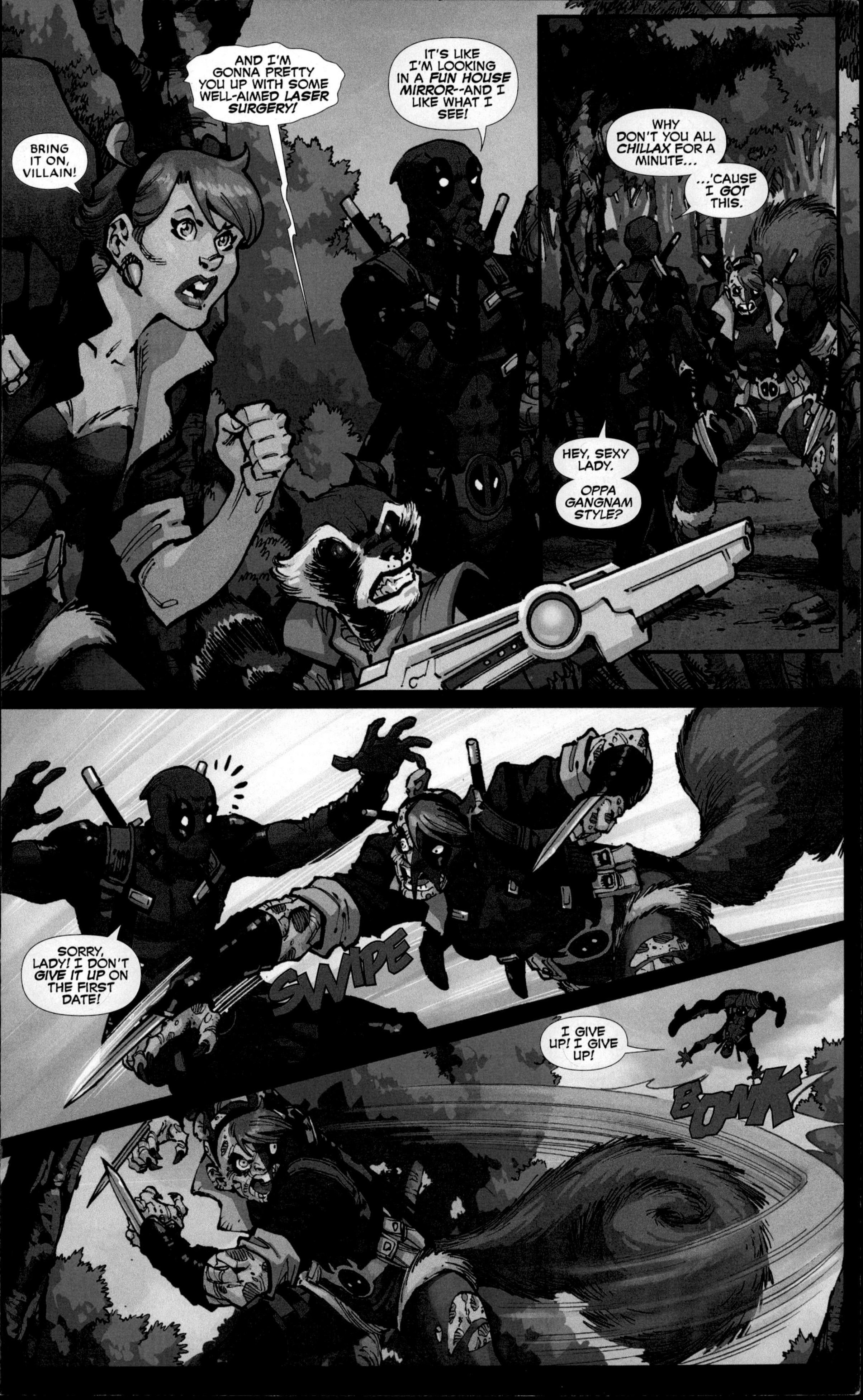
BRING IT ON, VILLAIN!
AND I'M GONNA PRETTY YOU UP WITH SOME WELL-AIMED LASER SURGERY!
IT'S LIKE I'M LOOKING IN A FUN HOUSE MIRROR--AND I LIKE WHAT I SEE!
WHY DON'T YOU ALL CHILLAX FOR A MINUTE...
...'CAUSE I GOT THIS.
HEY, SEXY LADY.
OPPA GANGNAM STYLE?
SORRY, LADY! I DON'T GIVE IT UP ON THE FIRST DATE!
SWIPE
I GIVE UP! I GIVE UP!
BONK

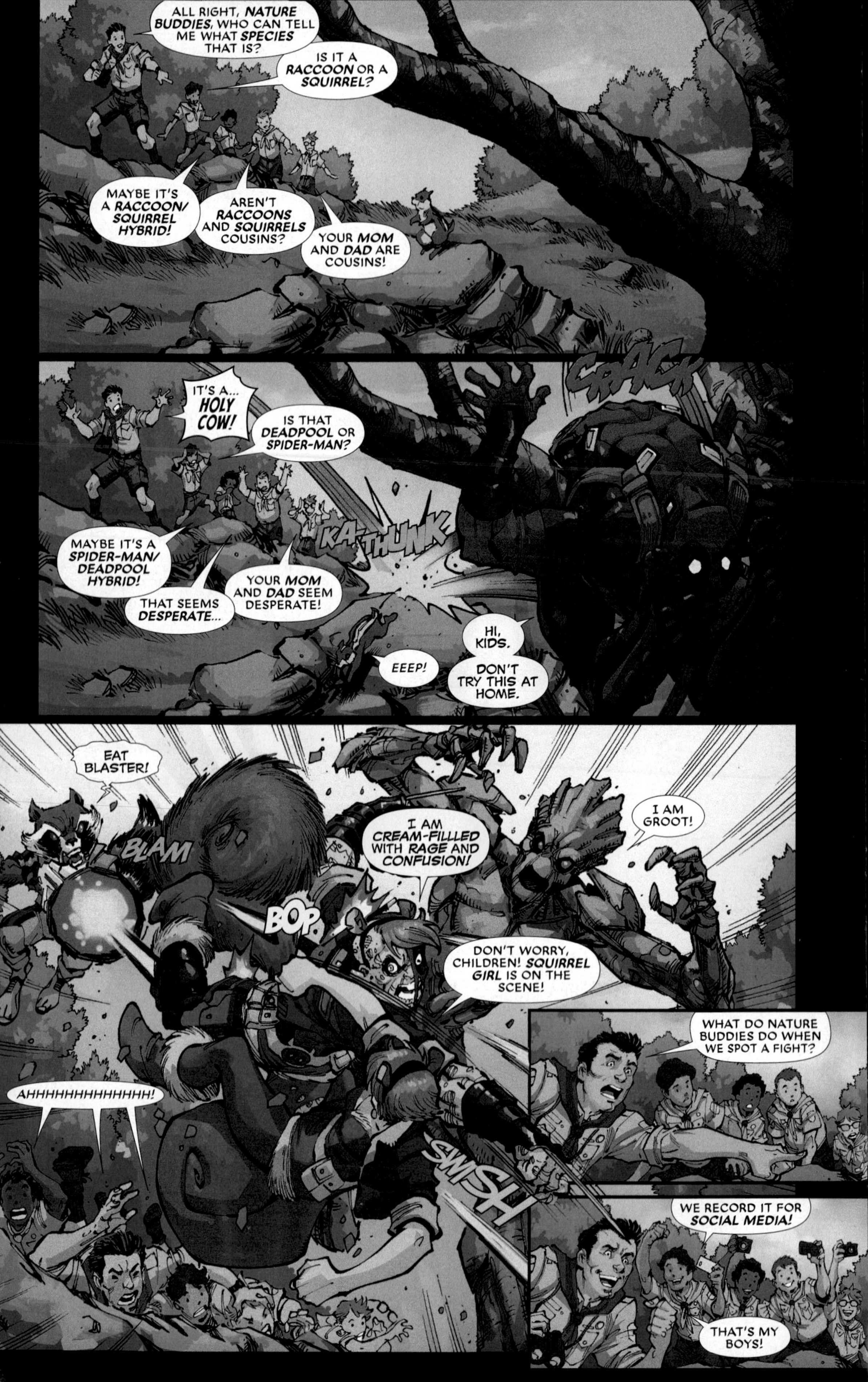
ALL RIGHT, NATURE BUDDIES, WHO CAN TELL ME WHAT SPECIES THAT IS?
IS IT A RACCOON OR A SQUIRREL?
MAYBE IT'S A RACCOON/ SQUIRREL HYBRID!
AREN'T RACCOONS AND SQUIRRELS COUSINS?
YOUR MOM AND DAD ARE COUSINS!
CRACK
IT'S A... HOLY COW!
IS THAT DEADPOOL OR SPIDER-MAN?
MAYBE IT'S A SPIDER-MAN/ DEADPOOL HYBRID!
THAT SEEMS DESPERATE...
YOUR MOM AND DAD SEEM DESPERATE!
KA-THUNK
EEEP!
HI, KIDS.
DON'T TRY THIS AT HOME.
EAT BLASTER!
BLAM
I AM CREAM-FILLED WITH RAGE AND CONFUSION!
I AM GROOT!
BOP
DON'T WORRY, CHILDREN! SQUIRREL GIRL IS ON THE SCENE!
AHHHHHHHHHHHHHH!
SWISH
WHAT DO NATURE BUDDIES DO WHEN WE SPOT A FIGHT?
WE RECORD IT FOR SOCIAL MEDIA!
THAT'S MY BOYS!

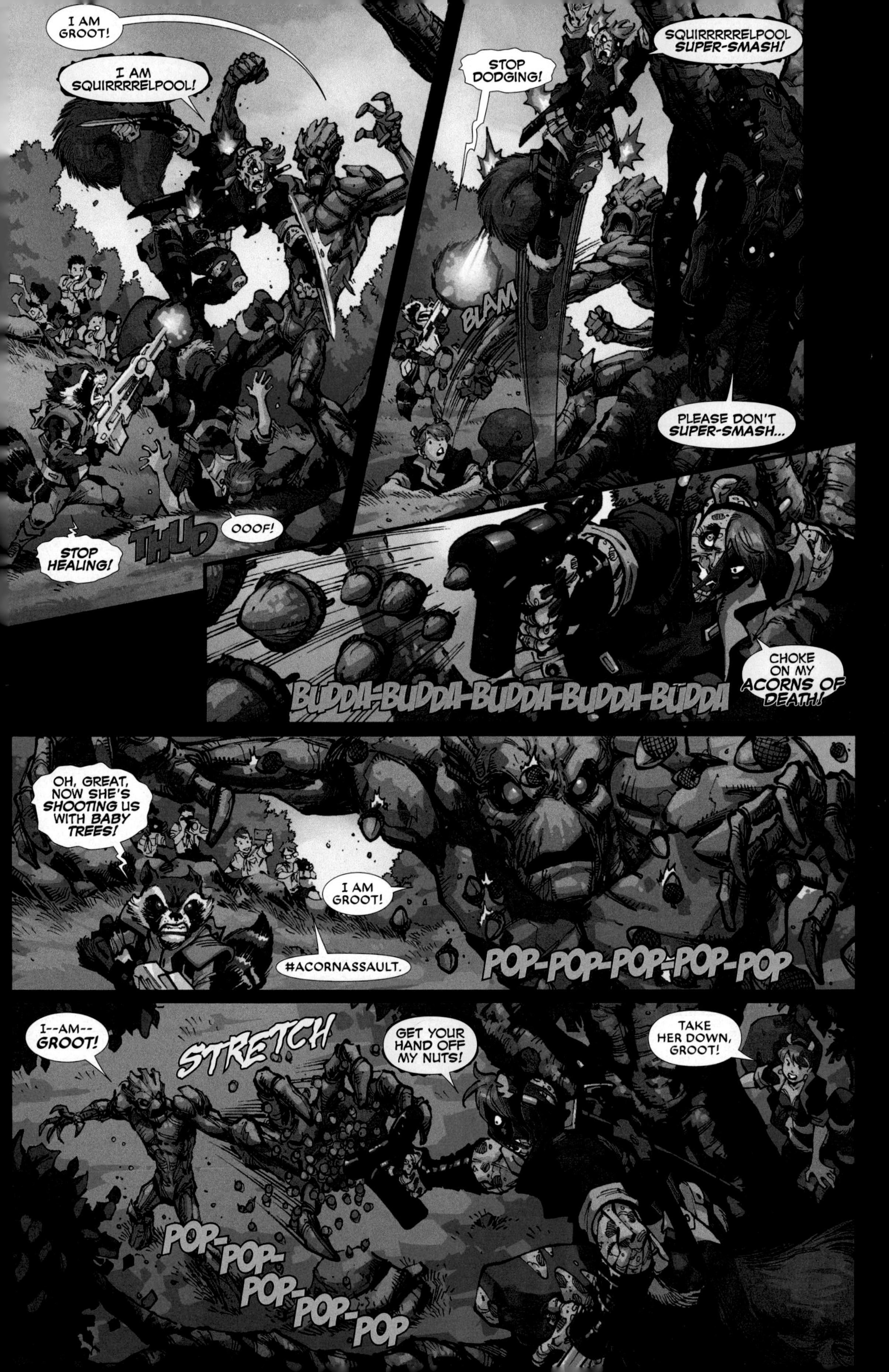
I AM GROOT!
I AM SQUIRRRRELPOOL!
STOP HEALING!
THUD
OOOF!
STOP DODGING!
SQUIRRRRRELPOOL SUPER-SMASH!
BLAM
PLEASE DON'T SUPER-SMASH...
BUDDA-BUDDA-BUDDA-BUDDA-BUDDA
CHOKE ON MY ACORNS OF DEATH!
OH, GREAT, NOW SHE'S SHOOTING US WITH BABY TREES!
I AM GROOT!
#ACORNASSAULT.
POP-POP-POP-POP-POP
I--AM--GROOT!
STRETCH
GET YOUR HAND OFF MY NUTS!
TAKE HER DOWN, GROOT!
POP-POP-POP-POP-POP

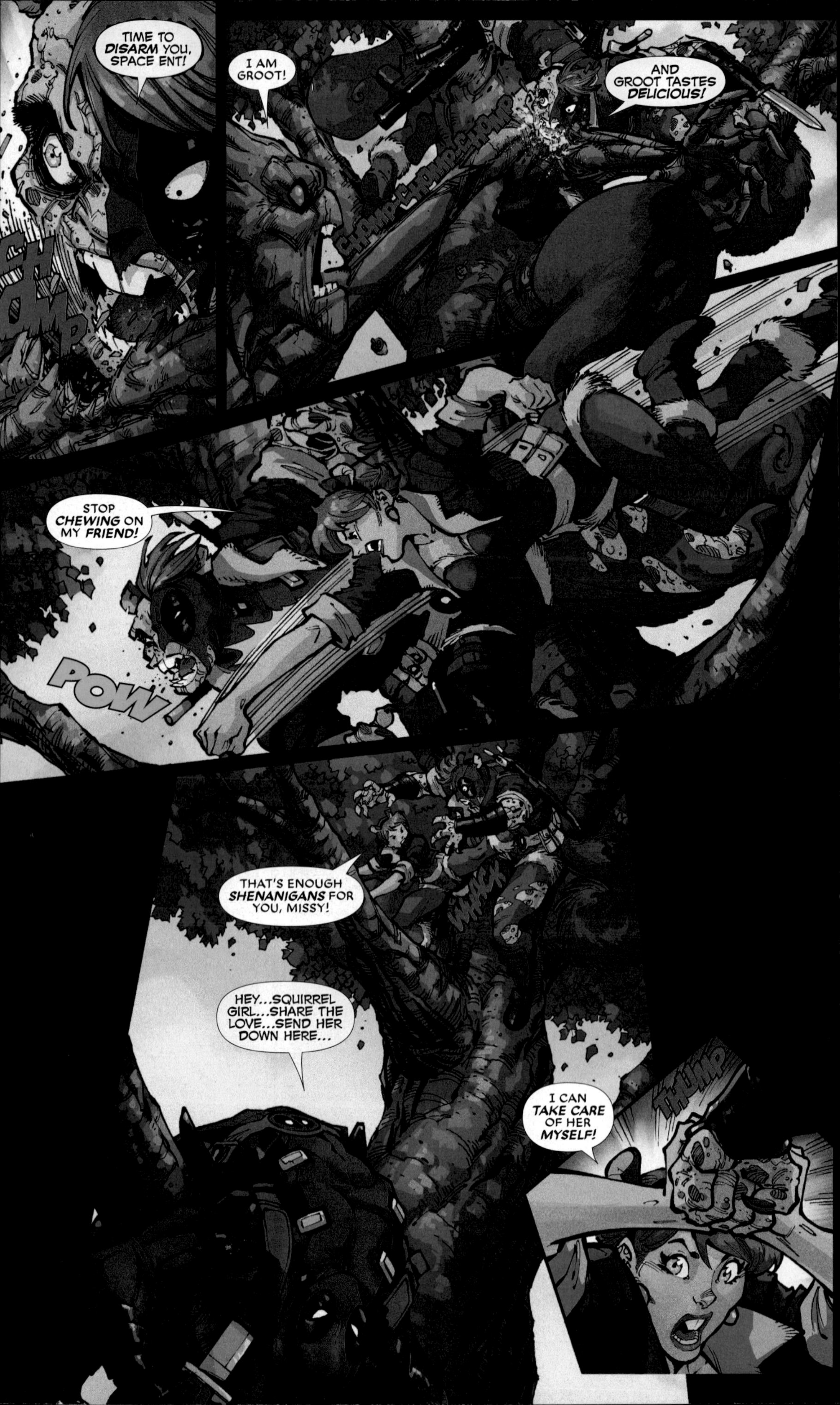

TIME TO DISARM YOU, SPACE ENT!
I AM GROOT!
CHOMP-CHOMP-CHOMP
AND GROOT TASTES DELICIOUS!
STOP CHEWING ON MY FRIEND!
POW!
THAT'S ENOUGH SHENANIGANS FOR YOU, MISSY!
HEY...SQUIRREL GIRL...SHARE THE LOVE...SEND HER DOWN HERE...
THUMP
I CAN TAKE CARE OF HER MYSELF!

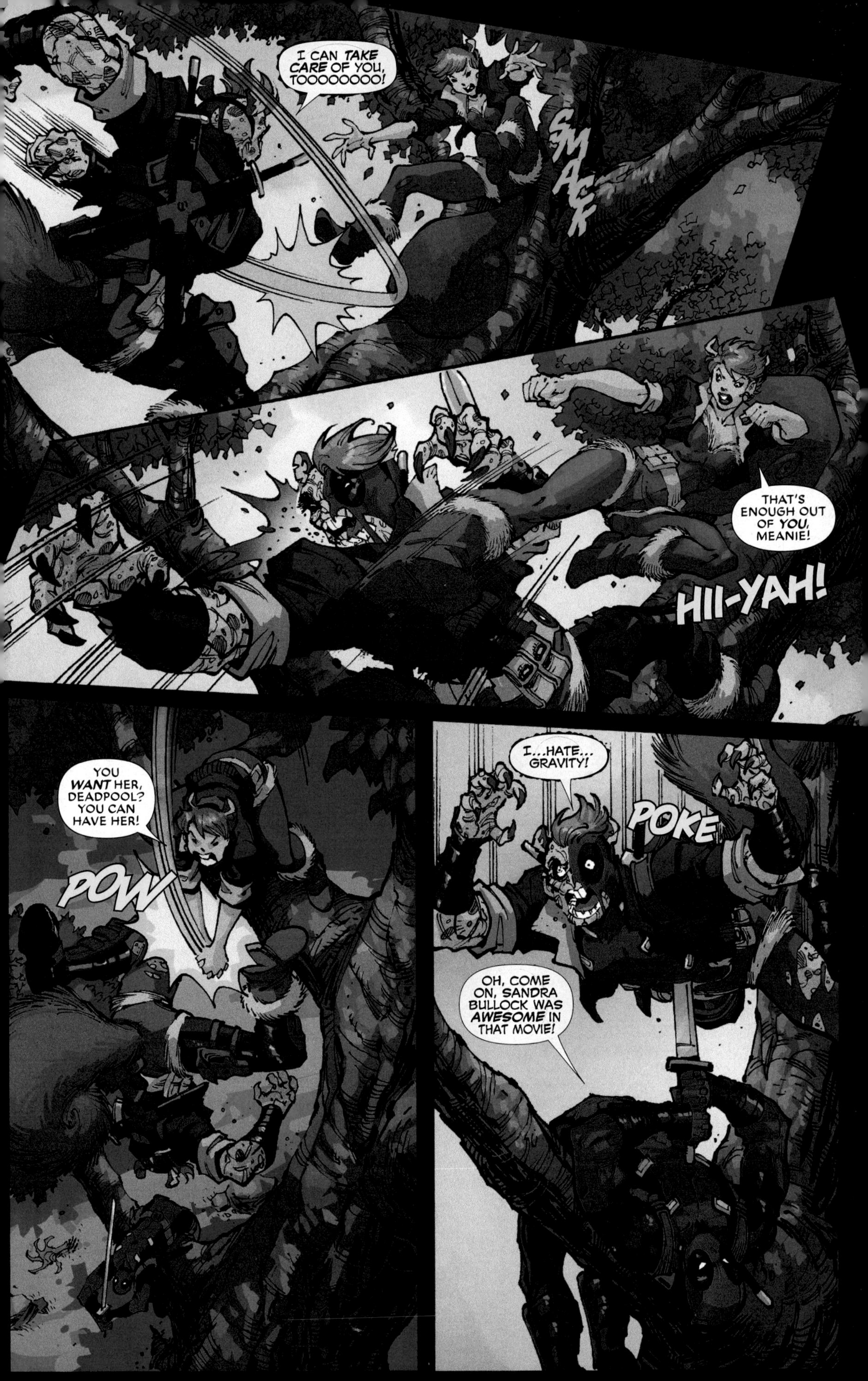
I CAN TAKE CARE OF YOU, TOOOOOOOOO!
SMACK
THAT'S ENOUGH OUT OF YOU, MEANIE!
HII-YAH!
YOU WANT HER, DEADPOOL? YOU CAN HAVE HER!
POW
I...HATE... GRAVITY!
POKE
OH, COME ON, SANDRA BULLOCK WAS AWESOME IN THAT MOVIE!

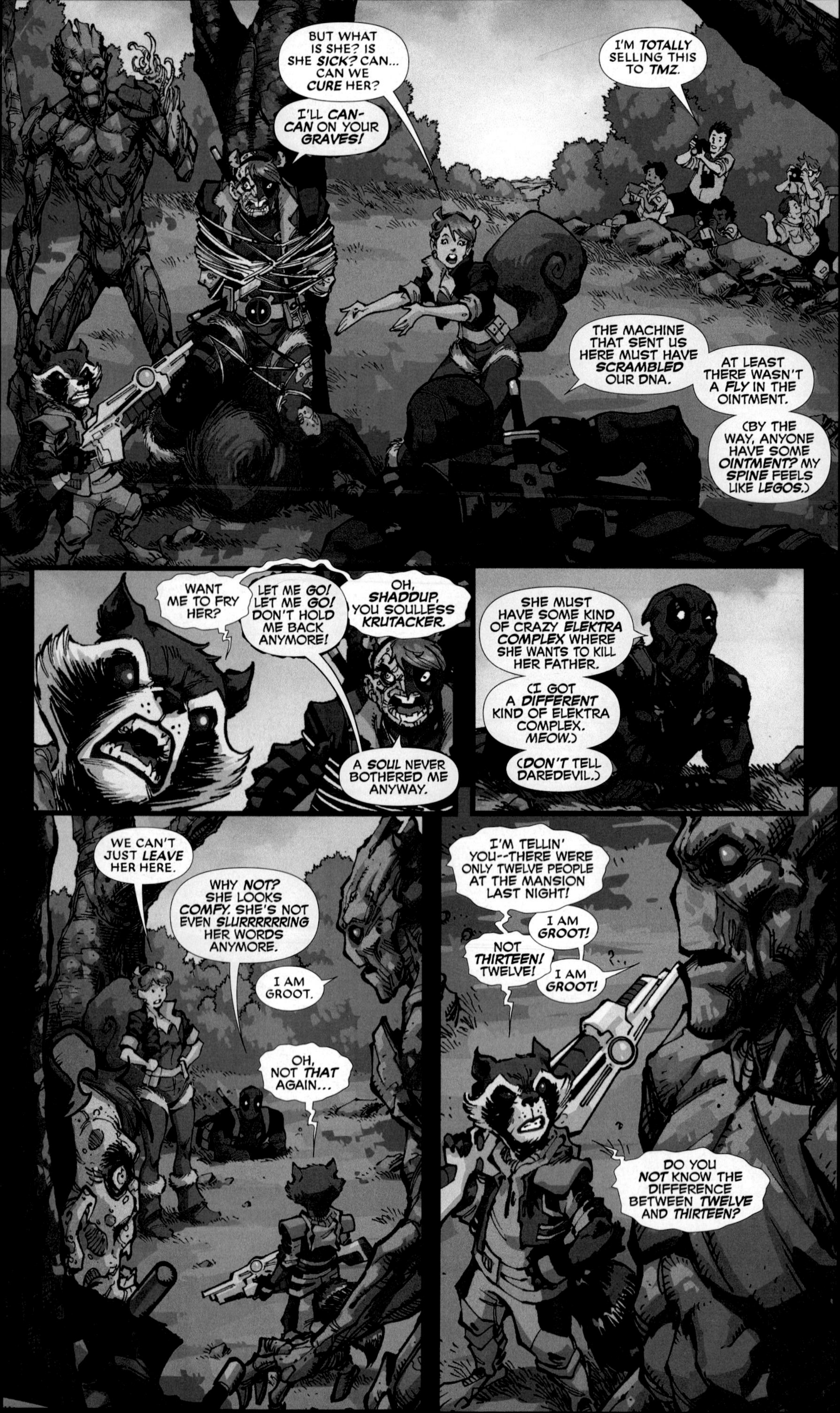
BUT WHAT IS SHE? IS SHE SICK? CAN... CAN WE CURE HER?
I'LL CAN-CAN ON YOUR GRAVES!
I'M TOTALLY SELLING THIS TO TMZ.
THE MACHINE THAT SENT US HERE MUST HAVE SCRAMBLED OUR DNA.
AT LEAST THERE WASN'T A FLY IN THE OINTMENT.
(BY THE WAY, ANYONE HAVE SOME OINTMENT? MY SPINE FEELS LIKE LEGOS.)
WANT ME TO FRY HER?
LET ME GO! LET ME GO! DON'T HOLD ME BACK ANYMORE!
OH, SHADDUP, YOU SOULLESS KRUTACKER.
A SOUL NEVER BOTHERED ME ANYWAY.
SHE MUST HAVE SOME KIND OF CRAZY ELEKTRA COMPLEX WHERE SHE WANTS TO KILL HER FATHER.
(I GOT A DIFFERENT KIND OF ELEKTRA COMPLEX. MEOW.)
(DON'T TELL DAREDEVIL.)
WE CAN'T JUST LEAVE HER HERE.
WHY NOT? SHE LOOKS COMFY. SHE'S NOT EVEN SLURRRRRRING HER WORDS ANYMORE.
I AM GROOT.
OH, NOT THAT AGAIN...
I'M TELLIN' YOU--THERE WERE ONLY TWELVE PEOPLE AT THE MANSION LAST NIGHT!
I AM GROOT!
NOT THIRTEEN! TWELVE!
I AM GROOT!
DO YOU NOT KNOW THE DIFFERENCE BETWEEN TWELVE AND THIRTEEN?

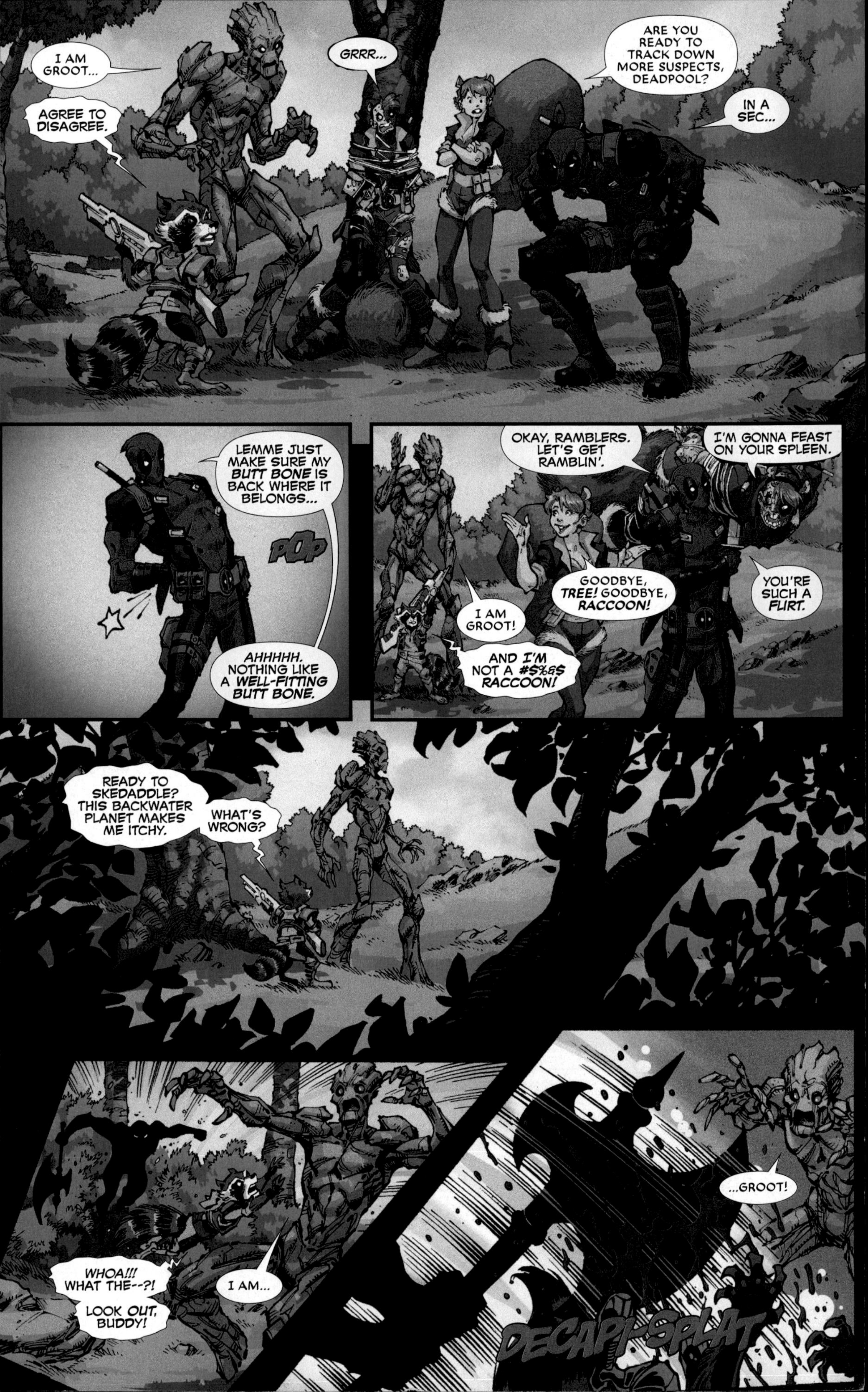
I AM GROOT...
AGREE TO DISAGREE.
GRRR...
ARE YOU READY TO TRACK DOWN MORE SUSPECTS, DEADPOOL?
IN A SEC...
LEMME JUST MAKE SURE MY BUTT BONE IS BACK WHERE IT BELONGS...
POP
AHHHHH. NOTHING LIKE A WELL-FITTING BUTT BONE.
OKAY, RAMBLERS. LET'S GET RAMBLIN'.
I'M GONNA FEAST ON YOUR SPLEEN.
GOODBYE, TREE! GOODBYE, RACCOON!
YOU'RE SUCH A FLIRT.
I AM GROOT!
AND I'M NOT A #$%&$ RACCOON!
READY TO SKEDADDLE? THIS BACKWATER PLANET MAKES ME ITCHY.
WHAT'S WRONG?
WHOA!!! WHAT THE--?!
LOOK OUT, BUDDY!
I AM...
...GROOT!
DECAPI-SPLAT

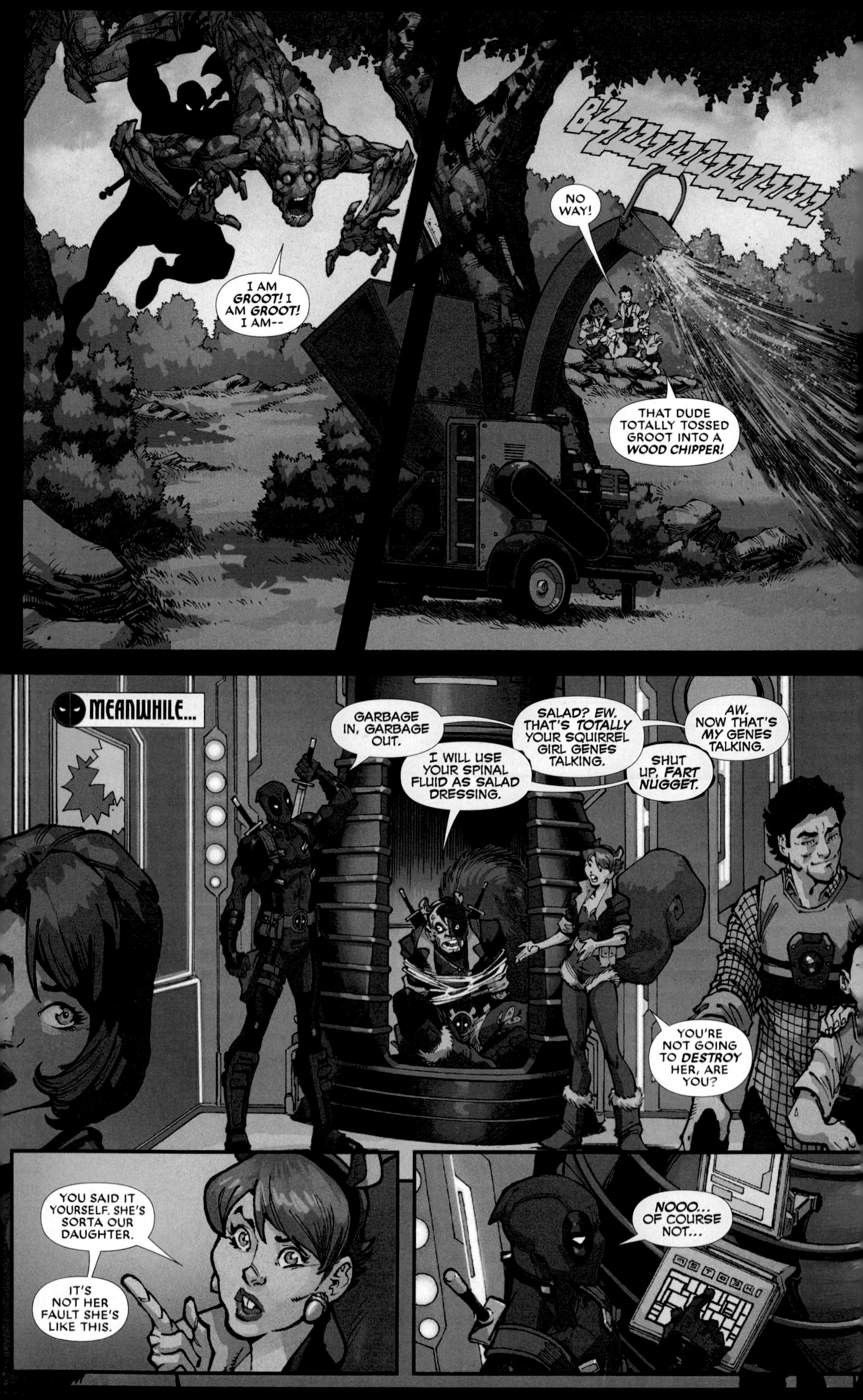
I AM GROOT! I AM GROOT! I AM--
BZZZZZZZZZZZZZZZZZZZ
NO WAY!
THAT DUDE TOTALLY TOSSED GROOT INTO A WOOD CHIPPER!
MEANWHILE...
GARBAGE IN, GARBAGE OUT.
I WILL USE YOUR SPINAL FLUID AS SALAD DRESSING.
SALAD? EW. THAT'S TOTALLY YOUR SQUIRREL GIRL GENES TALKING.
AW. NOW THAT'S MY GENES TALKING.
SHUT UP, FART NUGGET.
YOU'RE NOT GOING TO DESTROY HER, ARE YOU?
YOU SAID IT YOURSELF. SHE'S SORTA OUR DAUGHTER.
IT'S NOT HER FAULT SHE'S LIKE THIS.
NOOO... OF COURSE NOT...

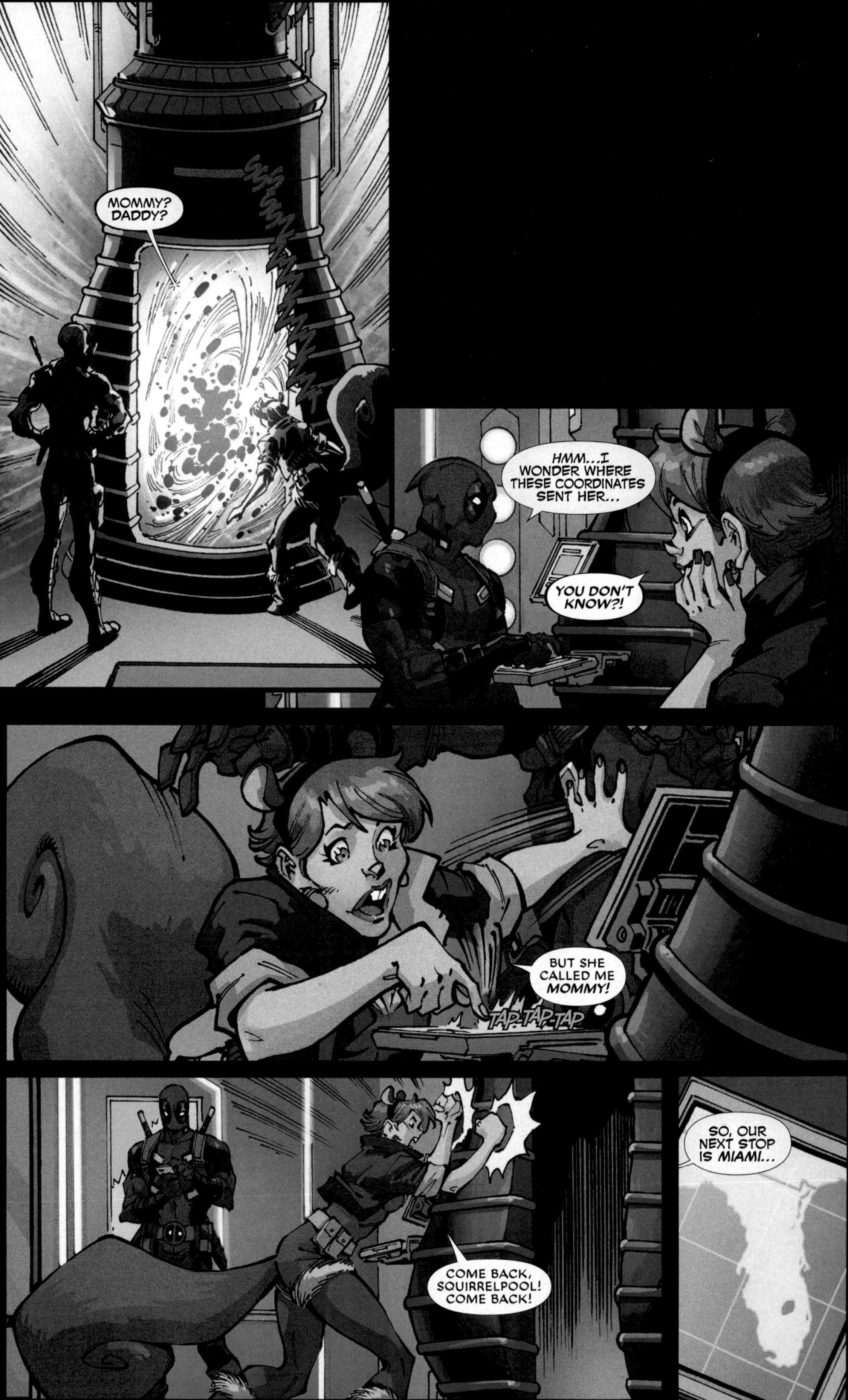
MOMMY? DADDY?
HMM...I WONDER WHERE THESE COORDINATES SENT HER...
YOU DON'T KNOW?!
BUT SHE CALLED ME MOMMY!
TAP-TAP-TAP
COME BACK, SQUIRRELPOOL! COME BACK!
SO, OUR NEXT STOP IS MIAMI...

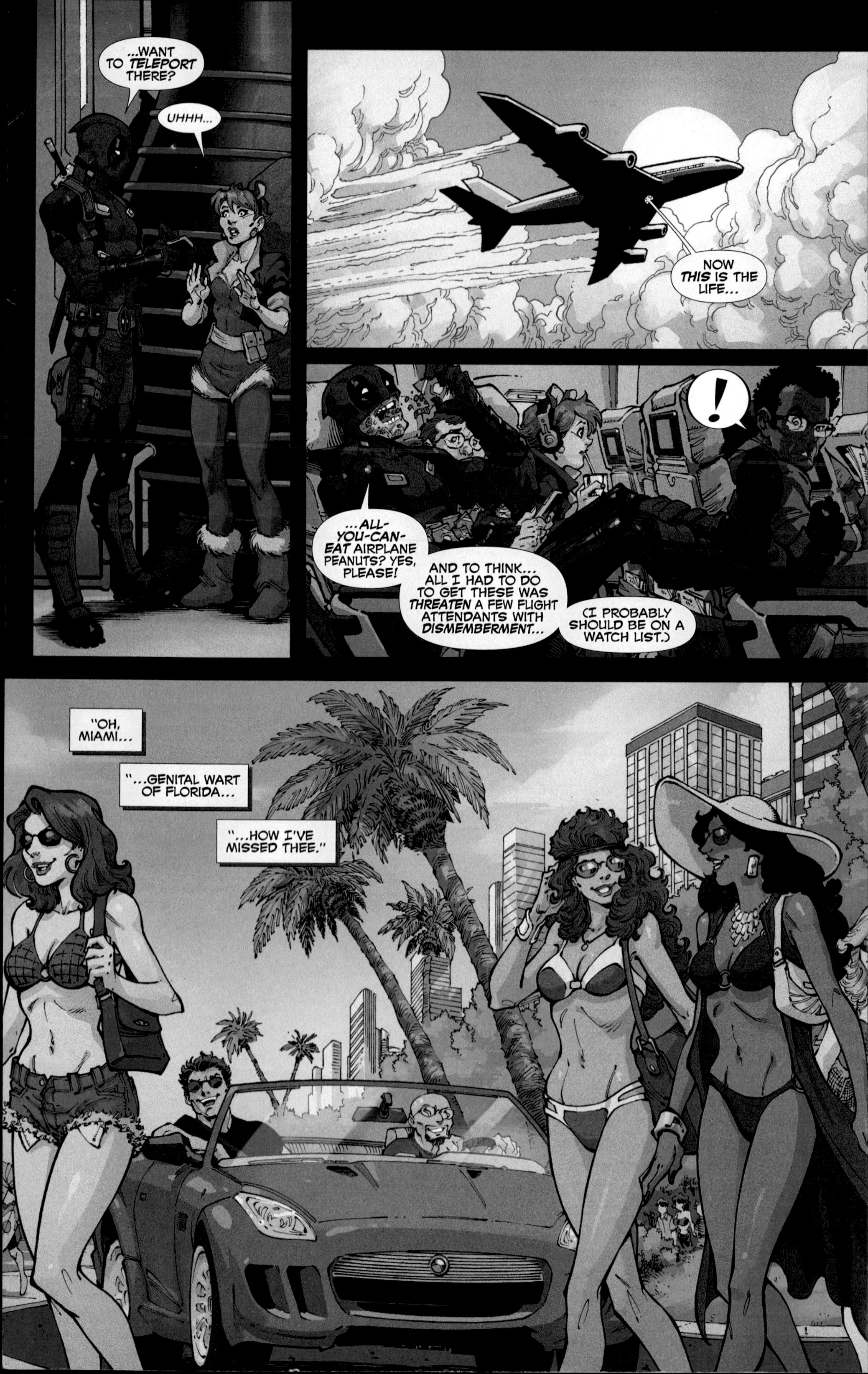
...WANT TO TELEPORT THERE?
UHHH...
NOW THIS IS THE LIFE...
!
...ALL-YOU-CAN-EAT AIRPLANE PEANUTS? YES, PLEASE!
AND TO THINK... ALL I HAD TO DO TO GET THESE WAS THREATEN A FEW FLIGHT ATTENDANTS WITH DISMEMBERMENT...
(I PROBABLY SHOULD BE ON A WATCH LIST.)
"OH, MIAMI...
"...GENITAL WART OF FLORIDA...
"...HOW I'VE MISSED THEE."

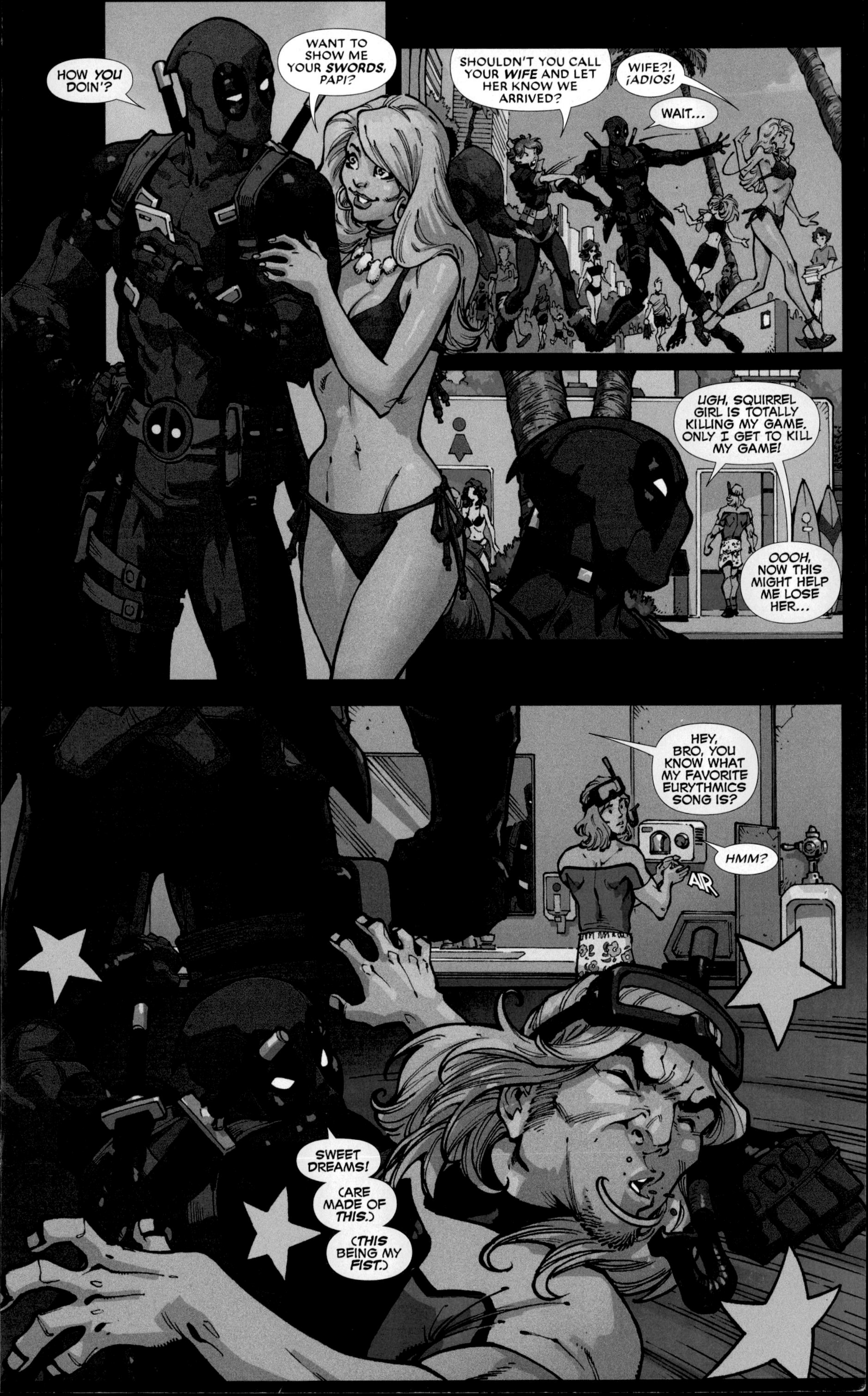
HOW *YOU* DOIN'?
WANT TO SHOW ME YOUR ***SWORDS***, PAPI?
SHOULDN'T YOU CALL YOUR ***WIFE*** AND LET HER KNOW WE ARRIVED?
WIFE?! ¡ADIOS!
WAIT...
UGH, SQUIRREL GIRL IS TOTALLY KILLING MY GAME. ONLY I GET TO KILL MY GAME!
OOOH, NOW THIS MIGHT HELP ME LOSE HER...
HEY, BRO, YOU KNOW WHAT MY FAVORITE EURYTHMICS SONG IS?
HMM?
AIR
SWEET DREAMS!
(ARE MADE OF *THIS*.)
(*THIS* BEING MY *FIST*.)

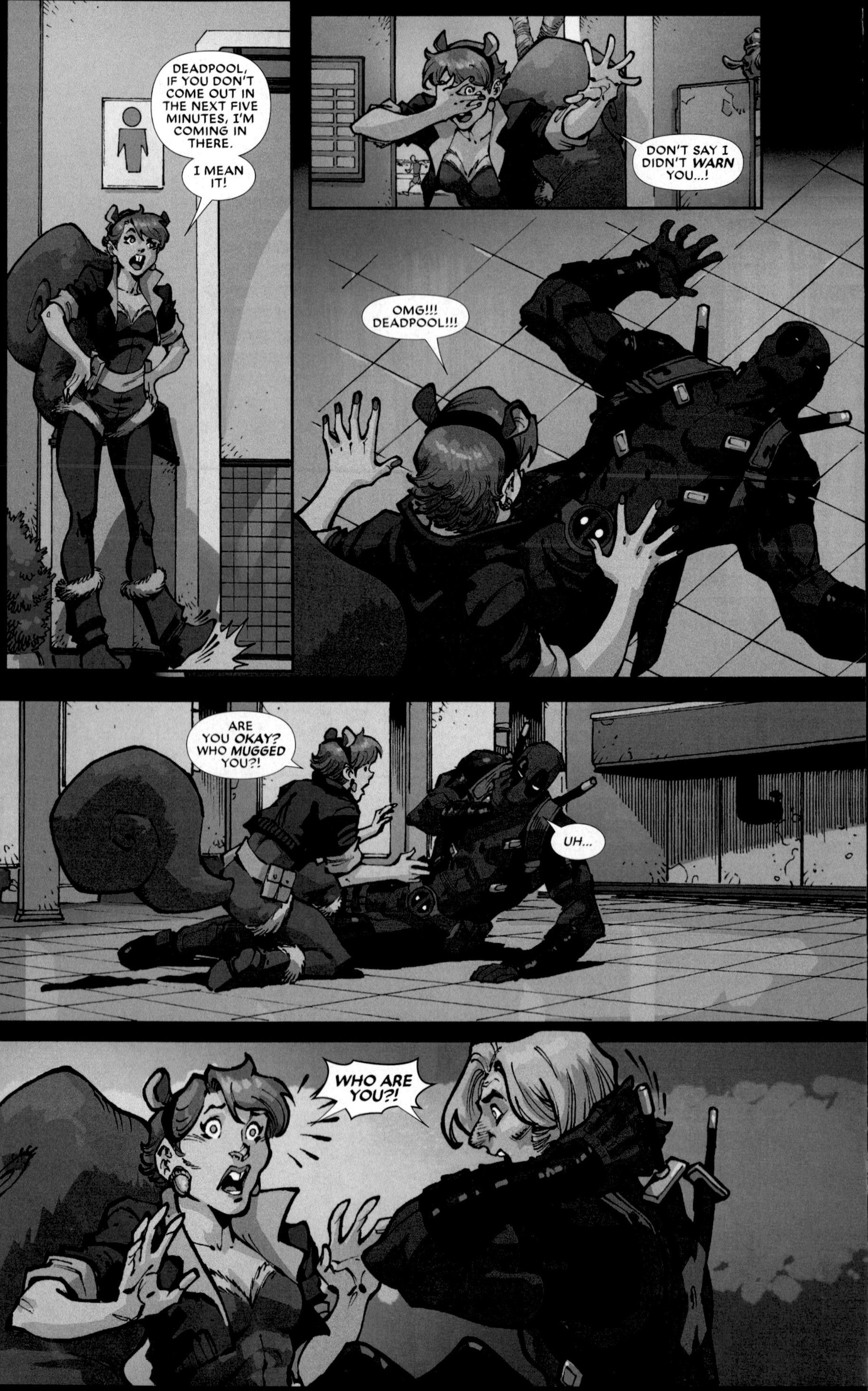
DEADPOOL, IF YOU DON'T COME OUT IN THE NEXT FIVE MINUTES, I'M COMING IN THERE.
I MEAN IT!
DON'T SAY I DIDN'T WARN YOU...!
OMG!!! DEADPOOL!!!
ARE YOU OKAY? WHO MUGGED YOU?!
UH...
WHO ARE YOU?!

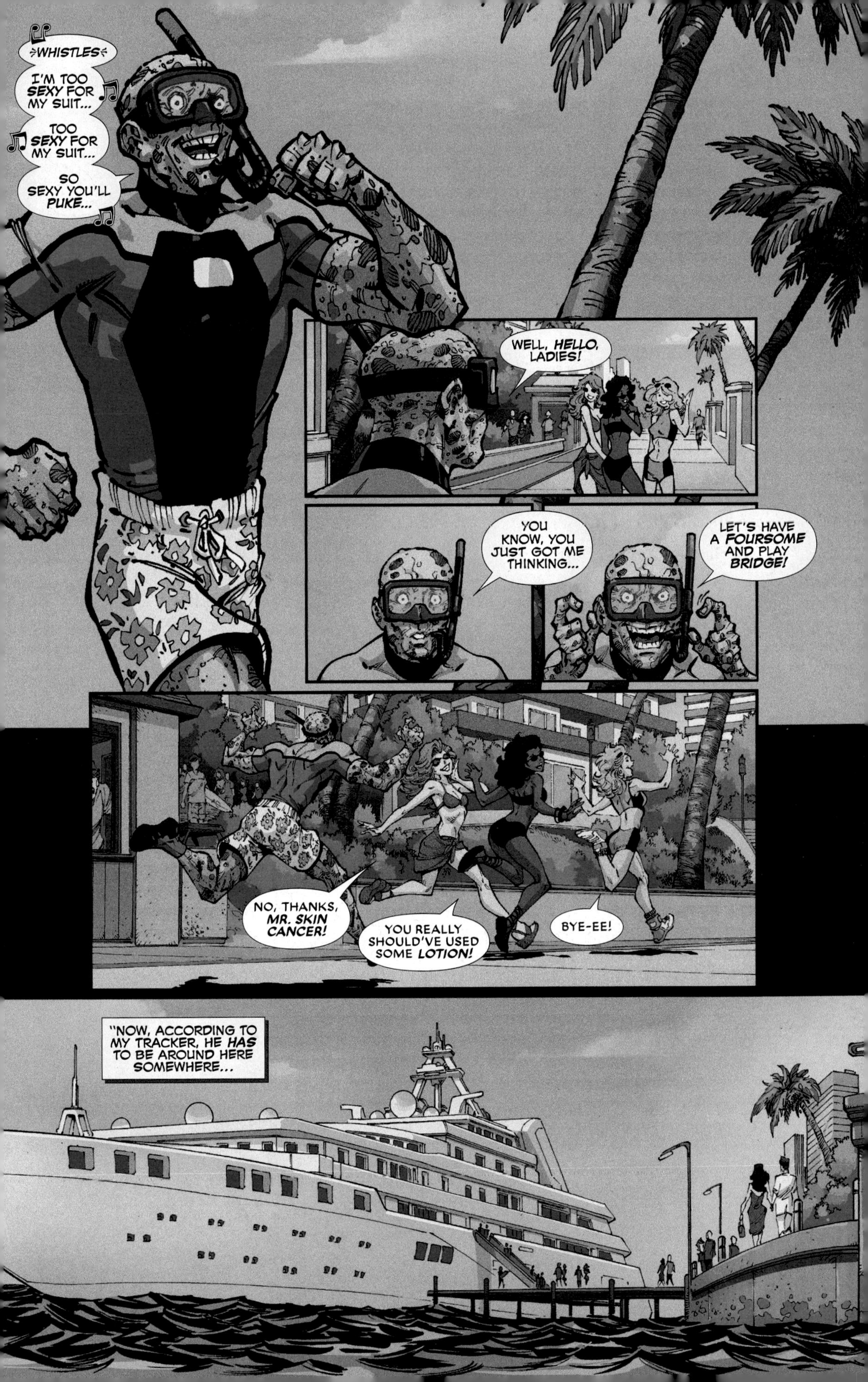
WHISTLES
I'M TOO SEXY FOR MY SUIT...
TOO SEXY FOR MY SUIT...
SO SEXY YOU'LL PUKE...
WELL, HELLO, LADIES!
YOU KNOW, YOU JUST GOT ME THINKING...
LET'S HAVE A FOURSOME AND PLAY BRIDGE!
NO, THANKS, MR. SKIN CANCER!
YOU REALLY SHOULD'VE USED SOME LOTION!
BYE-EE!
"NOW, ACCORDING TO MY TRACKER, HE HAS TO BE AROUND HERE SOMEWHERE...

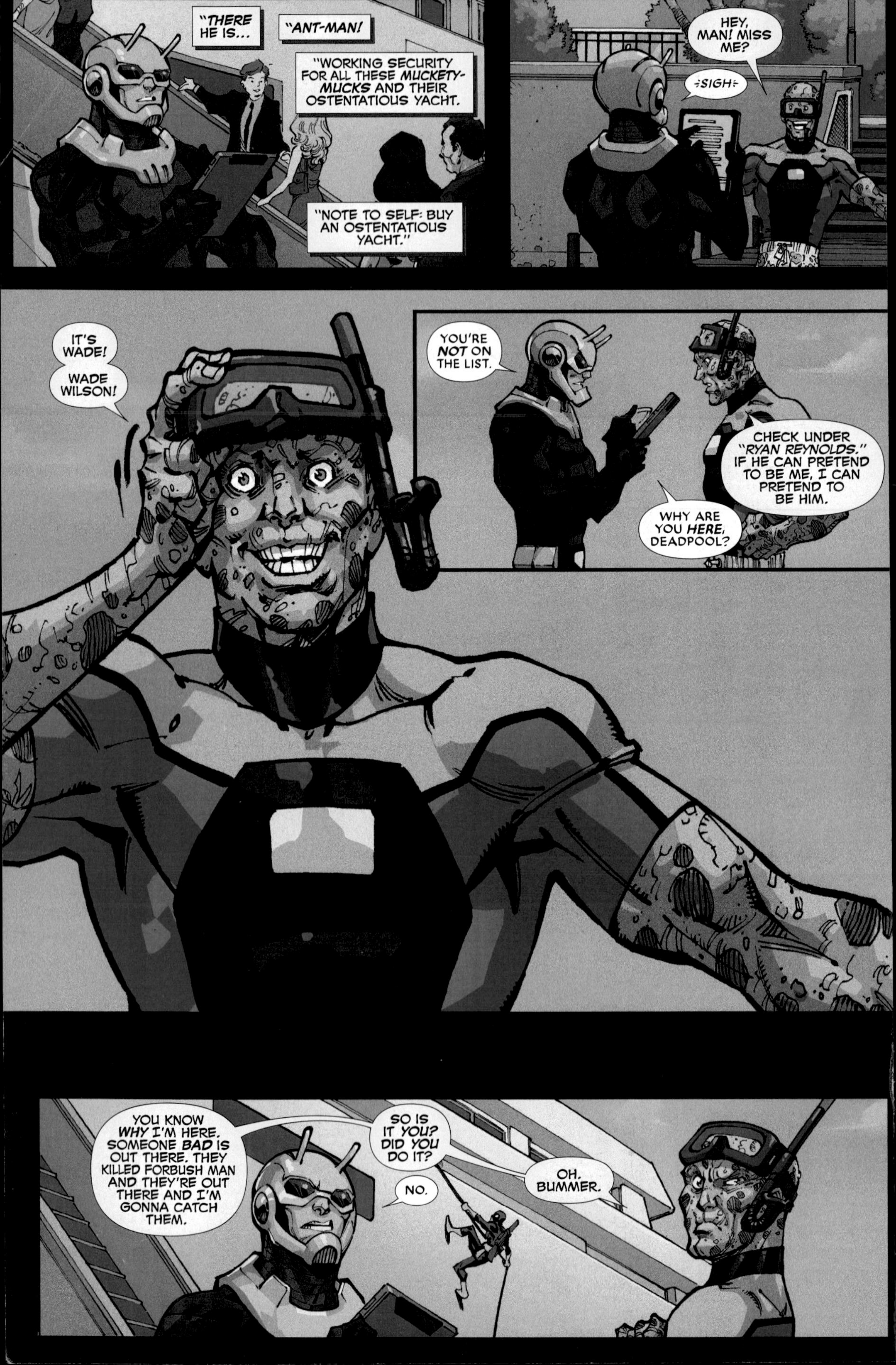

"THERE HE IS...
"ANT-MAN!
"WORKING SECURITY FOR ALL THESE MUCKETY-MUCKS AND THEIR OSTENTATIOUS YACHT.
"NOTE TO SELF: BUY AN OSTENTATIOUS YACHT."
HEY, MAN! MISS ME?
SIGH
IT'S WADE!
WADE WILSON!
YOU'RE NOT ON THE LIST.
CHECK UNDER "RYAN REYNOLDS." IF HE CAN PRETEND TO BE ME, I CAN PRETEND TO BE HIM.
WHY ARE YOU HERE, DEADPOOL?
YOU KNOW WHY I'M HERE. SOMEONE BAD IS OUT THERE. THEY KILLED FORBUSH MAN AND THEY'RE OUT THERE AND I'M GONNA CATCH THEM.
SO IS IT YOU? DID YOU DO IT?
NO.
OH. BUMMER.

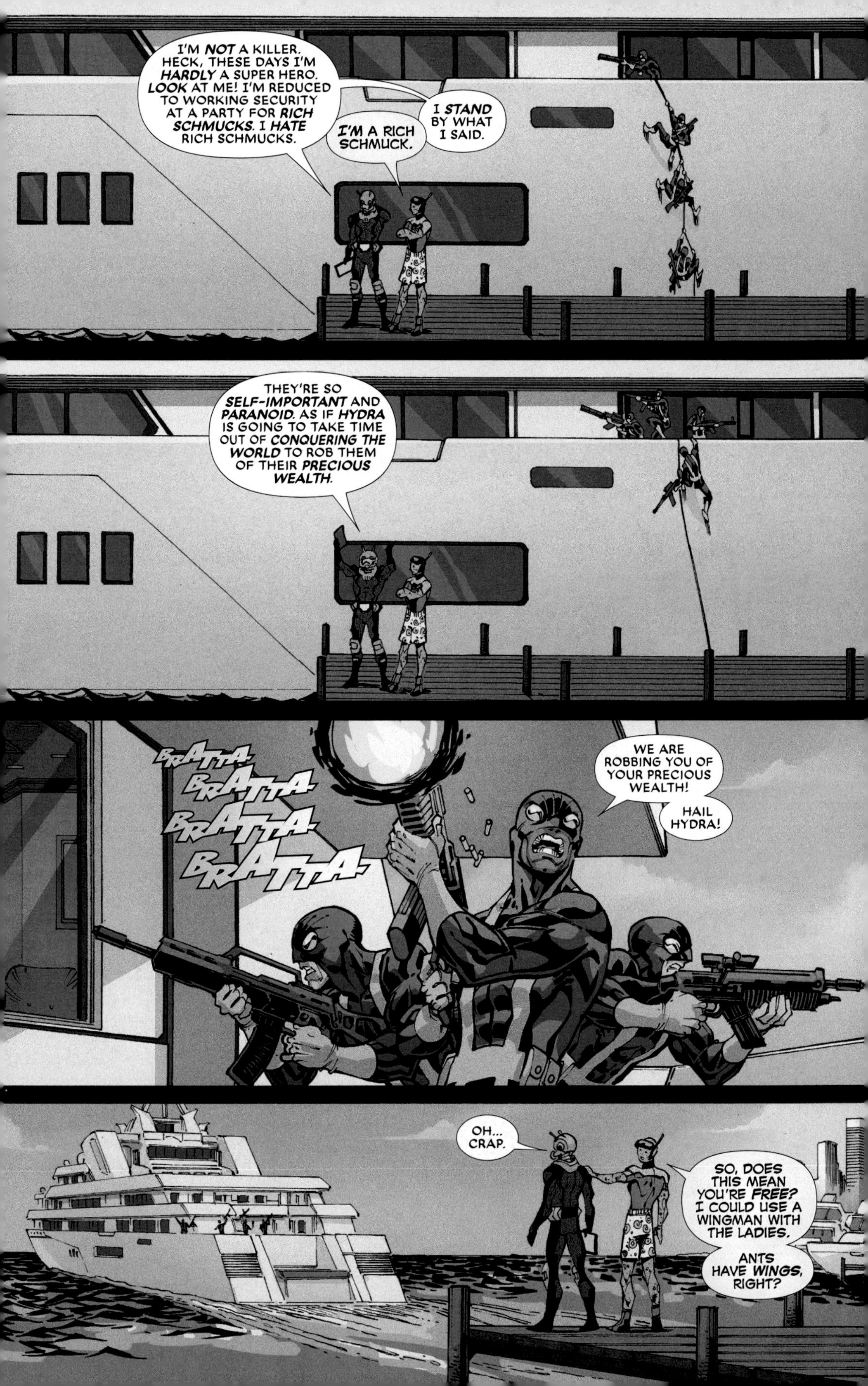
I'M NOT A KILLER. HECK, THESE DAYS I'M HARDLY A SUPER HERO. LOOK AT ME! I'M REDUCED TO WORKING SECURITY AT A PARTY FOR RICH SCHMUCKS. I HATE RICH SCHMUCKS.
I'M A RICH SCHMUCK.
I STAND BY WHAT I SAID.
THEY'RE SO SELF-IMPORTANT AND PARANOID. AS IF HYDRA IS GOING TO TAKE TIME OUT OF CONQUERING THE WORLD TO ROB THEM OF THEIR PRECIOUS WEALTH.
BRATTA BRATTA BRATTA BRATTA
WE ARE ROBBING YOU OF YOUR PRECIOUS WEALTH!
HAIL HYDRA!
OH... CRAP.
SO, DOES THIS MEAN YOU'RE FREE? I COULD USE A WINGMAN WITH THE LADIES.
ANTS HAVE WINGS, RIGHT?

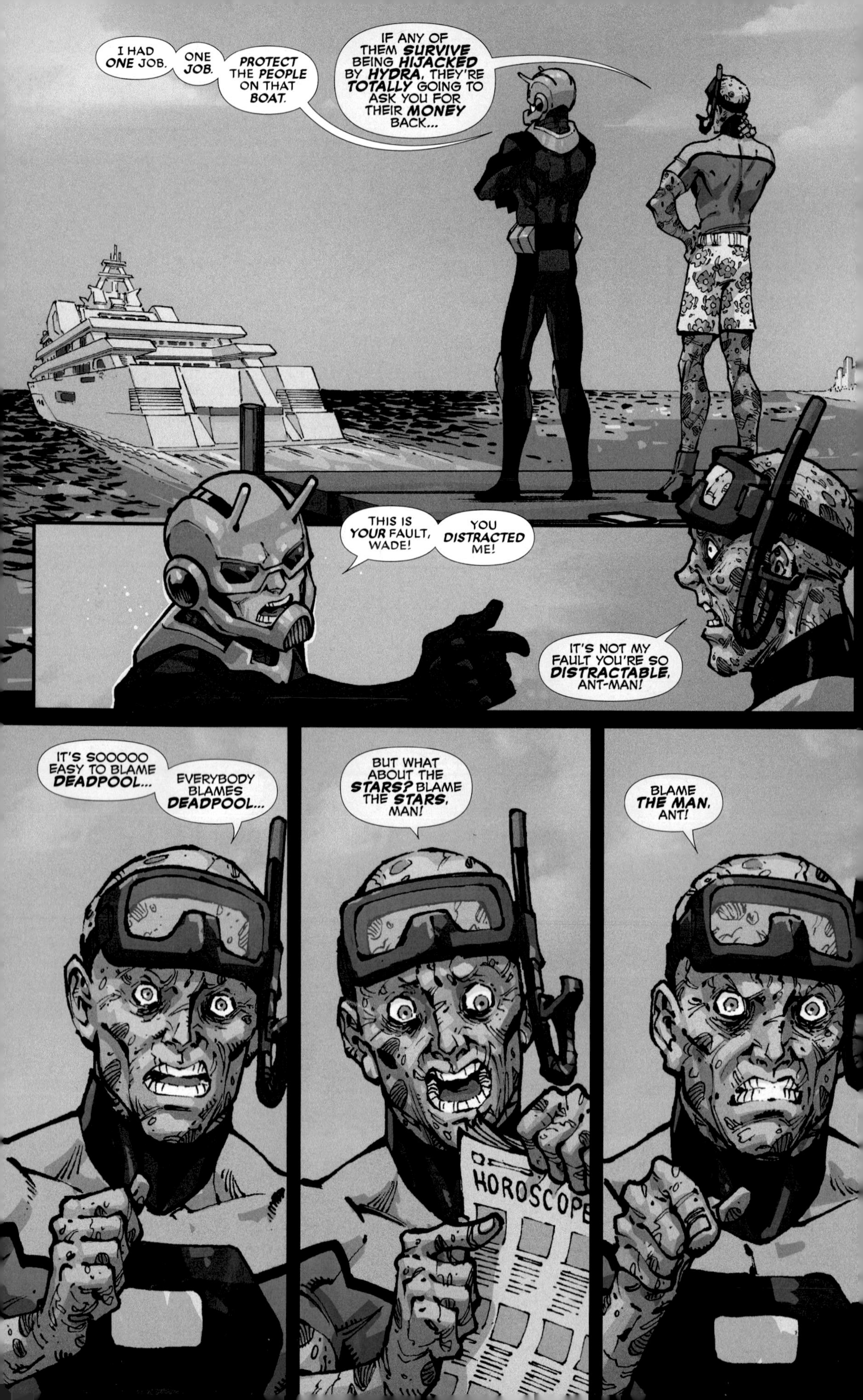

I HAD ONE JOB.
ONE JOB.
PROTECT THE PEOPLE ON THAT BOAT.
IF ANY OF THEM SURVIVE BEING HIJACKED BY HYDRA, THEY'RE TOTALLY GOING TO ASK YOU FOR THEIR MONEY BACK...
THIS IS YOUR FAULT, WADE!
YOU DISTRACTED ME!
IT'S NOT MY FAULT YOU'RE SO DISTRACTABLE, ANT-MAN!
IT'S SOOOOO EASY TO BLAME DEADPOOL...
EVERYBODY BLAMES DEADPOOL...
BUT WHAT ABOUT THE STARS? BLAME THE STARS, MAN!
HOROSCOPE
BLAME THE MAN, ANT!

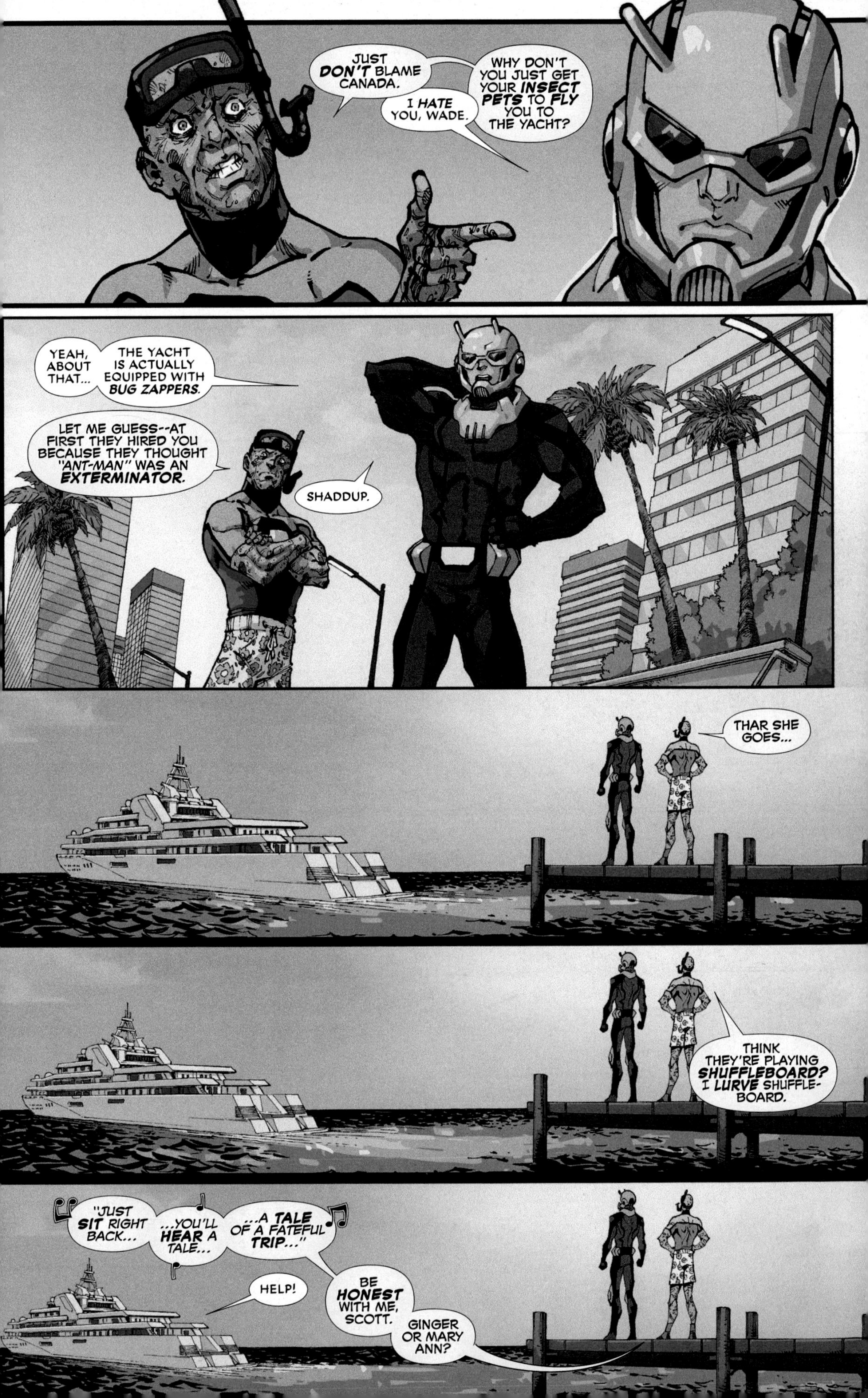
JUST **DON'T** BLAME CANADA.
WHY DON'T YOU JUST GET YOUR **INSECT PETS** TO **FLY** YOU TO THE YACHT?
I **HATE** YOU, WADE.
YEAH, ABOUT THAT...
THE YACHT IS ACTUALLY EQUIPPED WITH **BUG ZAPPERS**.
LET ME GUESS--AT FIRST THEY HIRED YOU BECAUSE THEY THOUGHT "ANT-MAN" WAS AN **EXTERMINATOR**.
SHADDUP.
THAR SHE GOES...
THINK THEY'RE PLAYING **SHUFFLEBOARD?** I **LURVE** SHUFFLE-BOARD.
"JUST **SIT** RIGHT BACK...
...YOU'LL **HEAR** A TALE...
...A **TALE** OF A FATEFUL **TRIP**..."
HELP!
BE **HONEST** WITH ME, SCOTT.
GINGER OR MARY ANN?

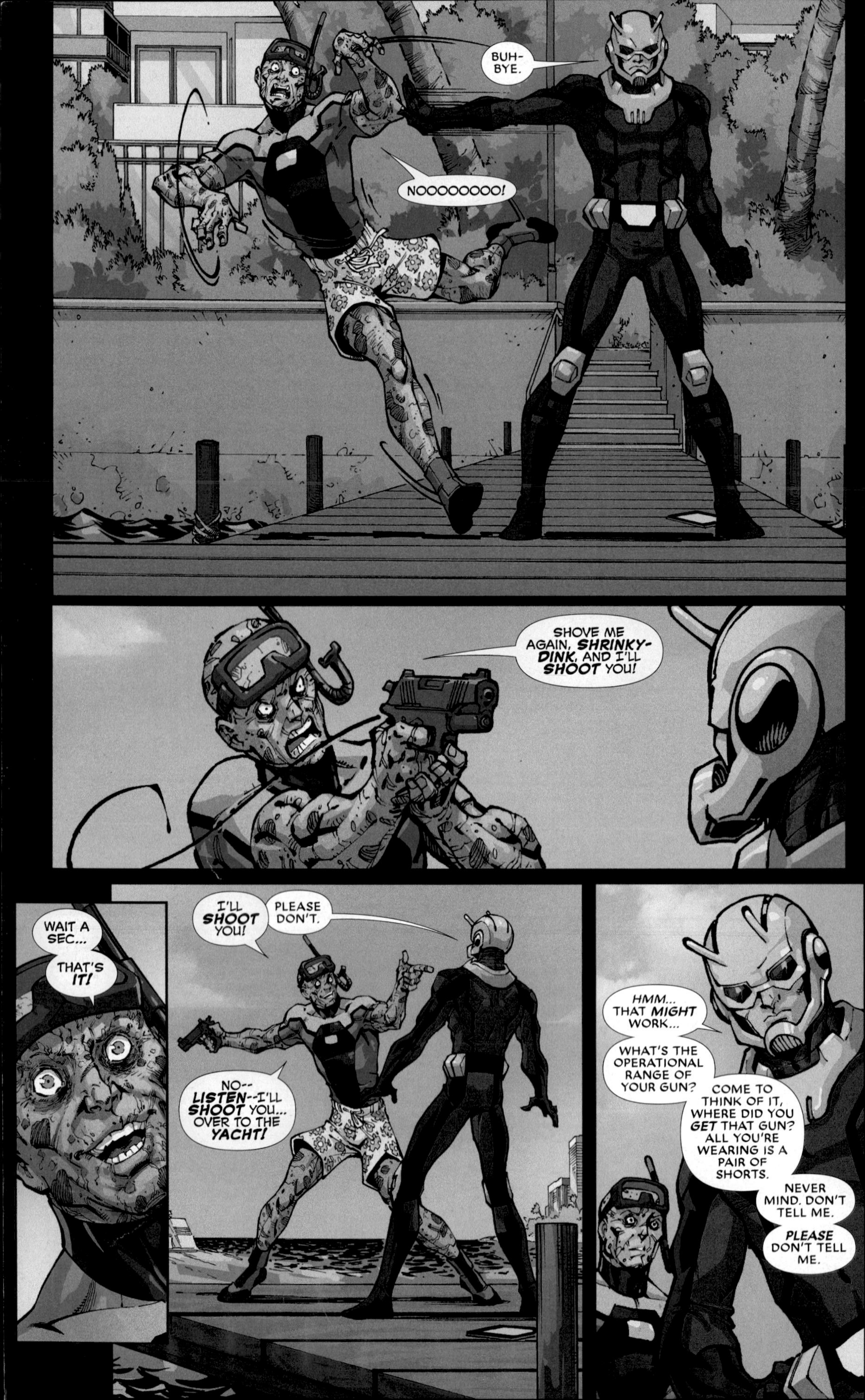
BUH-BYE.
NOOOOOOOO!
SHOVE ME AGAIN, SHRINKY-DINK, AND I'LL SHOOT YOU!
WAIT A SEC...
THAT'S IT!
I'LL SHOOT YOU!
PLEASE DON'T.
NO--LISTEN--I'LL SHOOT YOU... OVER TO THE YACHT!
HMM... THAT MIGHT WORK...
WHAT'S THE OPERATIONAL RANGE OF YOUR GUN?
COME TO THINK OF IT, WHERE DID YOU GET THAT GUN? ALL YOU'RE WEARING IS A PAIR OF SHORTS.
NEVER MIND. DON'T TELL ME.
PLEASE DON'T TELL ME.

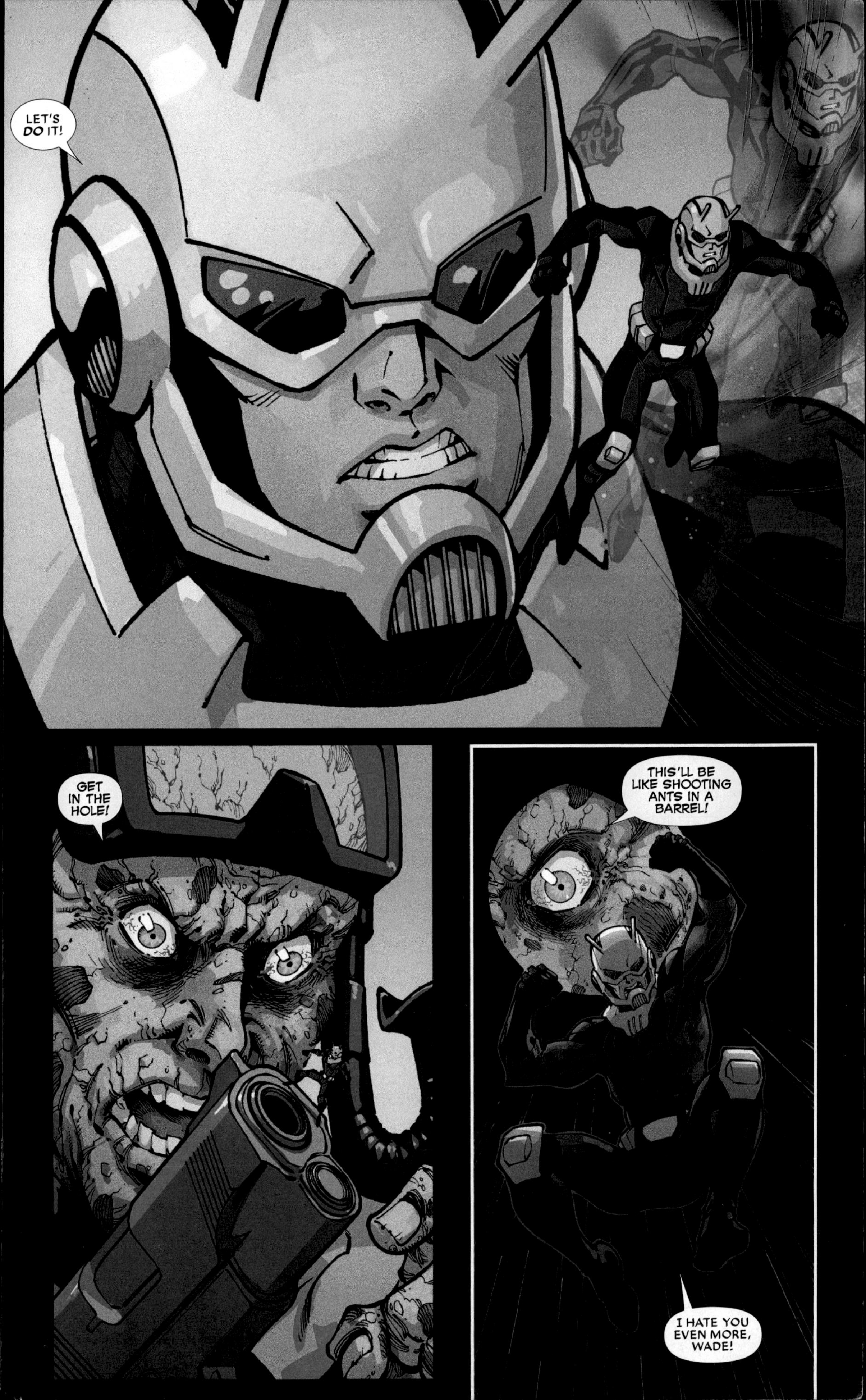
LET'S DO IT!
GET IN THE HOLE!
THIS'LL BE LIKE SHOOTING ANTS IN A BARREL!
I HATE YOU EVEN MORE, WADE!

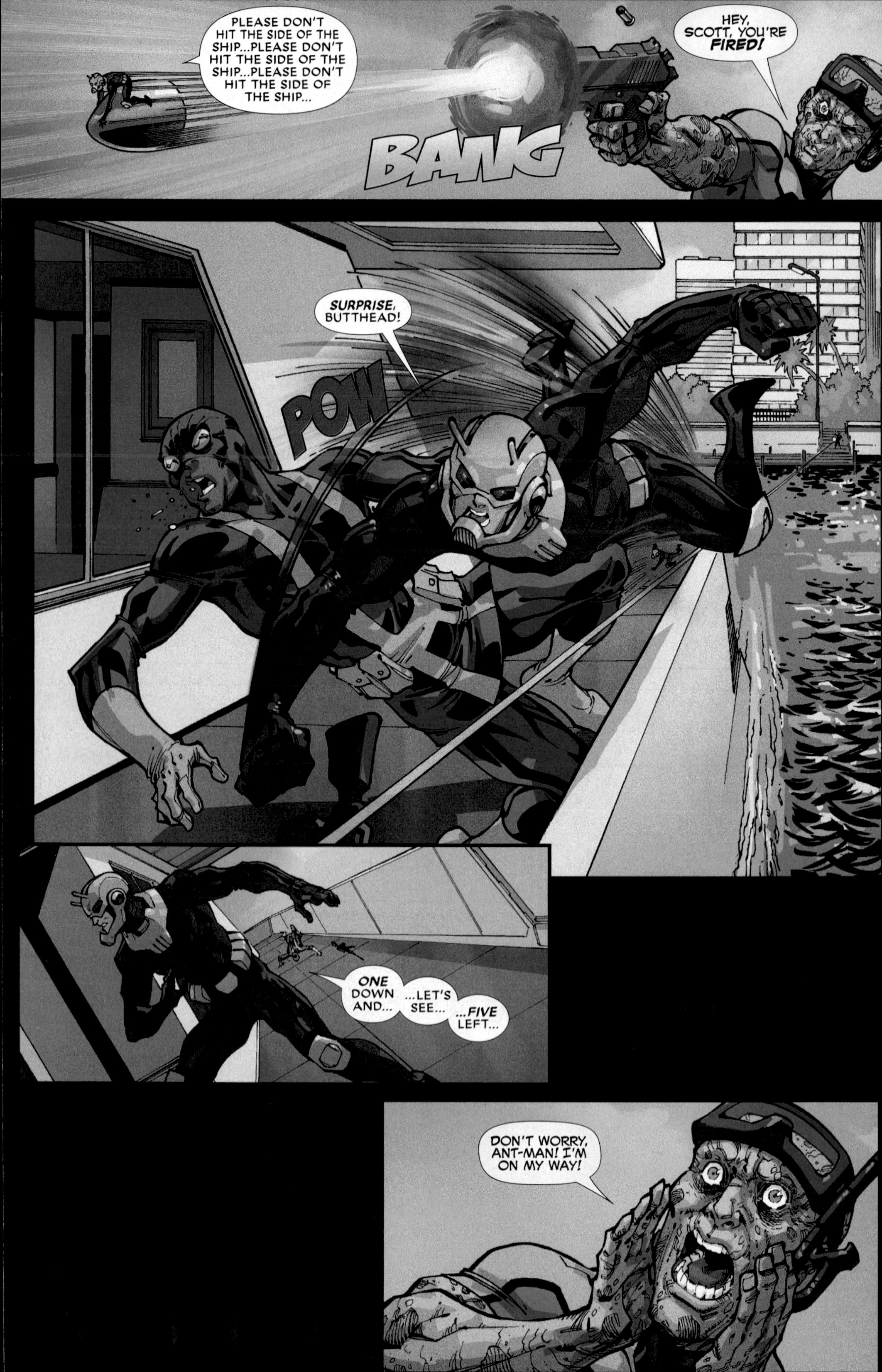

PLEASE DON'T HIT THE SIDE OF THE SHIP...PLEASE DON'T HIT THE SIDE OF THE SHIP...PLEASE DON'T HIT THE SIDE OF THE SHIP...
HEY, SCOTT, YOU'RE *FIRED!*
BANG
SURPRISE, BUTTHEAD!
POW
ONE DOWN AND...
...LET'S SEE...
...*FIVE* LEFT...
DON'T WORRY, ANT-MAN! I'M ON MY WAY!

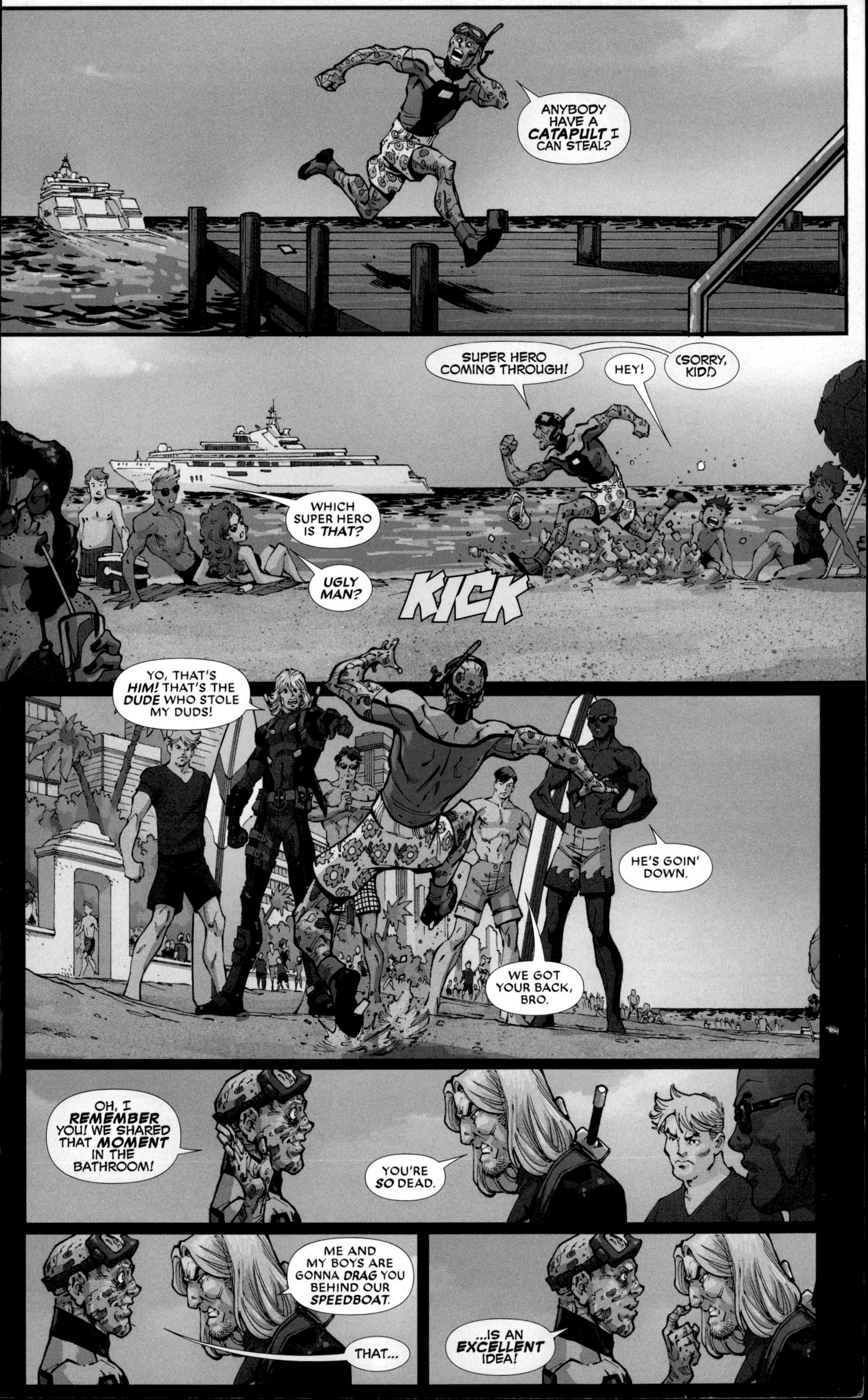
ANYBODY HAVE A CATAPULT I CAN STEAL?
SUPER HERO COMING THROUGH!
HEY!
(SORRY, KID!)
WHICH SUPER HERO IS THAT?
UGLY MAN?
KICK
YO, THAT'S HIM! THAT'S THE DUDE WHO STOLE MY DUDS!
HE'S GOIN' DOWN.
WE GOT YOUR BACK, BRO.
OH, I REMEMBER YOU! WE SHARED THAT MOMENT IN THE BATHROOM!
YOU'RE SO DEAD.
ME AND MY BOYS ARE GONNA DRAG YOU BEHIND OUR SPEEDBOAT.
THAT...
...IS AN EXCELLENT IDEA!

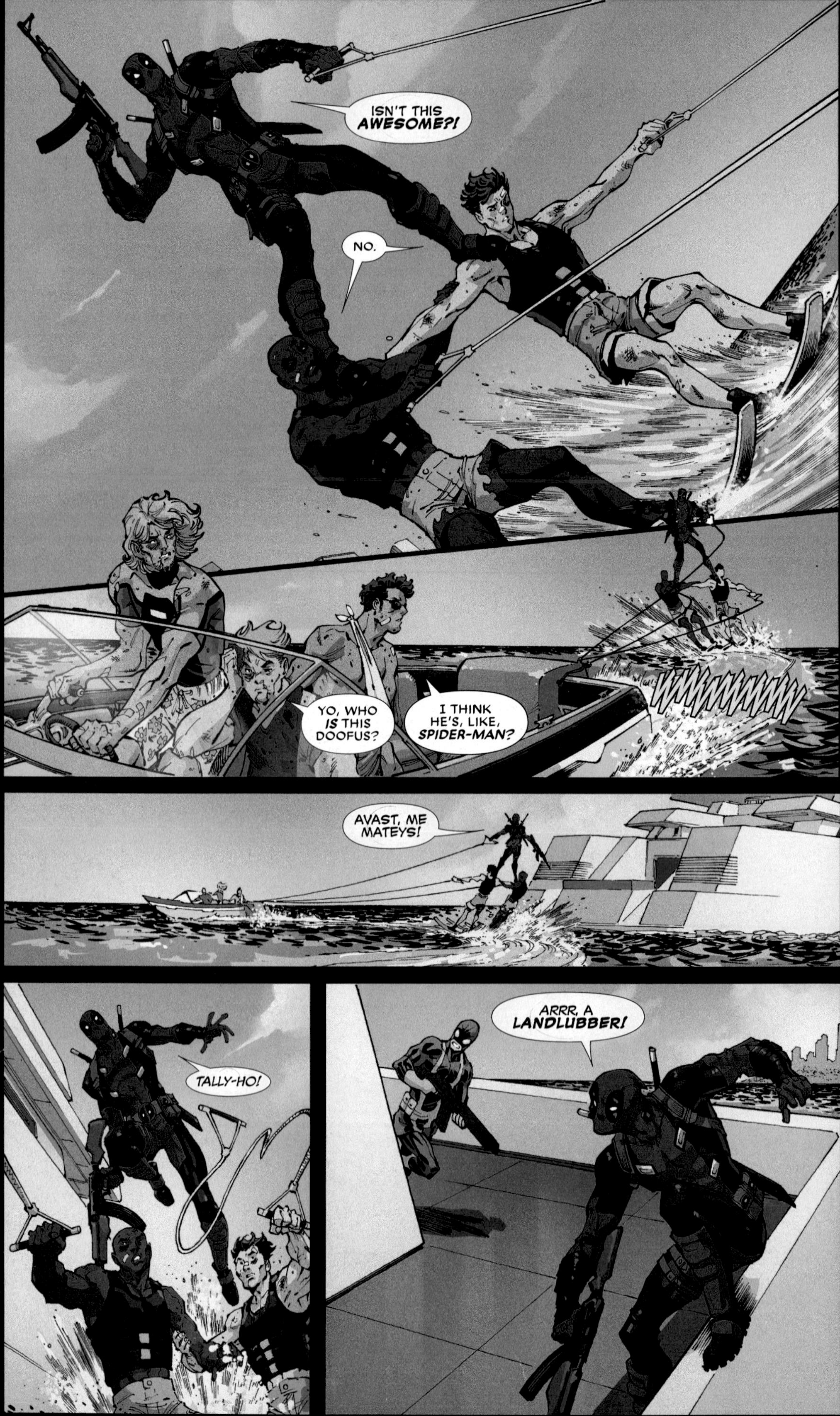
ISN'T THIS AWESOME?!
NO.
YO, WHO IS THIS DOOFUS?
I THINK HE'S, LIKE, SPIDER-MAN?
WWWWWWWWWW
AVAST, ME MATEYS!
TALLY-HO!
ARRR, A LANDLUBBER!

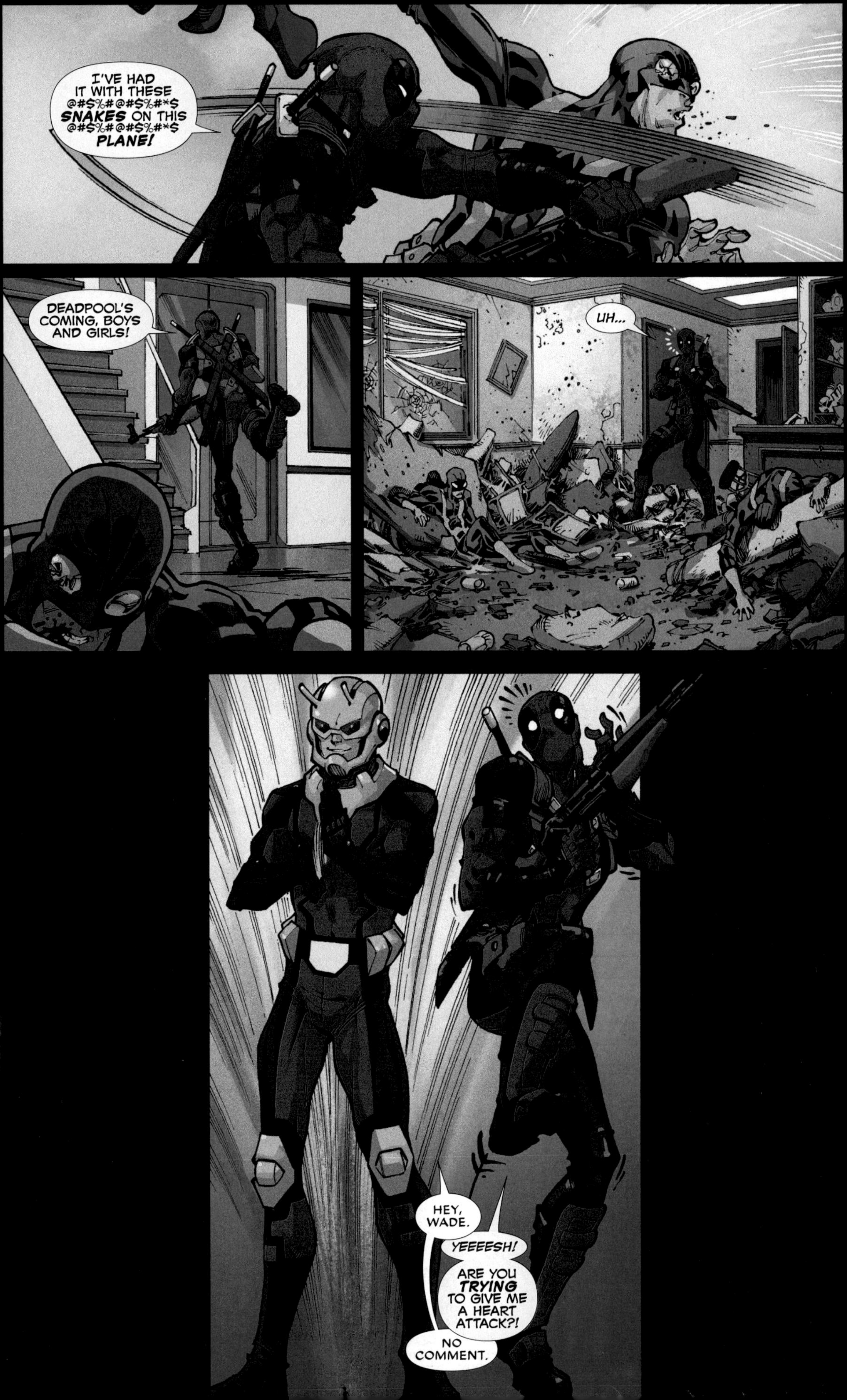
I'VE HAD IT WITH THESE @#$%#@#$%#*$ SNAKES ON THIS @#$%#@#$%#*$ PLANE!
DEADPOOL'S COMING, BOYS AND GIRLS!
UH...
HEY, WADE.
YEEEESH!
ARE YOU TRYING TO GIVE ME A HEART ATTACK?!
NO COMMENT.

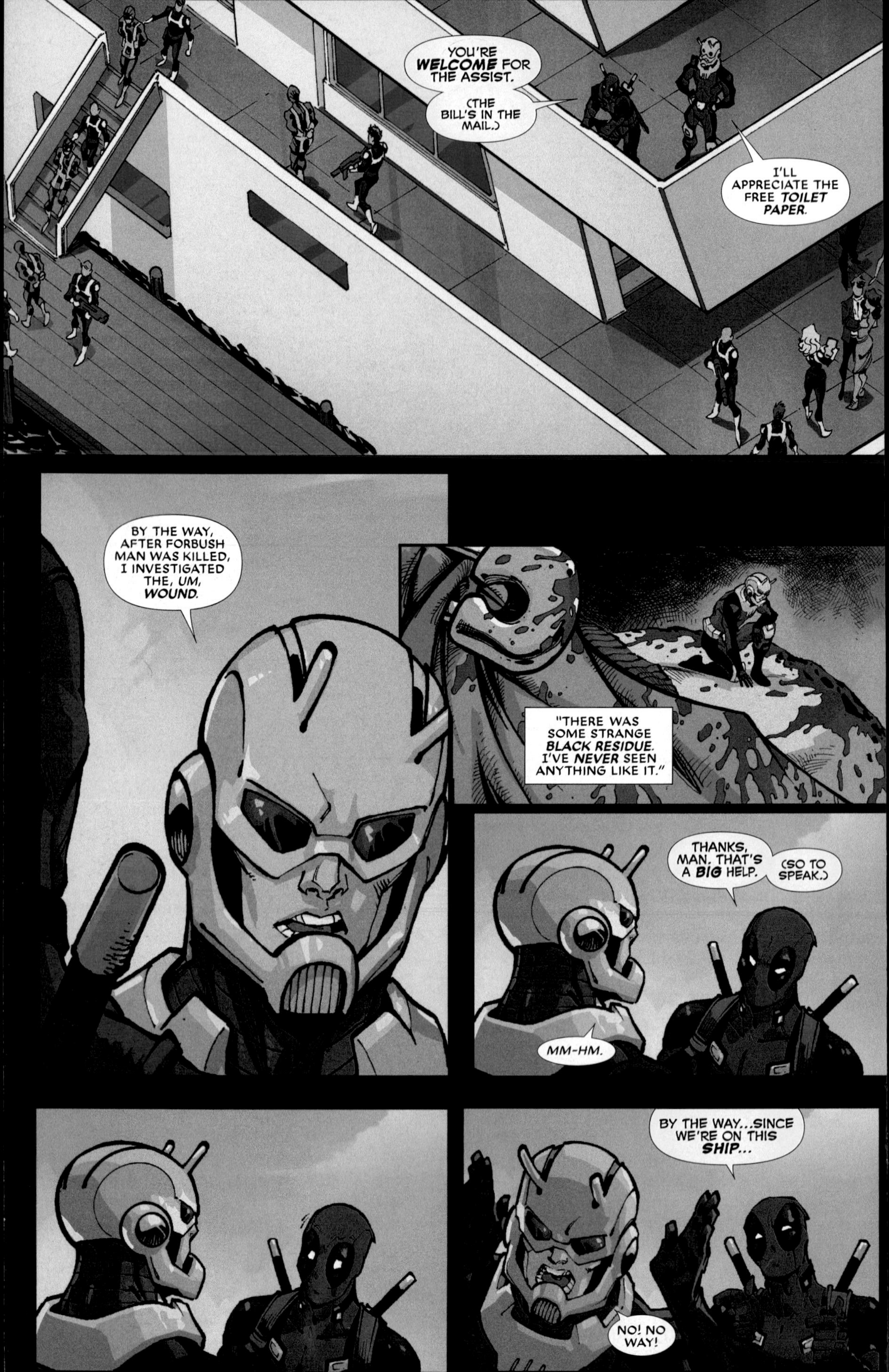
YOU'RE WELCOME FOR THE ASSIST.
(THE BILL'S IN THE MAIL.)
I'LL APPRECIATE THE FREE TOILET PAPER.
BY THE WAY, AFTER FORBUSH MAN WAS KILLED, I INVESTIGATED THE, UM, WOUND.
"THERE WAS SOME STRANGE BLACK RESIDUE. I'VE NEVER SEEN ANYTHING LIKE IT."
THANKS, MAN. THAT'S A BIG HELP.
(SO TO SPEAK.)
MM-HM.
BY THE WAY...SINCE WE'RE ON THIS SHIP...
NO! NO WAY!

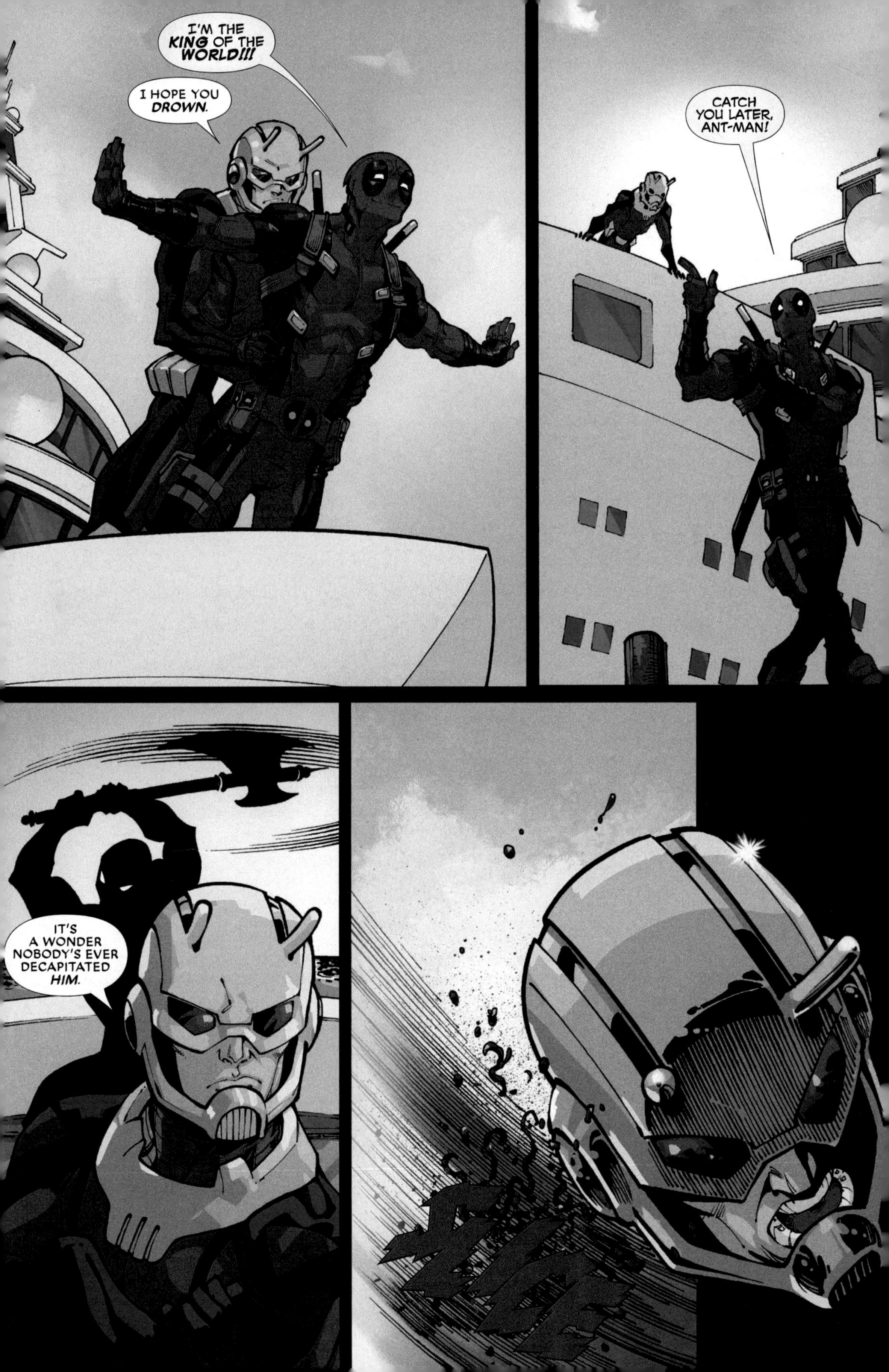
I'M THE KING OF THE WORLD!!!
I HOPE YOU DROWN.
CATCH YOU LATER, ANT-MAN!
IT'S A WONDER NOBODY'S EVER DECAPITATED HIM.

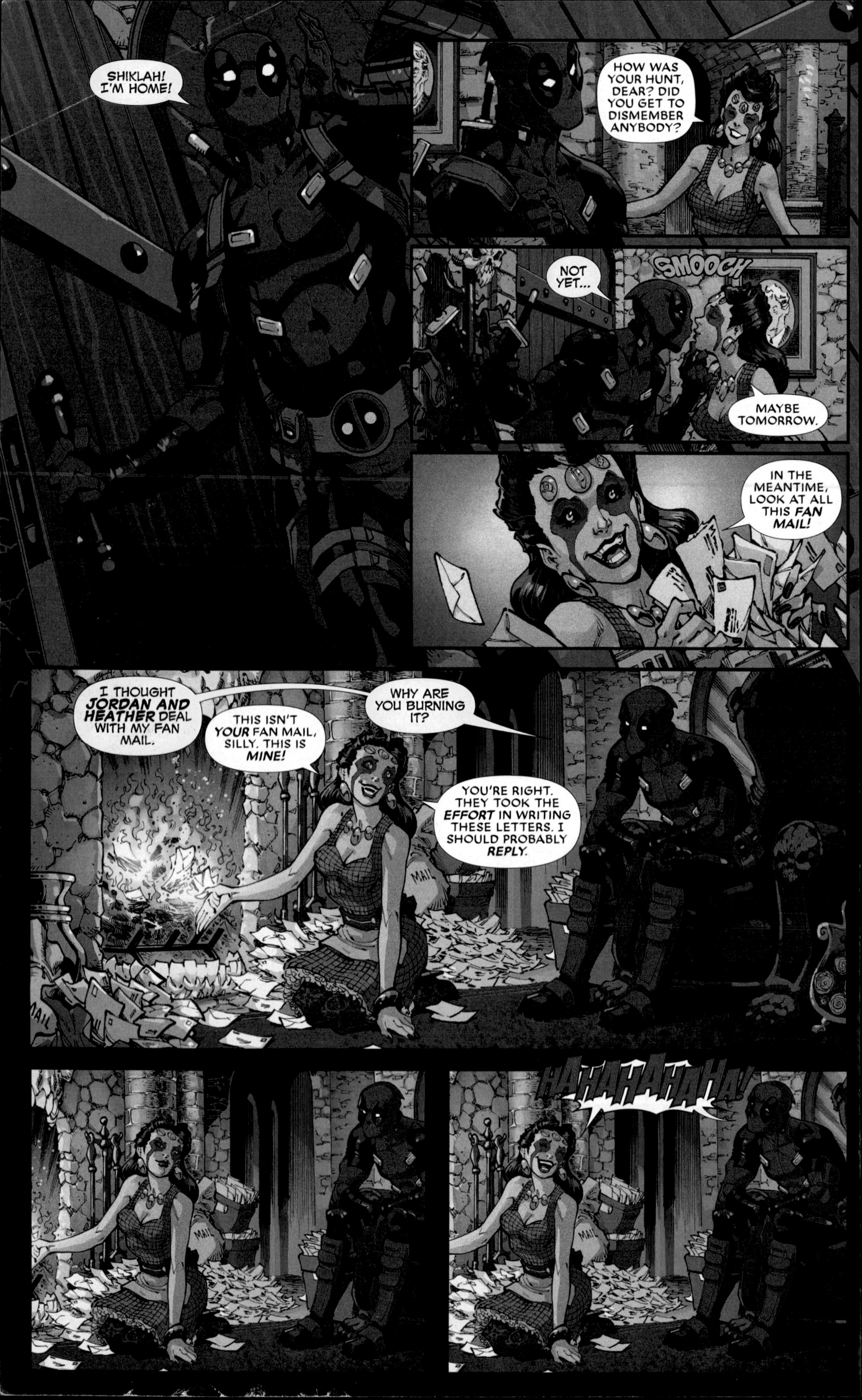
SHIKLAH! I'M HOME!
HOW WAS YOUR HUNT, DEAR? DID YOU GET TO DISMEMBER ANYBODY?
NOT YET...
SMOOCH
MAYBE TOMORROW.
IN THE MEANTIME, LOOK AT ALL THIS FAN MAIL!
I THOUGHT JORDAN AND HEATHER DEAL WITH MY FAN MAIL.
THIS ISN'T YOUR FAN MAIL, SILLY. THIS IS MINE!
WHY ARE YOU BURNING IT?
YOU'RE RIGHT. THEY TOOK THE EFFORT IN WRITING THESE LETTERS. I SHOULD PROBABLY REPLY.
MAIL
HAHAHAHAHAHA!

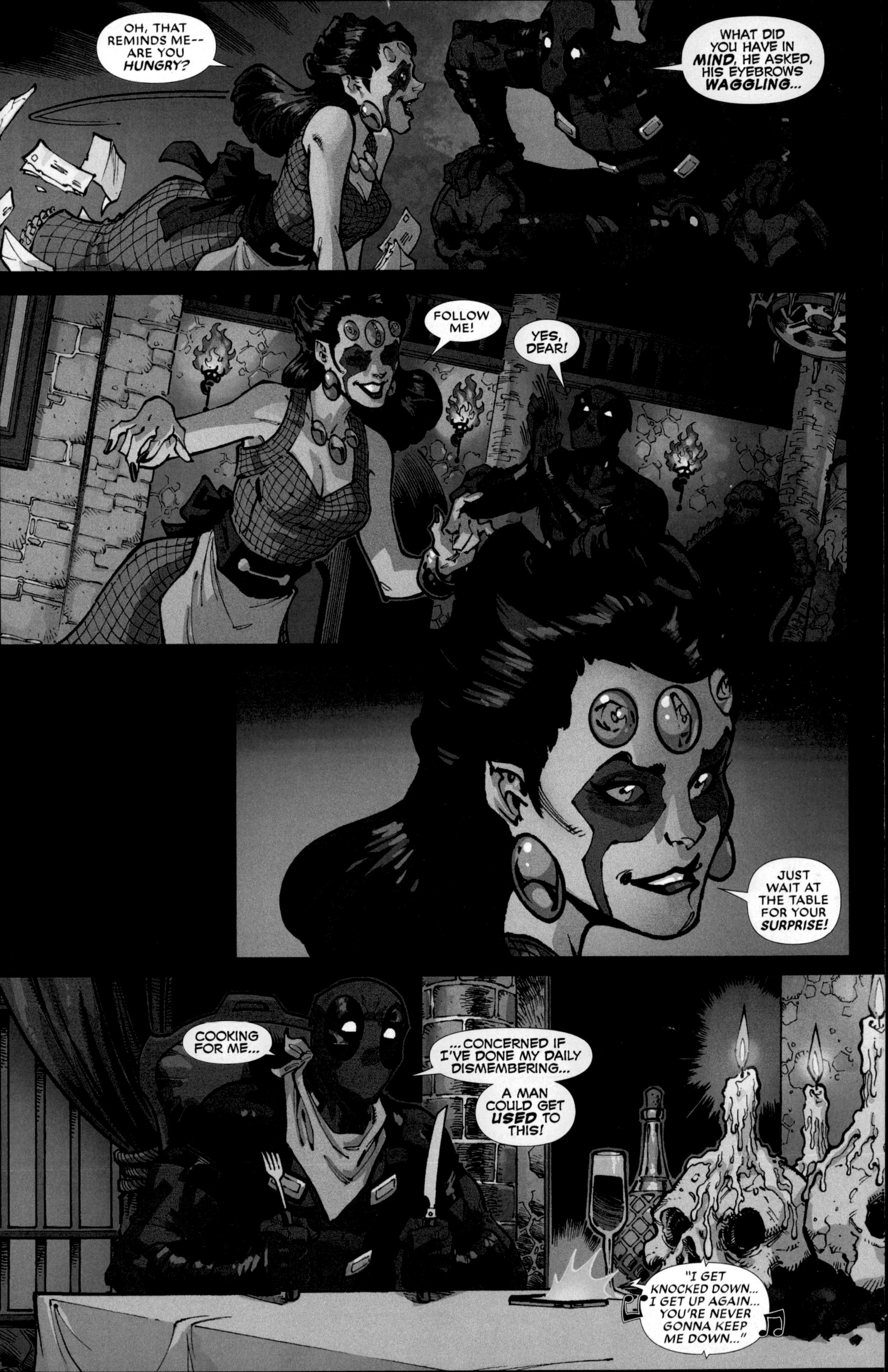

OH, THAT REMINDS ME-- ARE YOU HUNGRY?
WHAT DID YOU HAVE IN MIND, HE ASKED, HIS EYEBROWS WAGGLING...
FOLLOW ME!
YES, DEAR!
JUST WAIT AT THE TABLE FOR YOUR SURPRISE!
COOKING FOR ME...
...CONCERNED IF I'VE DONE MY DAILY DISMEMBERING...
A MAN COULD GET USED TO THIS!
"I GET KNOCKED DOWN... I GET UP AGAIN... YOU'RE NEVER GONNA KEEP ME DOWN..."

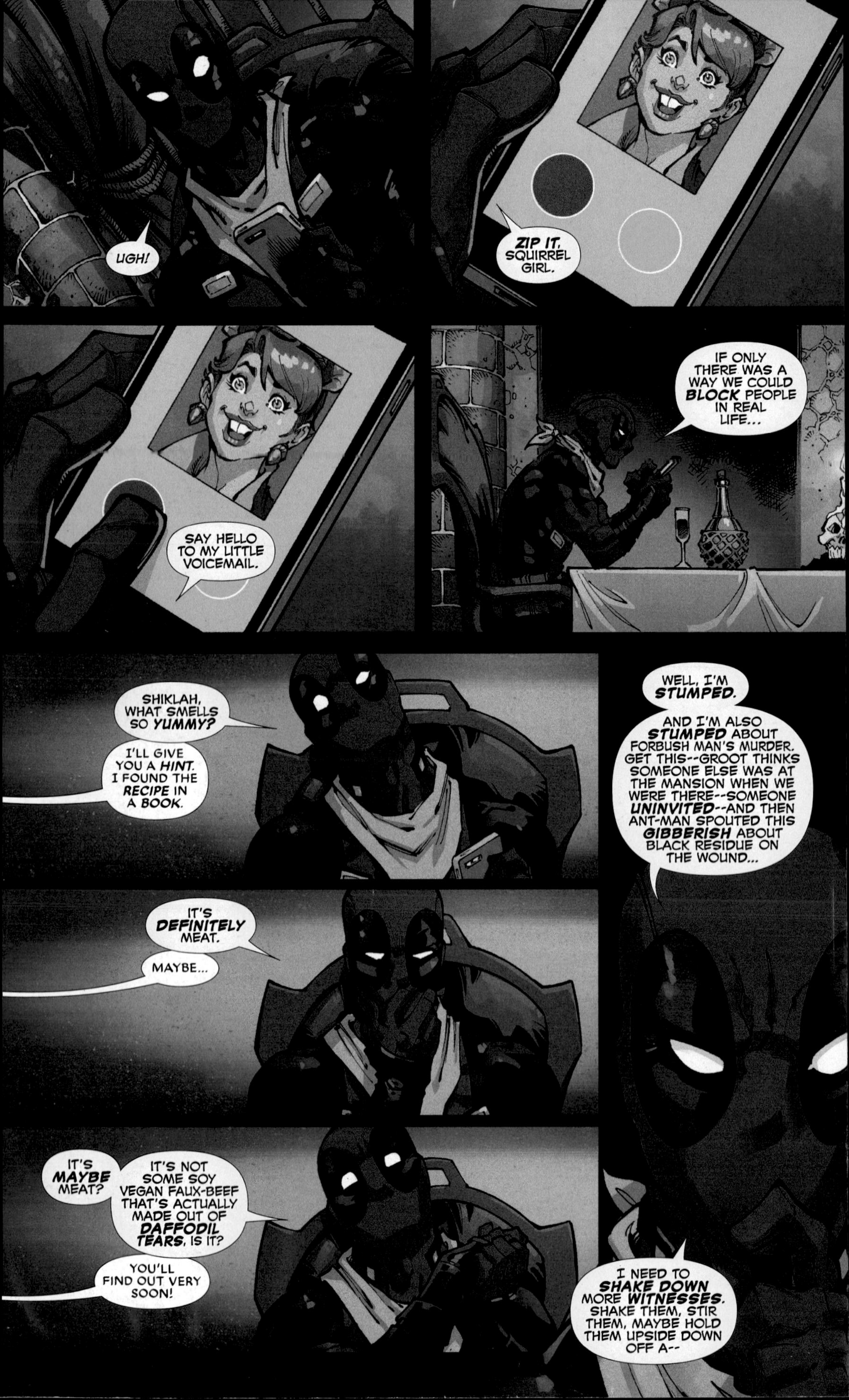
UGH!
ZIP IT, SQUIRREL GIRL.
SAY HELLO TO MY LITTLE VOICEMAIL.
IF ONLY THERE WAS A WAY WE COULD BLOCK PEOPLE IN REAL LIFE...
SHIKLAH, WHAT SMELLS SO YUMMY?
I'LL GIVE YOU A HINT. I FOUND THE RECIPE IN A BOOK.
IT'S DEFINITELY MEAT.
MAYBE...
IT'S MAYBE MEAT?
IT'S NOT SOME SOY VEGAN FAUX-BEEF THAT'S ACTUALLY MADE OUT OF DAFFODIL TEARS, IS IT?
YOU'LL FIND OUT VERY SOON!
WELL, I'M STUMPED.
AND I'M ALSO STUMPED ABOUT FORBUSH MAN'S MURDER. GET THIS--GROOT THINKS SOMEONE ELSE WAS AT THE MANSION WHEN WE WERE THERE--SOMEONE UNINVITED--AND THEN ANT-MAN SPOUTED THIS GIBBERISH ABOUT BLACK RESIDUE ON THE WOUND...
I NEED TO SHAKE DOWN MORE WITNESSES. SHAKE THEM, STIR THEM, MAYBE HOLD THEM UPSIDE DOWN OFF A--

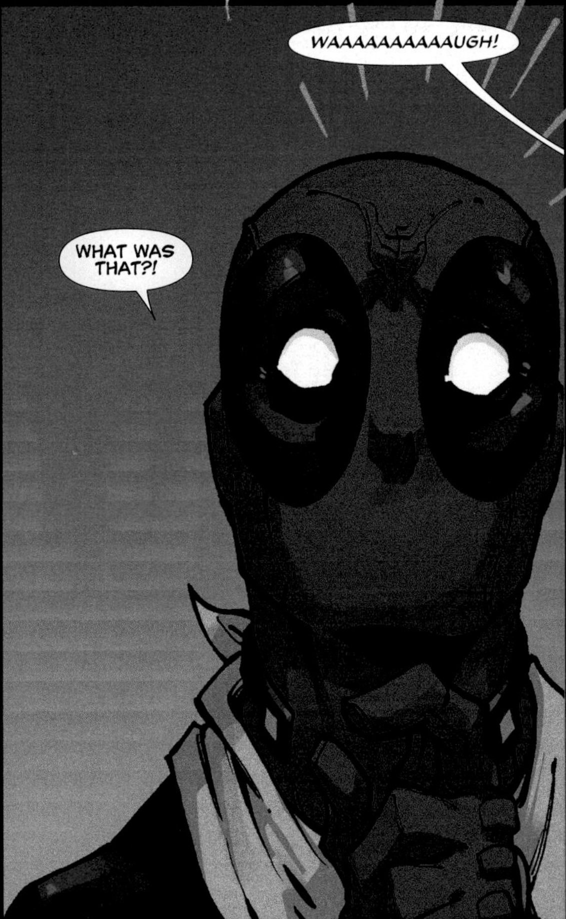
WAAAAAAAAAAUGH!
WHAT WAS THAT?!

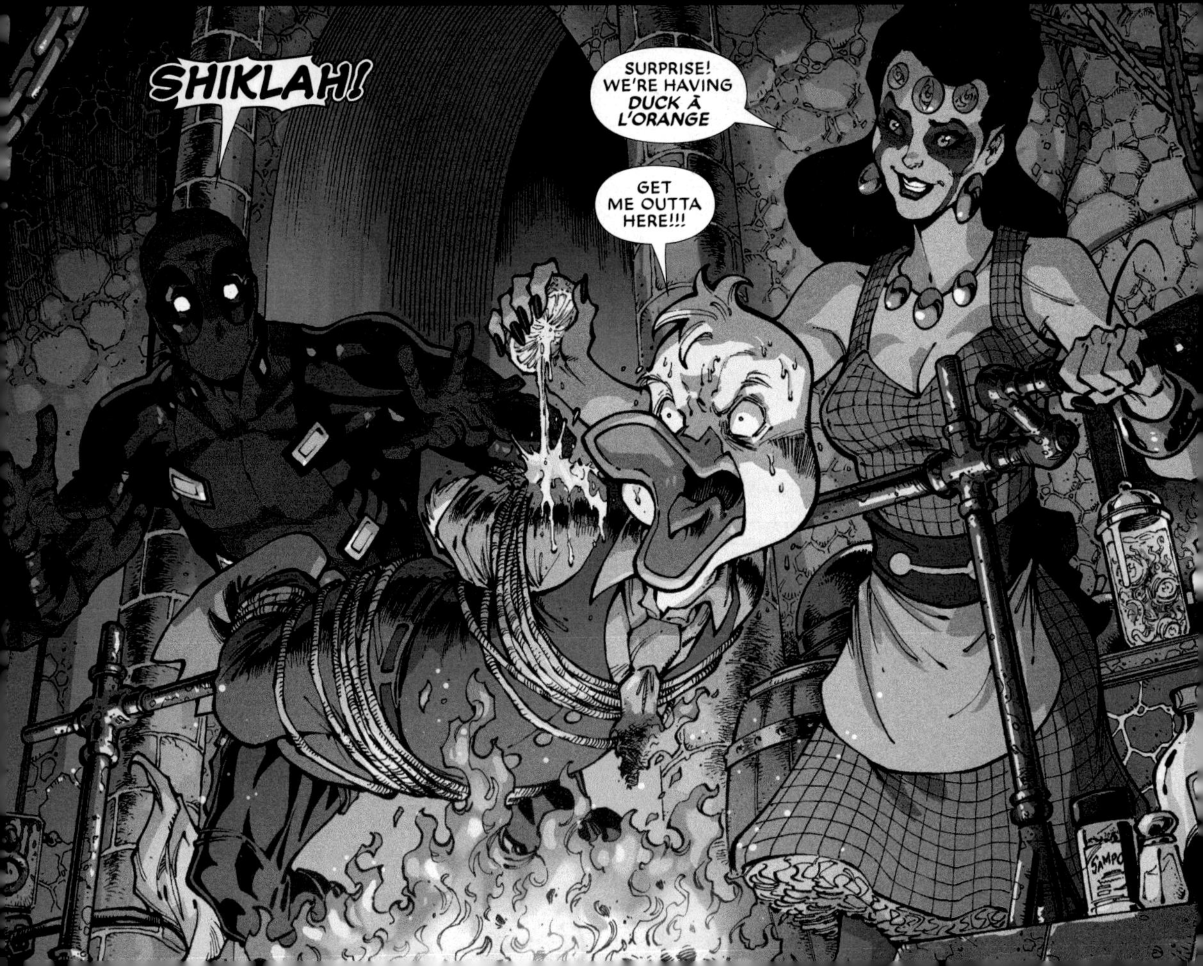
SHIKLAH!
SURPRISE! WE'RE HAVING *DUCK À L'ORANGE*
GET ME OUTTA HERE!!!

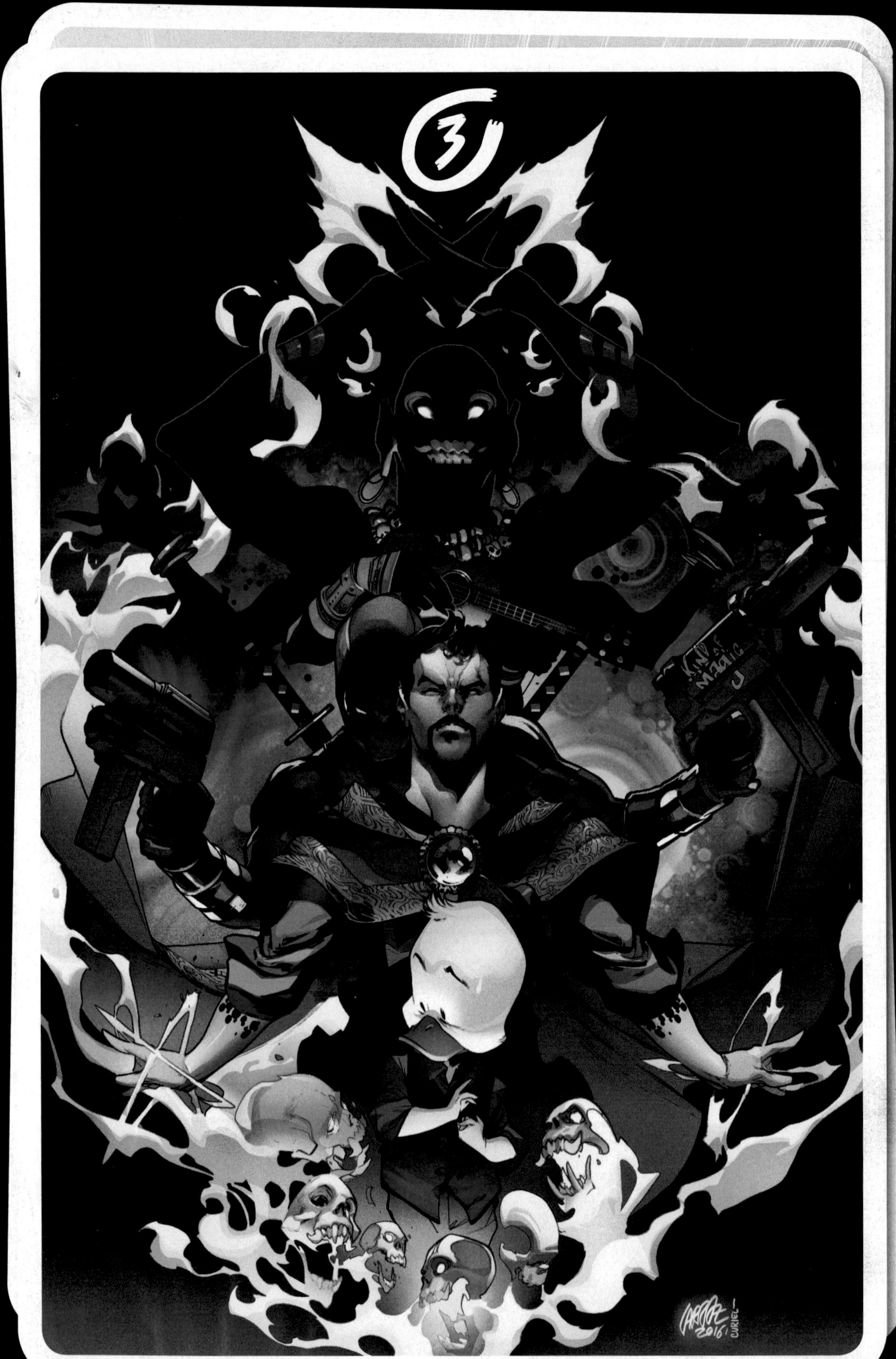
3

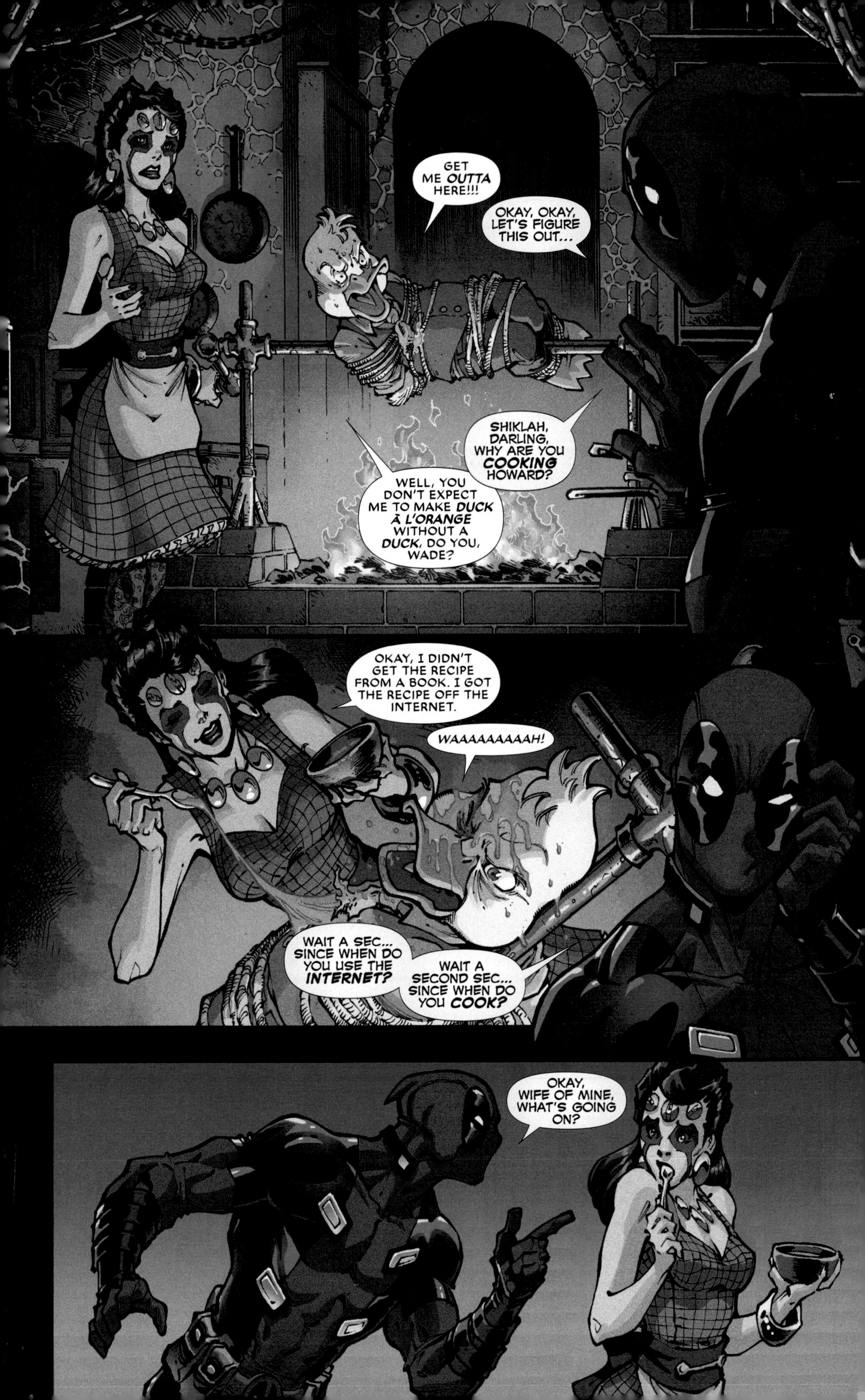
GET ME OUTTA HERE!!!
OKAY, OKAY, LET'S FIGURE THIS OUT...
SHIKLAH, DARLING, WHY ARE YOU COOKING HOWARD?
WELL, YOU DON'T EXPECT ME TO MAKE DUCK À L'ORANGE WITHOUT A DUCK, DO YOU, WADE?
OKAY, I DIDN'T GET THE RECIPE FROM A BOOK. I GOT THE RECIPE OFF THE INTERNET.
WAAAAAAAAAH!
WAIT A SEC... SINCE WHEN DO YOU USE THE INTERNET?
WAIT A SECOND SEC... SINCE WHEN DO YOU COOK?
OKAY, WIFE OF MINE, WHAT'S GOING ON?

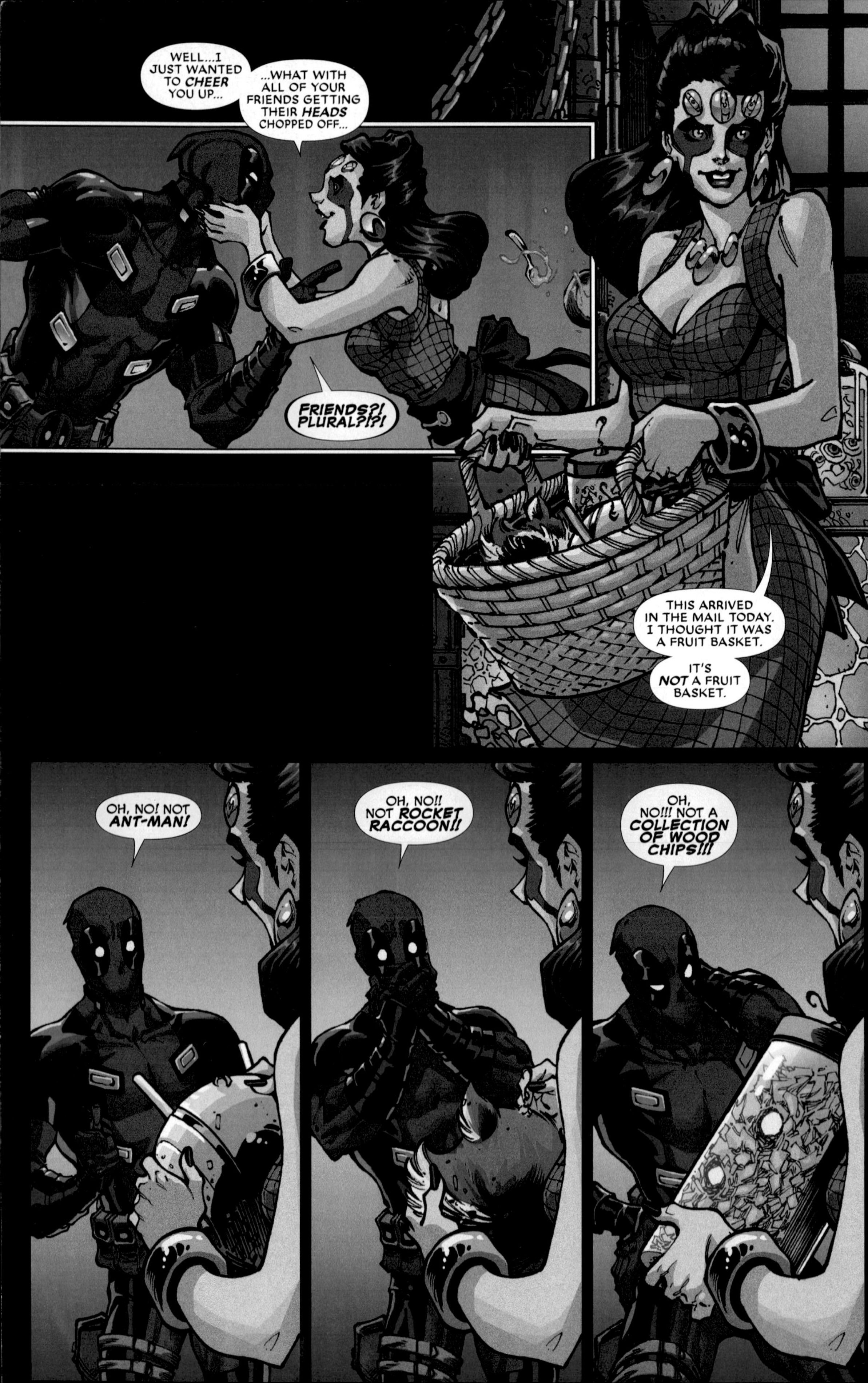
WELL...I JUST WANTED TO CHEER YOU UP...
...WHAT WITH ALL OF YOUR FRIENDS GETTING THEIR HEADS CHOPPED OFF...
FRIENDS?! PLURAL?!?!
THIS ARRIVED IN THE MAIL TODAY. I THOUGHT IT WAS A FRUIT BASKET.
IT'S NOT A FRUIT BASKET.
OH, NO! NOT ANT-MAN!
OH, NO!! NOT ROCKET RACCOON!!
OH, NO!!! NOT A COLLECTION OF WOOD CHIPS!!!

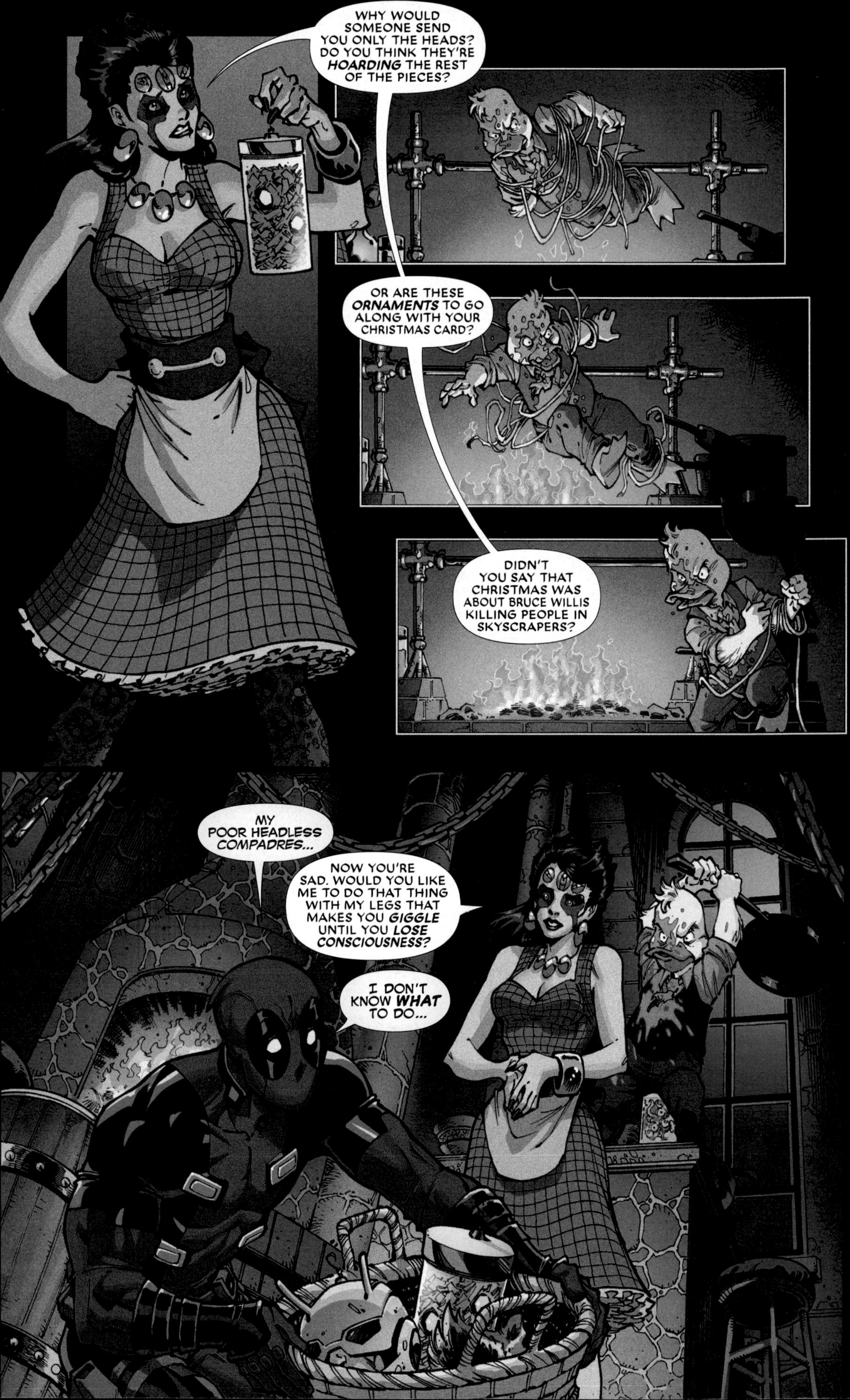

WHY WOULD SOMEONE SEND YOU ONLY THE HEADS? DO YOU THINK THEY'RE *HOARDING* THE REST OF THE PIECES?
OR ARE THESE *ORNAMENTS* TO GO ALONG WITH YOUR CHRISTMAS CARD?
DIDN'T YOU SAY THAT CHRISTMAS WAS ABOUT BRUCE WILLIS KILLING PEOPLE IN SKYSCRAPERS?
MY POOR HEADLESS *COMPADRES...*
NOW YOU'RE SAD. WOULD YOU LIKE ME TO DO THAT THING WITH MY LEGS THAT MAKES YOU *GIGGLE* UNTIL YOU *LOSE CONSCIOUSNESS?*
I DON'T KNOW *WHAT* TO DO...

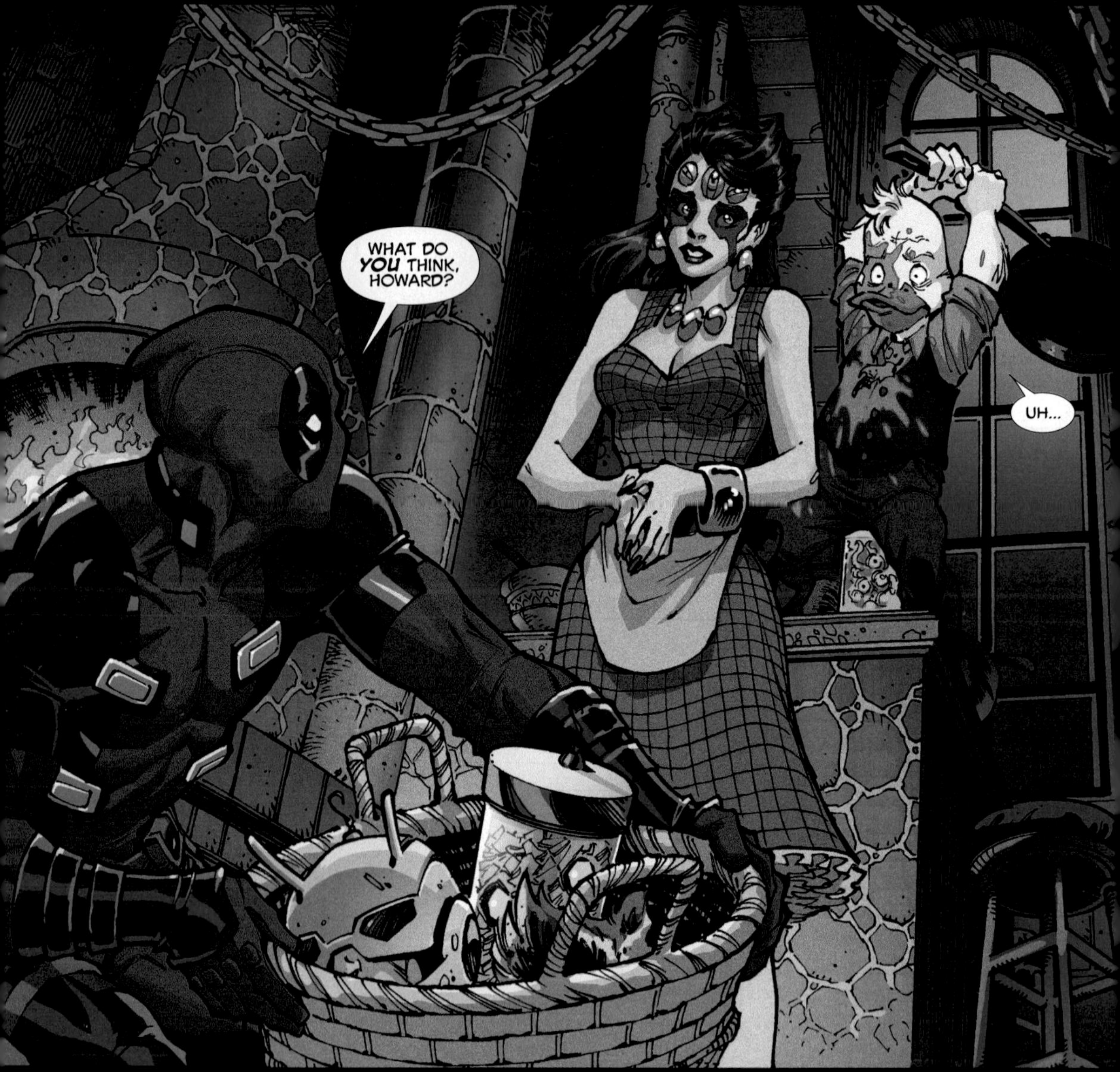
WHAT DO *YOU* THINK, HOWARD?
UH...

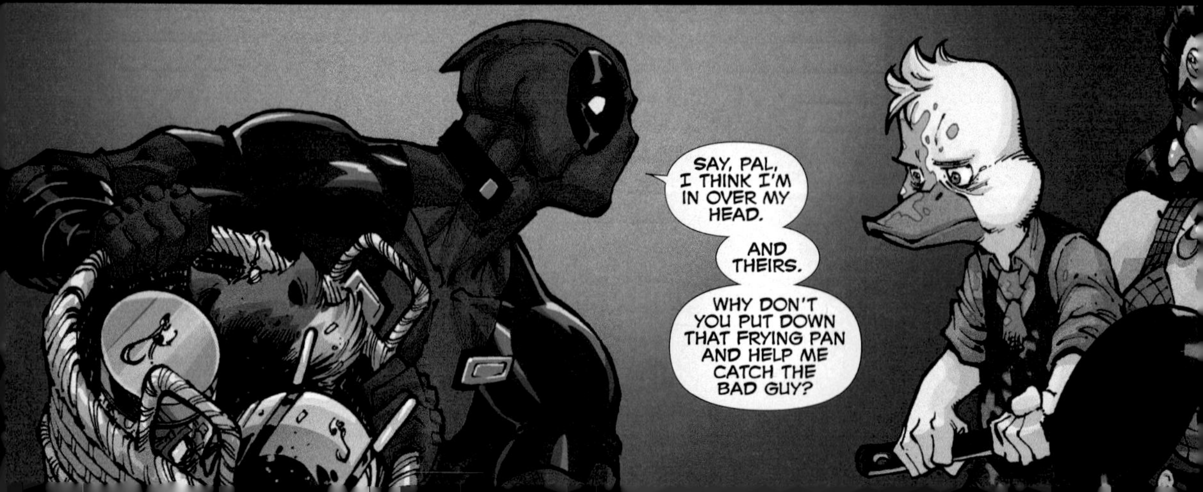
SAY, PAL, I THINK I'M IN OVER MY HEAD.
AND THEIRS.
WHY DON'T YOU PUT DOWN THAT FRYING PAN AND HELP ME CATCH THE BAD GUY?

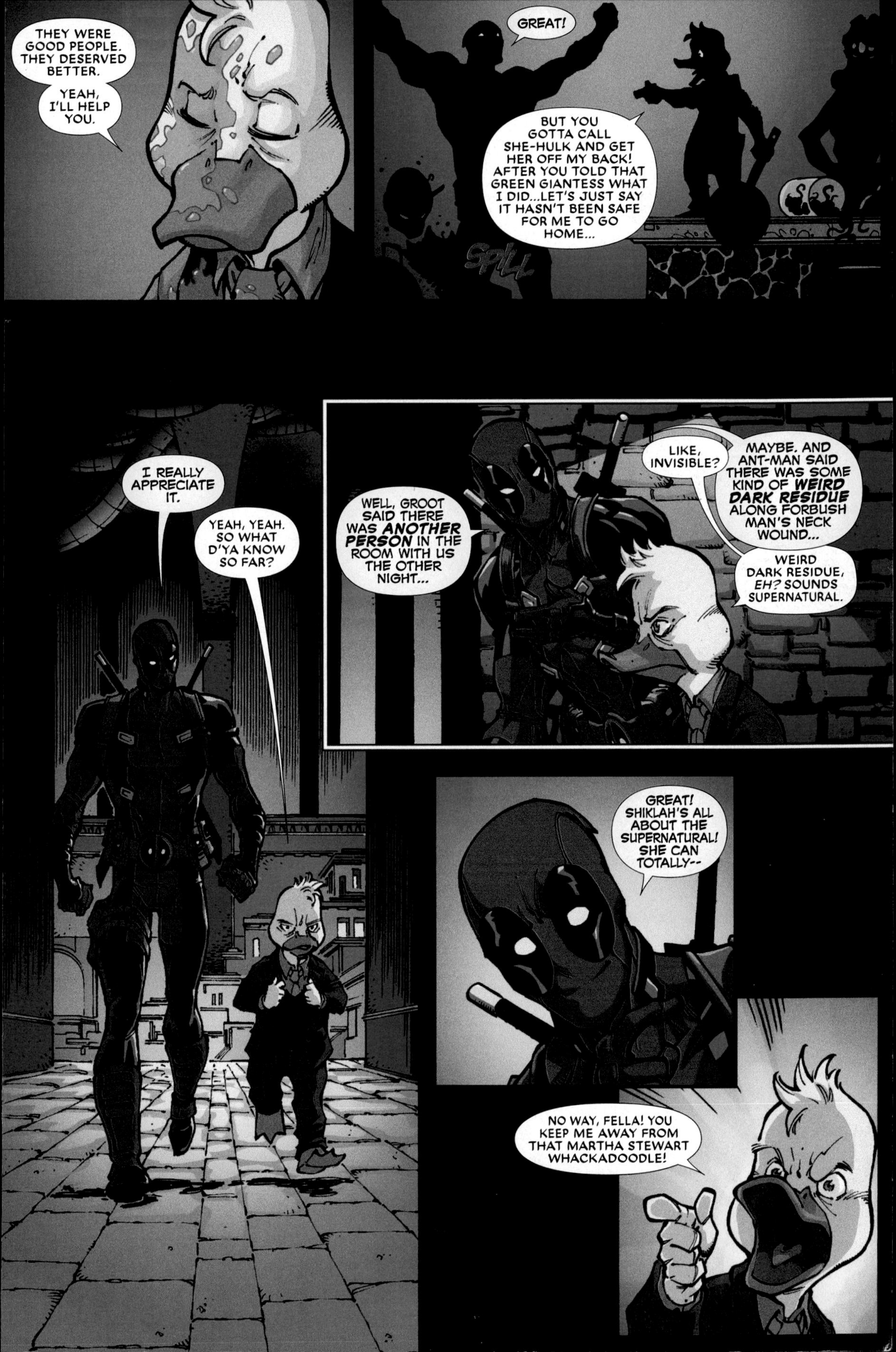
THEY WERE GOOD PEOPLE. THEY DESERVED BETTER.
YEAH, I'LL HELP YOU.
GREAT!
BUT YOU GOTTA CALL SHE-HULK AND GET HER OFF MY BACK! AFTER YOU TOLD THAT GREEN GIANTESS WHAT I DID...LET'S JUST SAY IT HASN'T BEEN SAFE FOR ME TO GO HOME...
SPILL
I REALLY APPRECIATE IT.
YEAH, YEAH. SO WHAT D'YA KNOW SO FAR?
WELL, GROOT SAID THERE WAS ANOTHER PERSON IN THE ROOM WITH US THE OTHER NIGHT...
LIKE, INVISIBLE?
MAYBE. AND ANT-MAN SAID THERE WAS SOME KIND OF WEIRD DARK RESIDUE ALONG FORBUSH MAN'S NECK WOUND...
WEIRD DARK RESIDUE, EH? SOUNDS SUPERNATURAL.
GREAT! SHIKLAH'S ALL ABOUT THE SUPERNATURAL! SHE CAN TOTALLY--
NO WAY, FELLA! YOU KEEP ME AWAY FROM THAT MARTHA STEWART WHACKADOODLE!

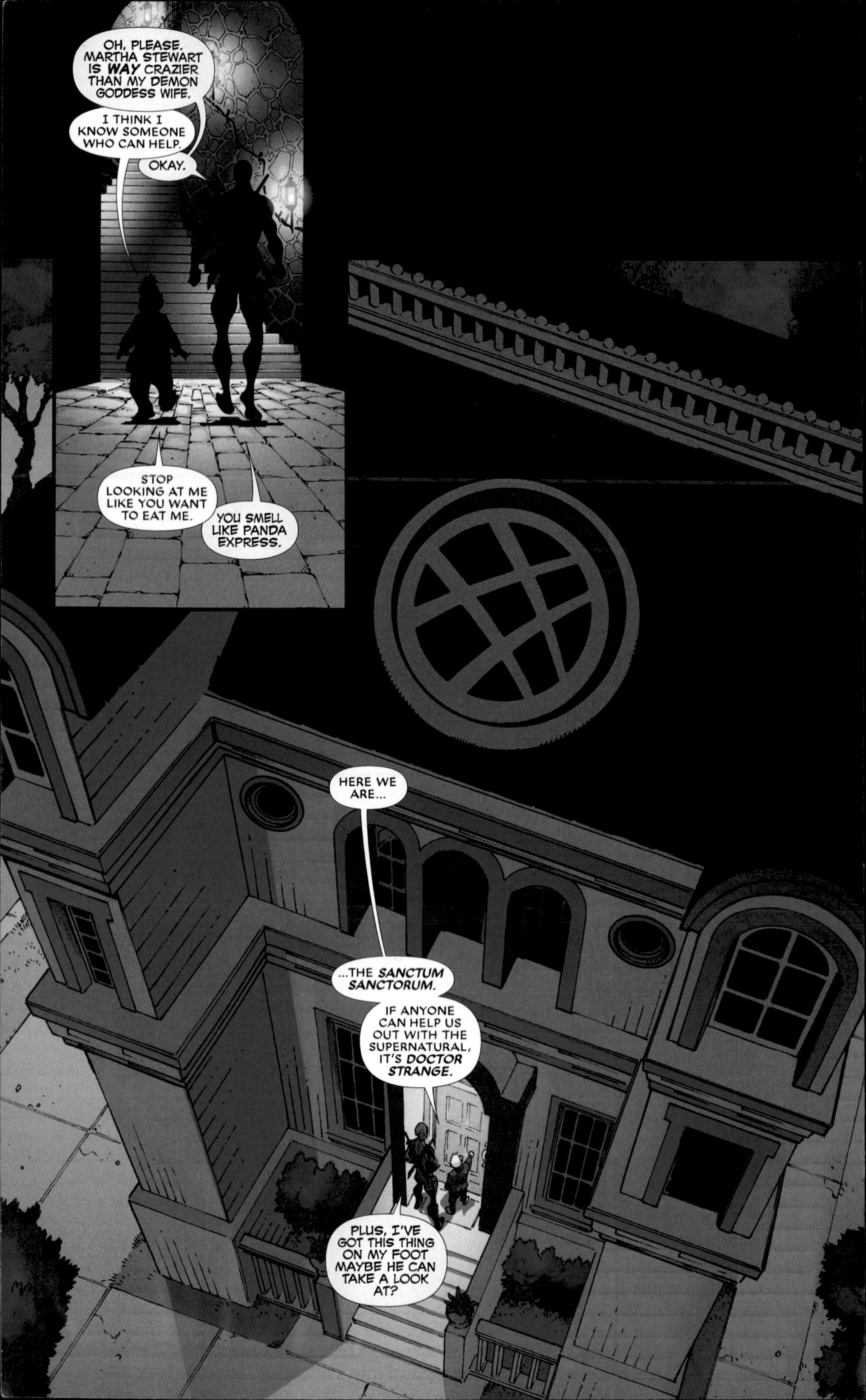
OH, PLEASE. MARTHA STEWART IS WAY CRAZIER THAN MY DEMON GODDESS WIFE.
I THINK I KNOW SOMEONE WHO CAN HELP.
OKAY.
STOP LOOKING AT ME LIKE YOU WANT TO EAT ME.
YOU SMELL LIKE PANDA EXPRESS.
HERE WE ARE...
...THE SANCTUM SANCTORUM.
IF ANYONE CAN HELP US OUT WITH THE SUPERNATURAL, IT'S DOCTOR STRANGE.
PLUS, I'VE GOT THIS THING ON MY FOOT MAYBE HE CAN TAKE A LOOK AT?

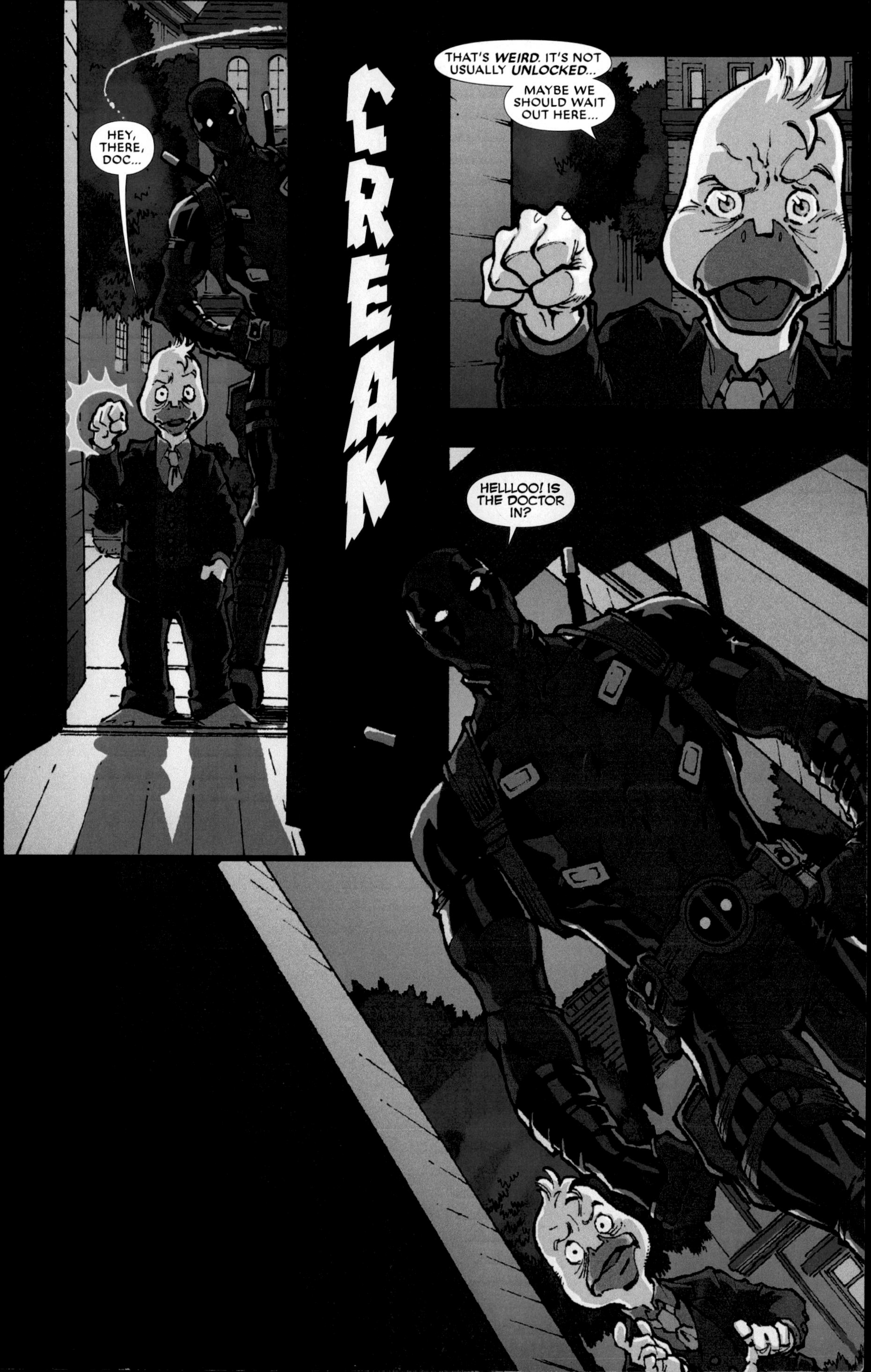
HEY, THERE, DOC...
CREAK
THAT'S WEIRD. IT'S NOT USUALLY UNLOCKED...
MAYBE WE SHOULD WAIT OUT HERE...
HELLLOO! IS THE DOCTOR IN?

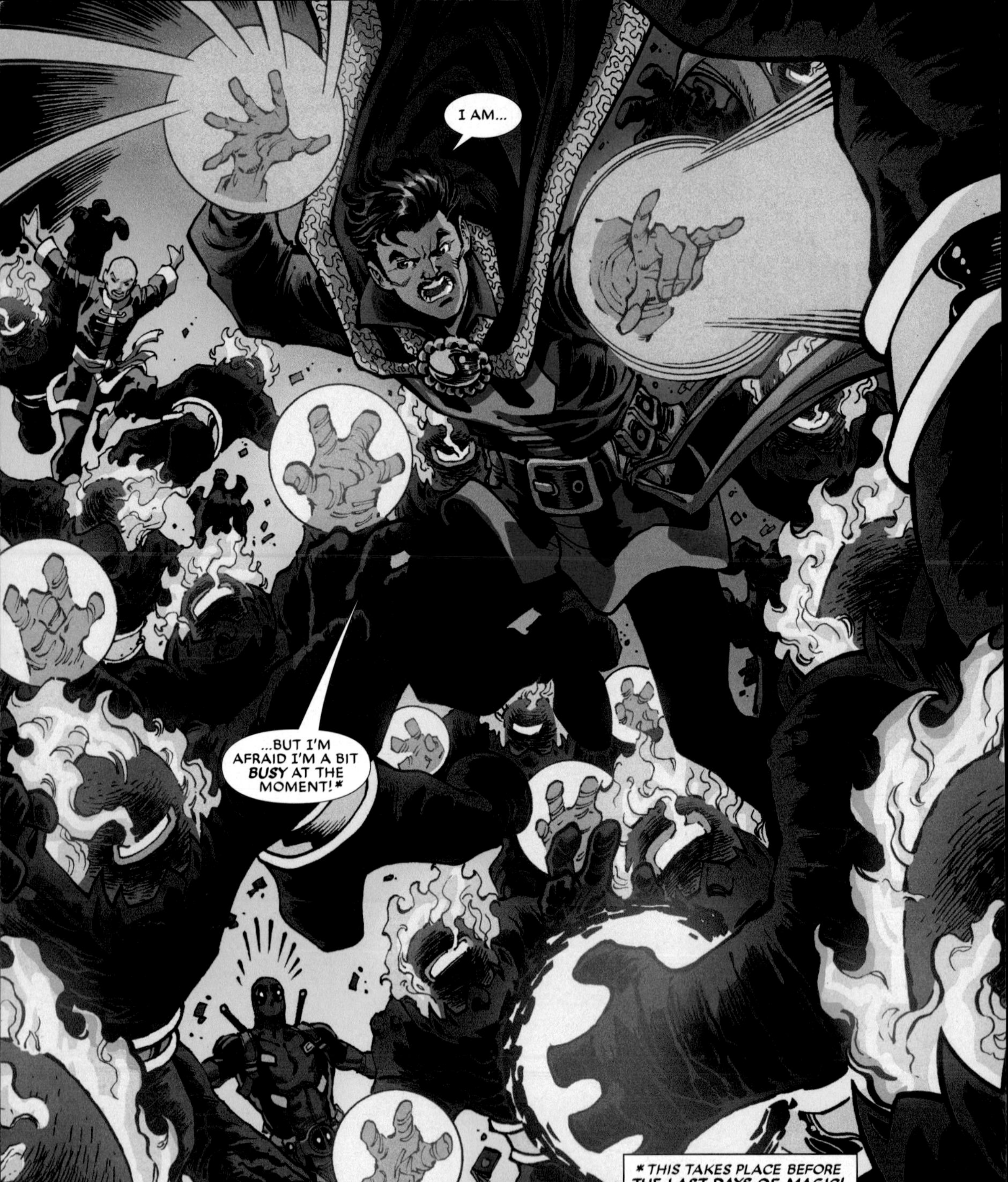
I AM...
...BUT I'M AFRAID I'M A BIT BUSY AT THE MOMENT!*
*THIS TAKES PLACE BEFORE THE LAST DAYS OF MAGIC! -JORDAN "DEMONIC" WHITE

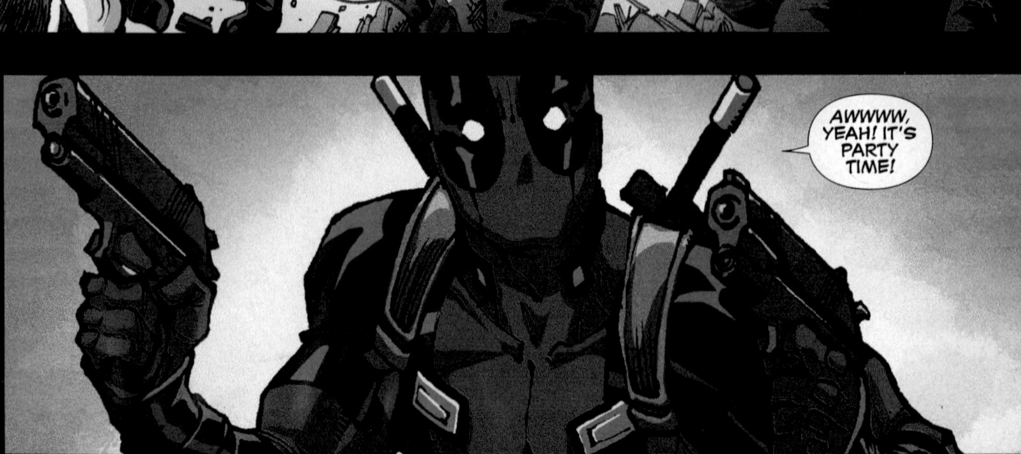
AWWWW, YEAH! IT'S PARTY TIME!

ONE RABBIT STEW COMING RIGHT UP!

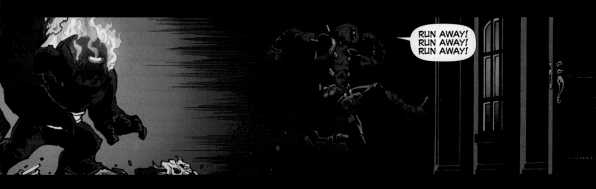

RUN AWAY! RUN AWAY! RUN AWAY!

OKAY! NEW PLAN! YOU HAPPEN TO KNOW MAGIK'S PHONE NUMBER? SHE CAN HELP US, RIGHT? OR MAYBE DAIMON HELLSTROM?

I TOLD YOU NOT TO JUST WALK IN THERE! WHAT HAPPENED?

SLAM

OH, NOTHING. I JUST LIKE TO KEEP MY OPTIONS OPEN.

IMPLOSION!

HOUSTON, WE HAVE A PROBLEM.

Y'THINK?

YANK

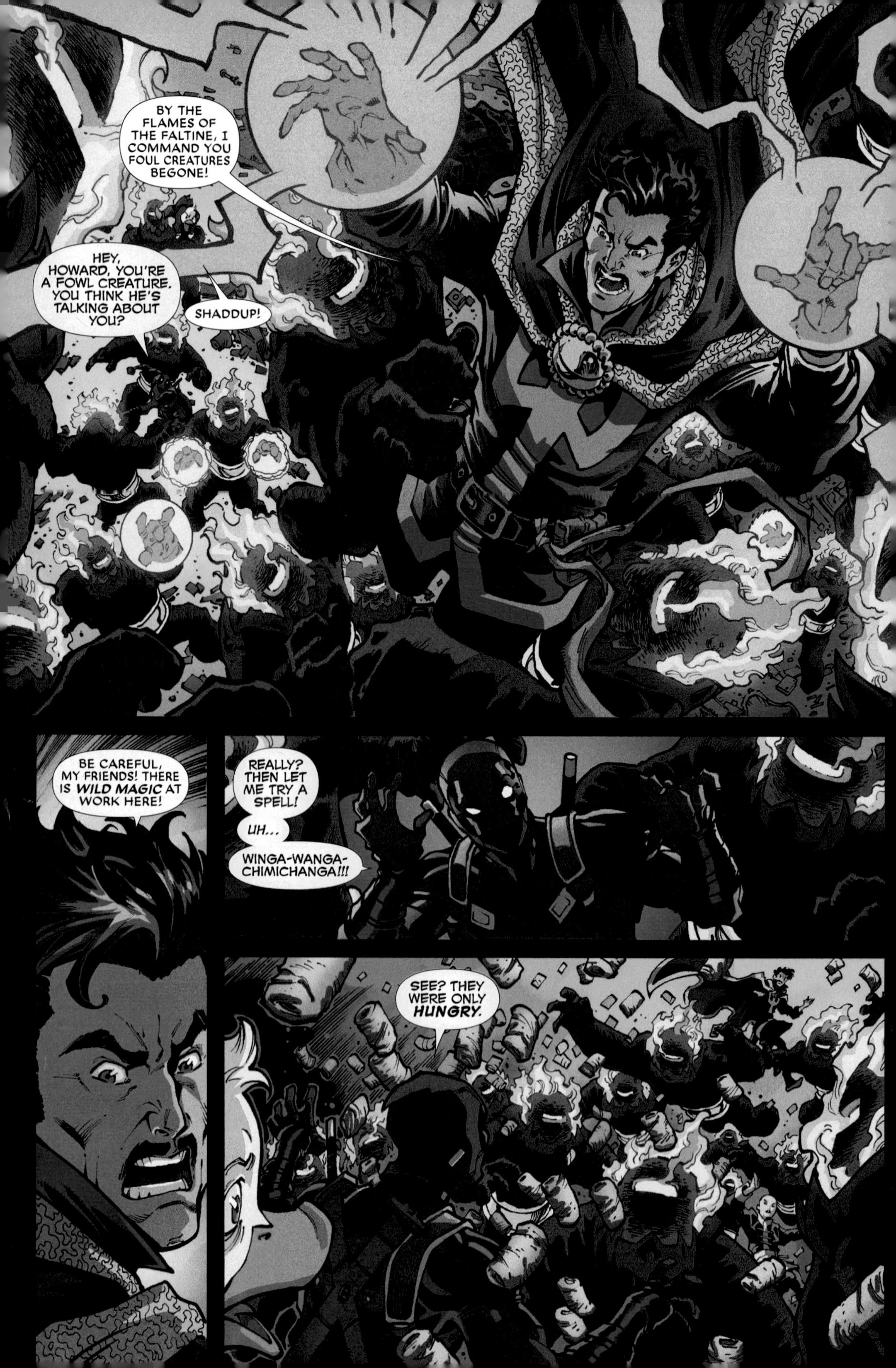
BY THE FLAMES OF THE FALTINE, I COMMAND YOU FOUL CREATURES BEGONE!
HEY, HOWARD, YOU'RE A FOWL CREATURE. YOU THINK HE'S TALKING ABOUT YOU?
SHADDUP!
BE CAREFUL, MY FRIENDS! THERE IS WILD MAGIC AT WORK HERE!
REALLY? THEN LET ME TRY A SPELL!
UH...
WINGA-WANGA-CHIMICHANGA!!!
SEE? THEY WERE ONLY HUNGRY.

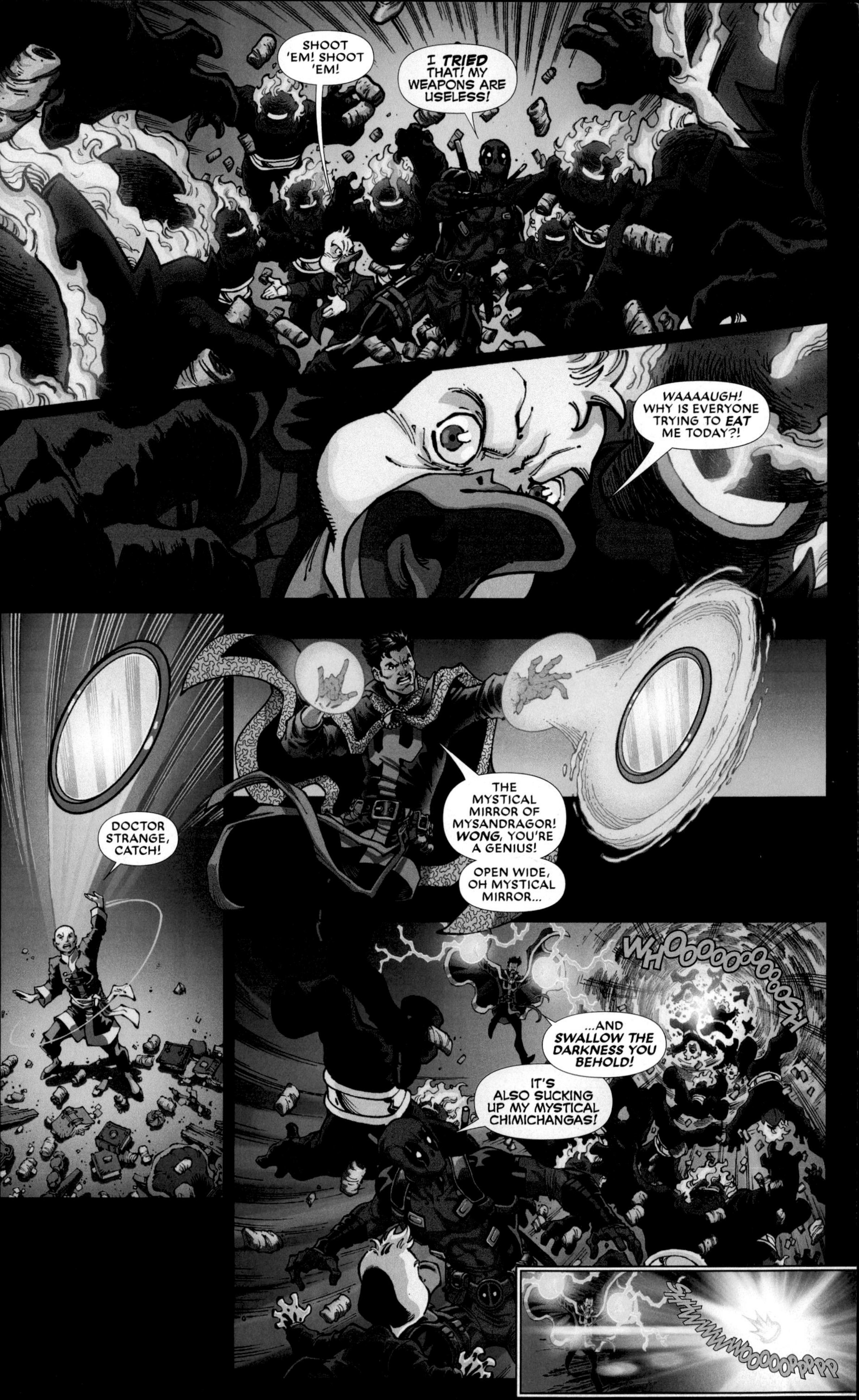
SHOOT 'EM! SHOOT 'EM!
I TRIED THAT! MY WEAPONS ARE USELESS!
WAAAAUGH! WHY IS EVERYONE TRYING TO EAT ME TODAY?!
DOCTOR STRANGE, CATCH!
THE MYSTICAL MIRROR OF MYSANDRAGOR! WONG, YOU'RE A GENIUS!
OPEN WIDE, OH MYSTICAL MIRROR...
WHOOOOOOOOOOOSH
...AND SWALLOW THE DARKNESS YOU BEHOLD!
IT'S ALSO SUCKING UP MY MYSTICAL CHIMICHANGAS!
SHWWWWOOOOORPPPP

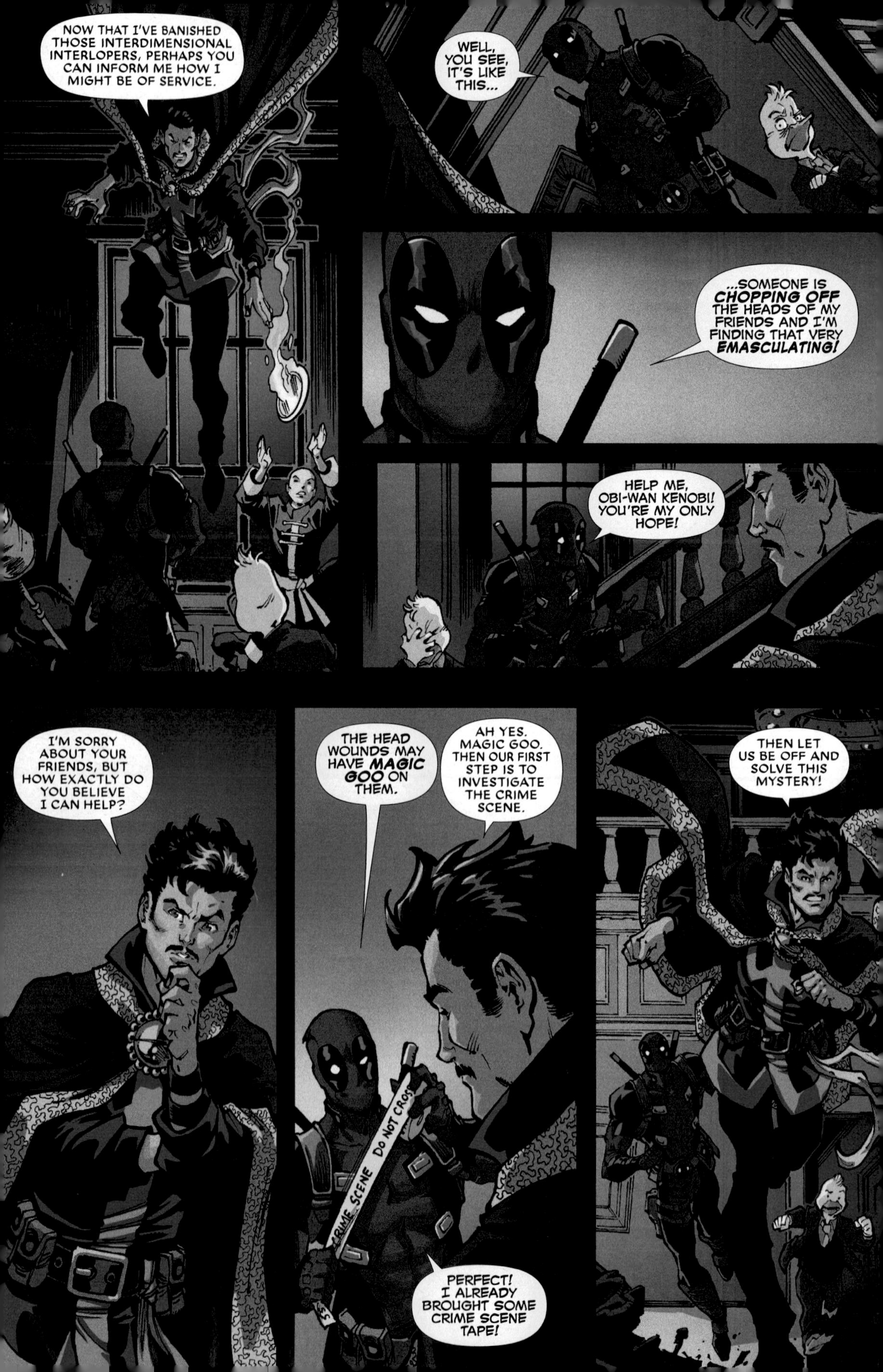
NOW THAT I'VE BANISHED THOSE INTERDIMENSIONAL INTERLOPERS, PERHAPS YOU CAN INFORM ME HOW I MIGHT BE OF SERVICE.
WELL, YOU SEE, IT'S LIKE THIS...
...SOMEONE IS CHOPPING OFF THE HEADS OF MY FRIENDS AND I'M FINDING THAT VERY EMASCULATING!
HELP ME, OBI-WAN KENOBI! YOU'RE MY ONLY HOPE!
I'M SORRY ABOUT YOUR FRIENDS, BUT HOW EXACTLY DO YOU BELIEVE I CAN HELP?
THE HEAD WOUNDS MAY HAVE MAGIC GOO ON THEM.
AH YES. MAGIC GOO. THEN OUR FIRST STEP IS TO INVESTIGATE THE CRIME SCENE.
CRIME SCENE DO NOT CROS
PERFECT! I ALREADY BROUGHT SOME CRIME SCENE TAPE!
THEN LET US BE OFF AND SOLVE THIS MYSTERY!

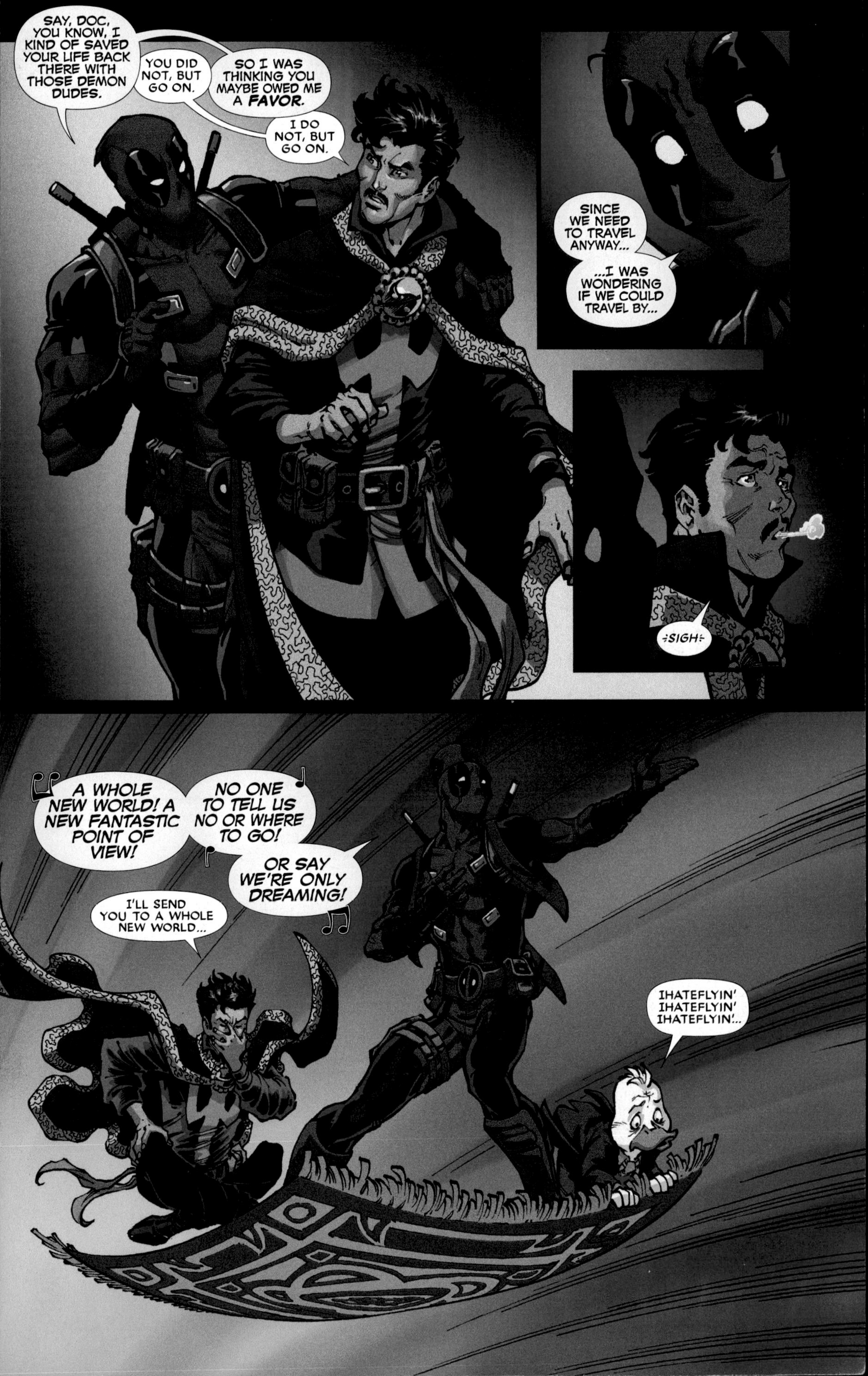
SAY, DOC, YOU KNOW, I KIND OF SAVED YOUR LIFE BACK THERE WITH THOSE DEMON DUDES.
YOU DID NOT, BUT GO ON.
SO I WAS THINKING YOU MAYBE OWED ME A FAVOR.
I DO NOT, BUT GO ON.
SINCE WE NEED TO TRAVEL ANYWAY...
...I WAS WONDERING IF WE COULD TRAVEL BY...
SIGH
A WHOLE NEW WORLD! A NEW FANTASTIC POINT OF VIEW!
NO ONE TO TELL US NO OR WHERE TO GO!
OR SAY WE'RE ONLY DREAMING!
I'LL SEND YOU TO A WHOLE NEW WORLD...
IHATEFLYIN' IHATEFLYIN' IHATEFLYIN'...

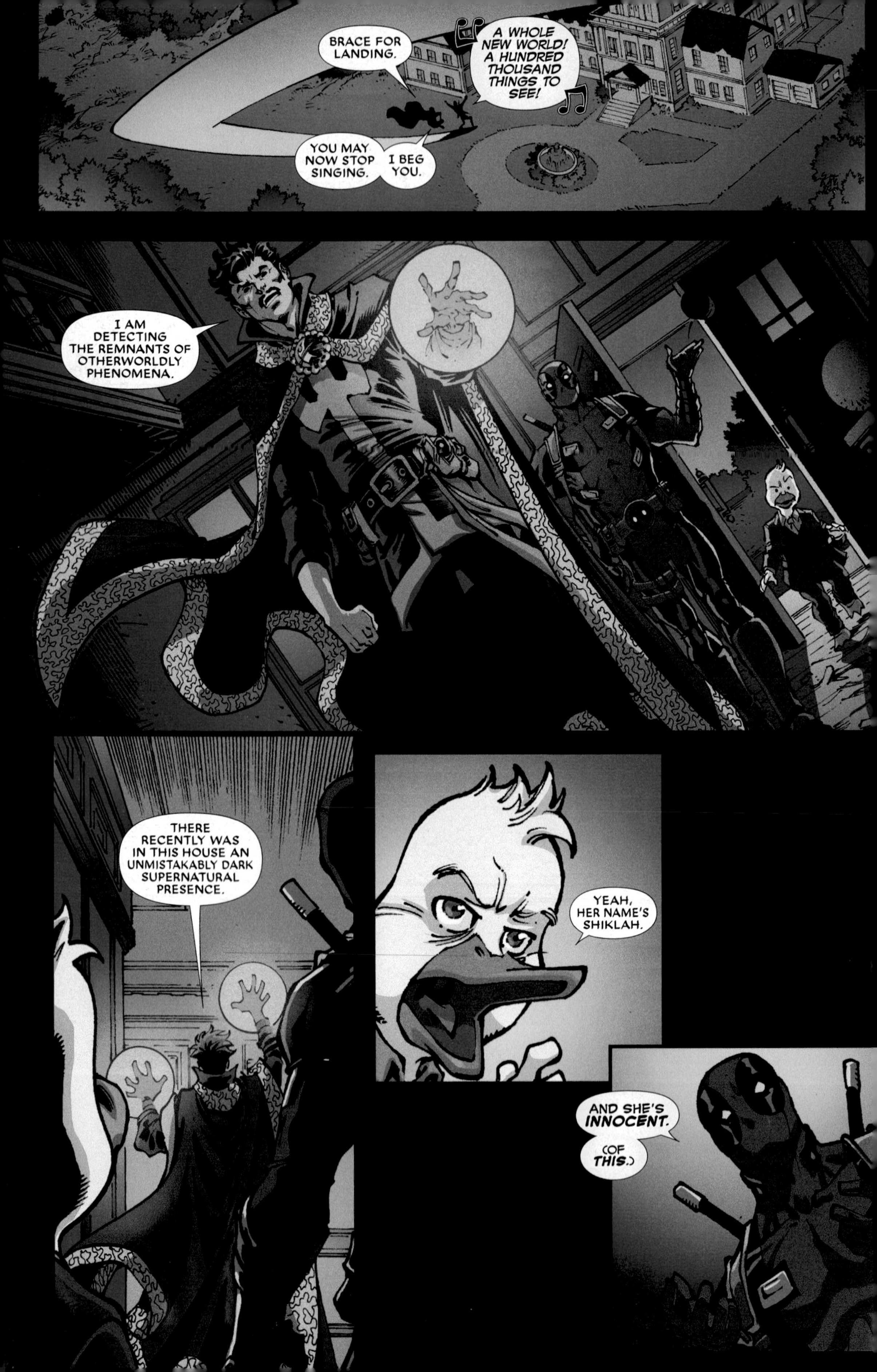
BRACE FOR LANDING.
A WHOLE NEW WORLD! A HUNDRED THOUSAND THINGS TO SEE!
YOU MAY NOW STOP SINGING.
I BEG YOU.
I AM DETECTING THE REMNANTS OF OTHERWORLDLY PHENOMENA.
THERE RECENTLY WAS IN THIS HOUSE AN UNMISTAKABLY DARK SUPERNATURAL PRESENCE.
YEAH, HER NAME'S SHIKLAH.
AND SHE'S ***INNOCENT***.
(OF ***THIS***.)

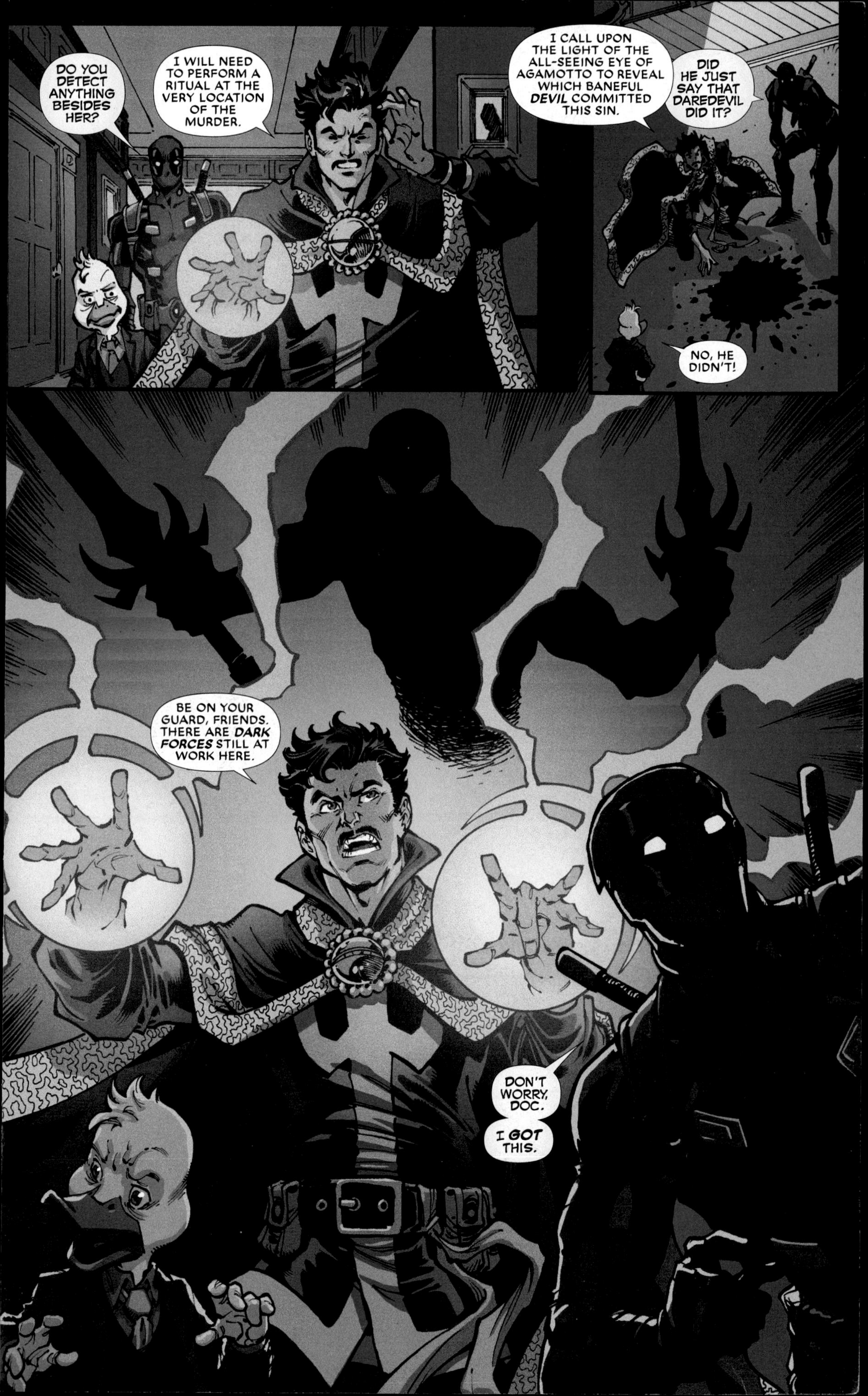
DO YOU DETECT ANYTHING BESIDES HER?
I WILL NEED TO PERFORM A RITUAL AT THE VERY LOCATION OF THE MURDER.
I CALL UPON THE LIGHT OF THE ALL-SEEING EYE OF AGAMOTTO TO REVEAL WHICH BANEFUL DEVIL COMMITTED THIS SIN.
DID HE JUST SAY THAT DAREDEVIL DID IT?
NO, HE DIDN'T!
BE ON YOUR GUARD, FRIENDS. THERE ARE DARK FORCES STILL AT WORK HERE.
DON'T WORRY, DOC.
I GOT THIS.

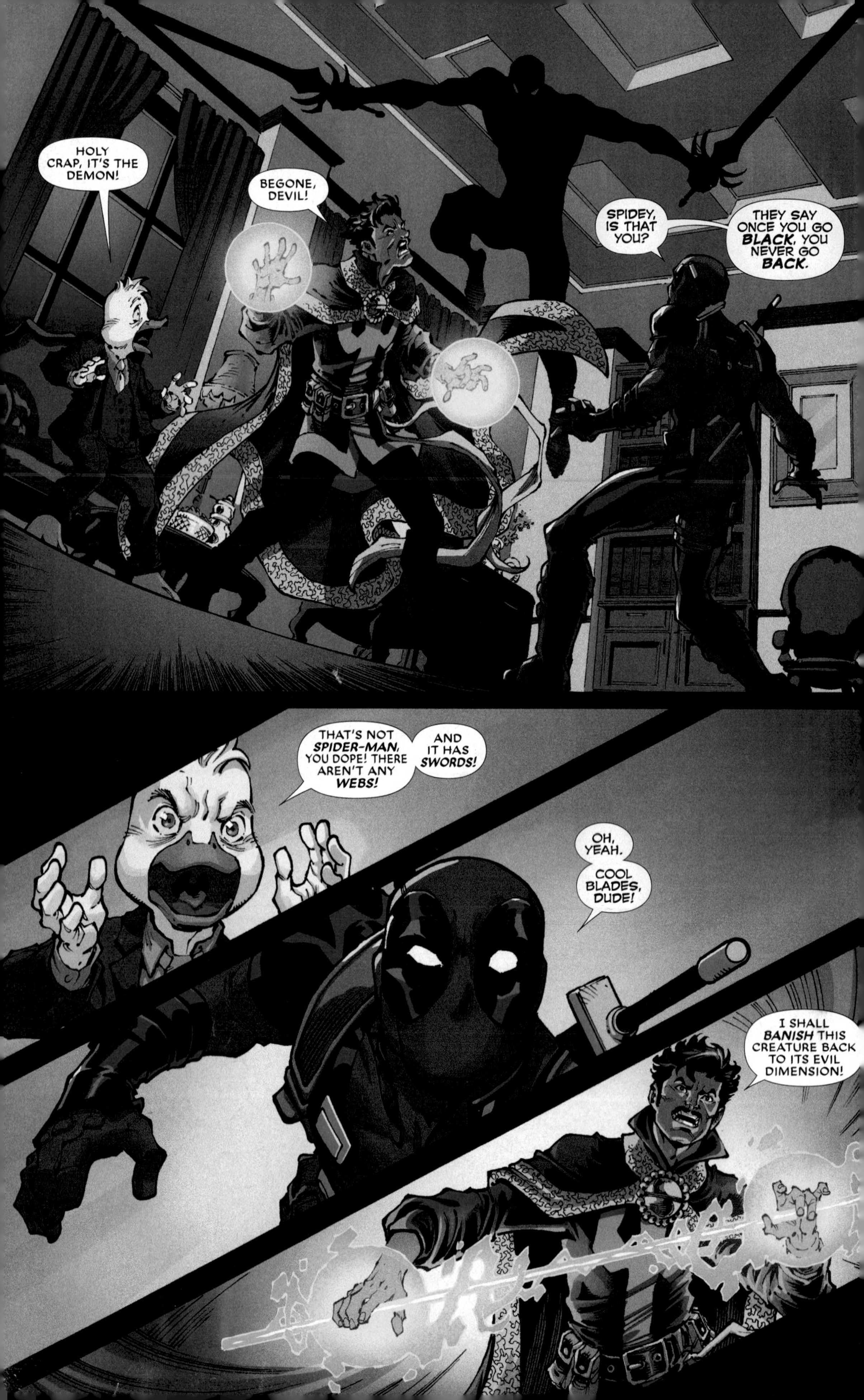
HOLY CRAP, IT'S THE DEMON!
BEGONE, DEVIL!
SPIDEY, IS THAT YOU?
THEY SAY ONCE YOU GO BLACK, YOU NEVER GO BACK.
THAT'S NOT SPIDER-MAN, YOU DOPE! THERE AREN'T ANY WEBS!
AND IT HAS SWORDS!
OH, YEAH.
COOL BLADES, DUDE!
I SHALL BANISH THIS CREATURE BACK TO ITS EVIL DIMENSION!

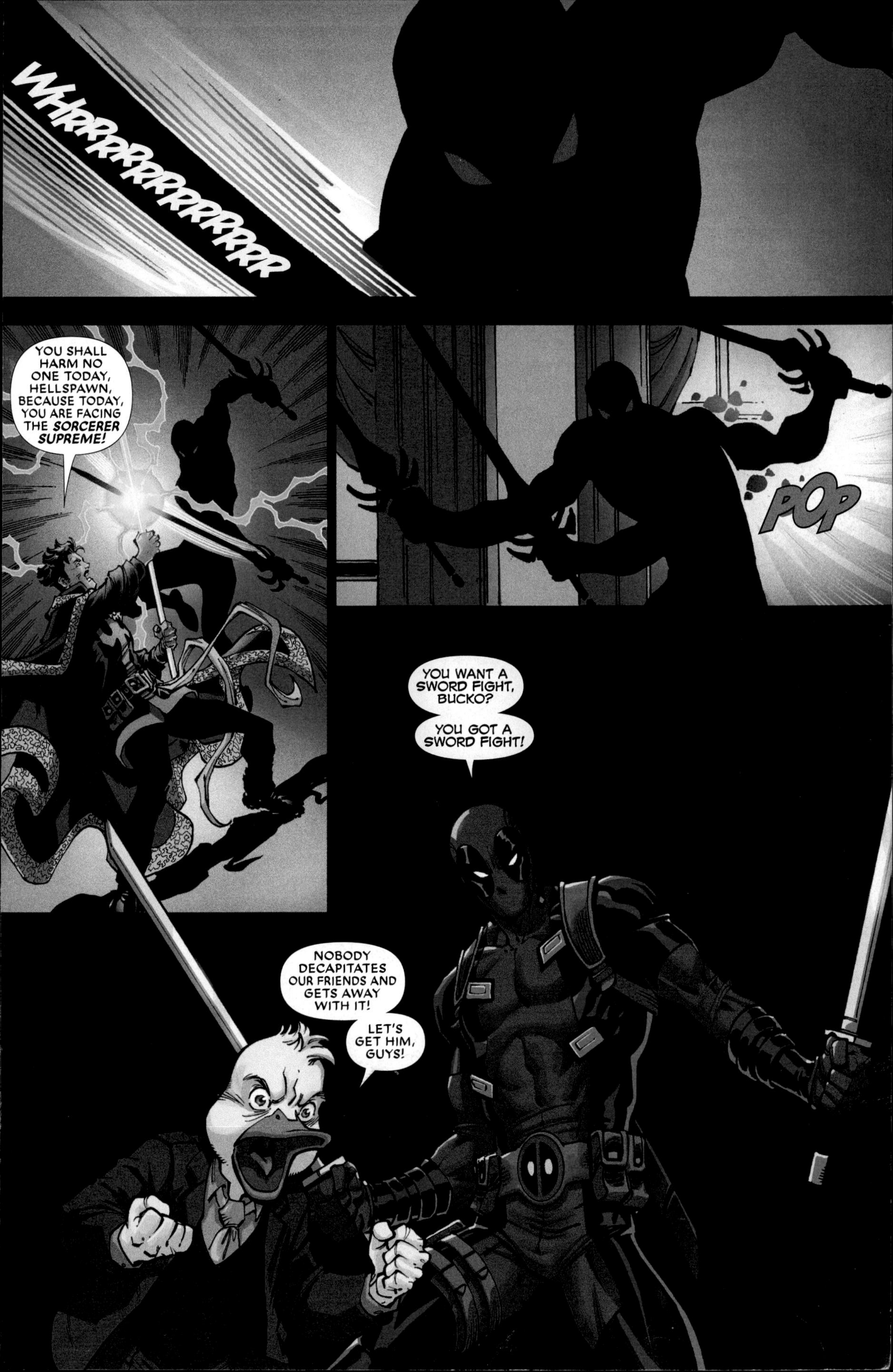
WHRRRRRRRRRRRR
YOU SHALL HARM NO ONE TODAY, HELLSPAWN, BECAUSE TODAY, YOU ARE FACING THE *SORCERER SUPREME!*
POP
YOU WANT A SWORD FIGHT, BUCKO?
YOU GOT A SWORD FIGHT!
NOBODY DECAPITATES OUR FRIENDS AND GETS AWAY WITH IT!
LET'S GET HIM, GUYS!

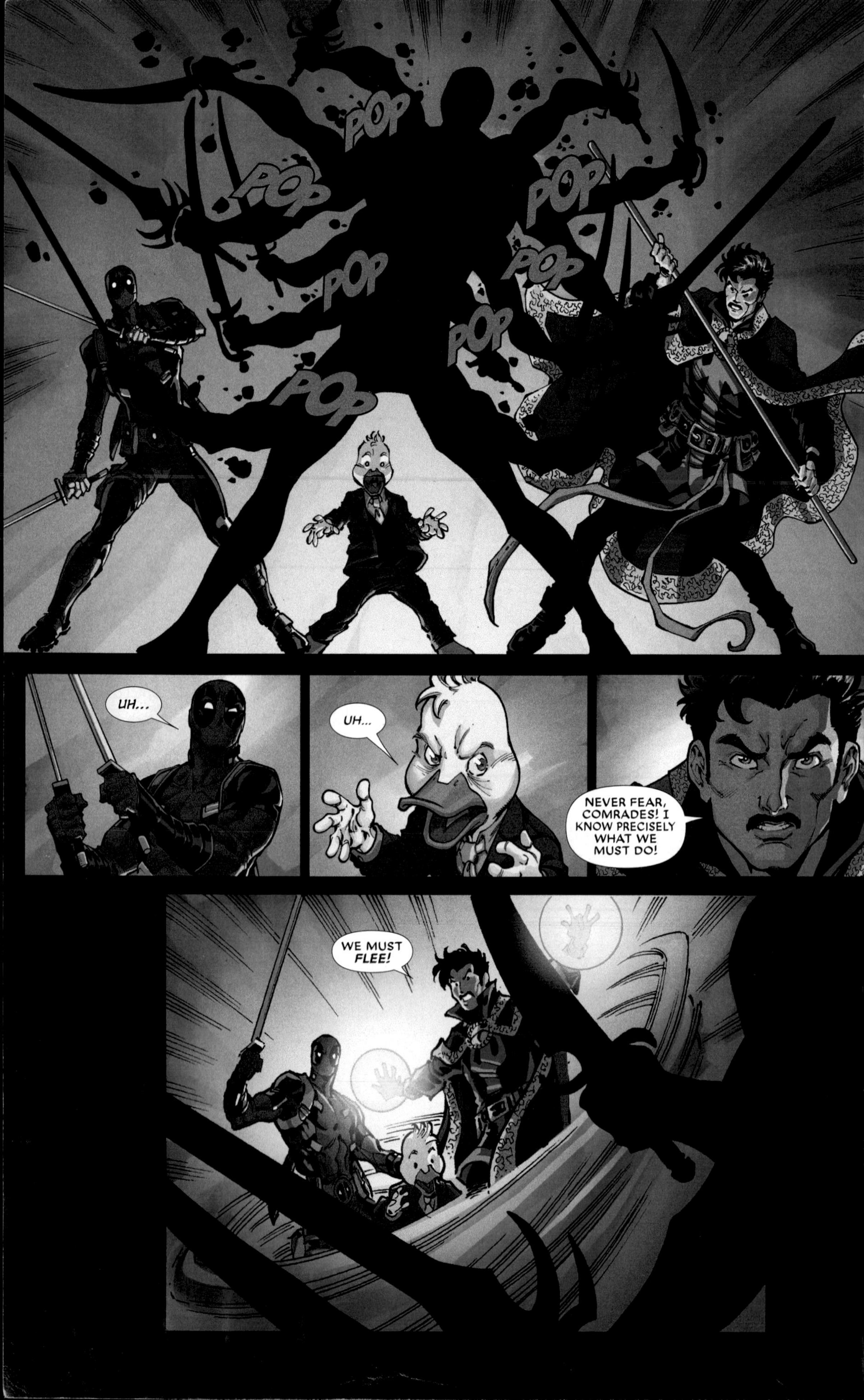
POP
POP
POP
POP
POP
POP
POP
POP
UH...
UH...
NEVER FEAR, COMRADES! I KNOW PRECISELY WHAT WE MUST DO!
WE MUST FLEE!

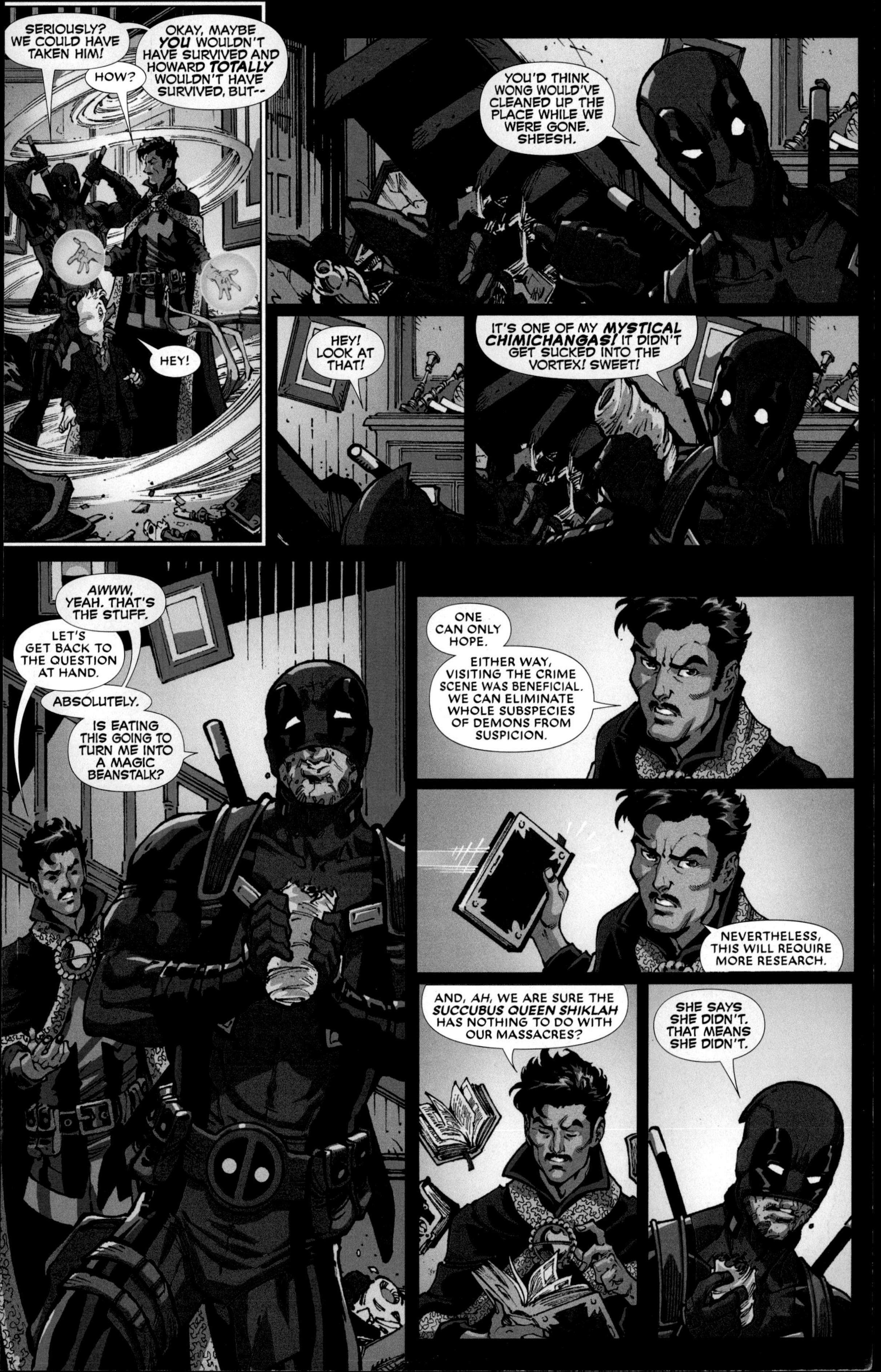
SERIOUSLY? WE COULD HAVE TAKEN HIM!
OKAY, MAYBE *YOU* WOULDN'T HAVE SURVIVED AND HOWARD ***TOTALLY*** WOULDN'T HAVE SURVIVED, BUT--
HOW?
HEY!
YOU'D THINK WONG WOULD'VE CLEANED UP THE PLACE WHILE WE WERE GONE. SHEESH.
HEY! LOOK AT THAT!
IT'S ONE OF MY ***MYSTICAL CHIMICHANGAS!*** IT DIDN'T GET SUCKED INTO THE VORTEX! SWEET!
AWWW, YEAH. THAT'S THE STUFF.
LET'S GET BACK TO THE QUESTION AT HAND.
ABSOLUTELY.
IS EATING THIS GOING TO TURN ME INTO A MAGIC BEANSTALK?
ONE CAN ONLY HOPE.
EITHER WAY, VISITING THE CRIME SCENE WAS BENEFICIAL. WE CAN ELIMINATE WHOLE SUBSPECIES OF DEMONS FROM SUSPICION.
NEVERTHELESS, THIS WILL REQUIRE MORE RESEARCH.
AND, *AH,* WE ARE SURE THE ***SUCCUBUS QUEEN SHIKLAH*** HAS NOTHING TO DO WITH OUR MASSACRES?
SHE SAYS SHE DIDN'T. THAT MEANS SHE DIDN'T.

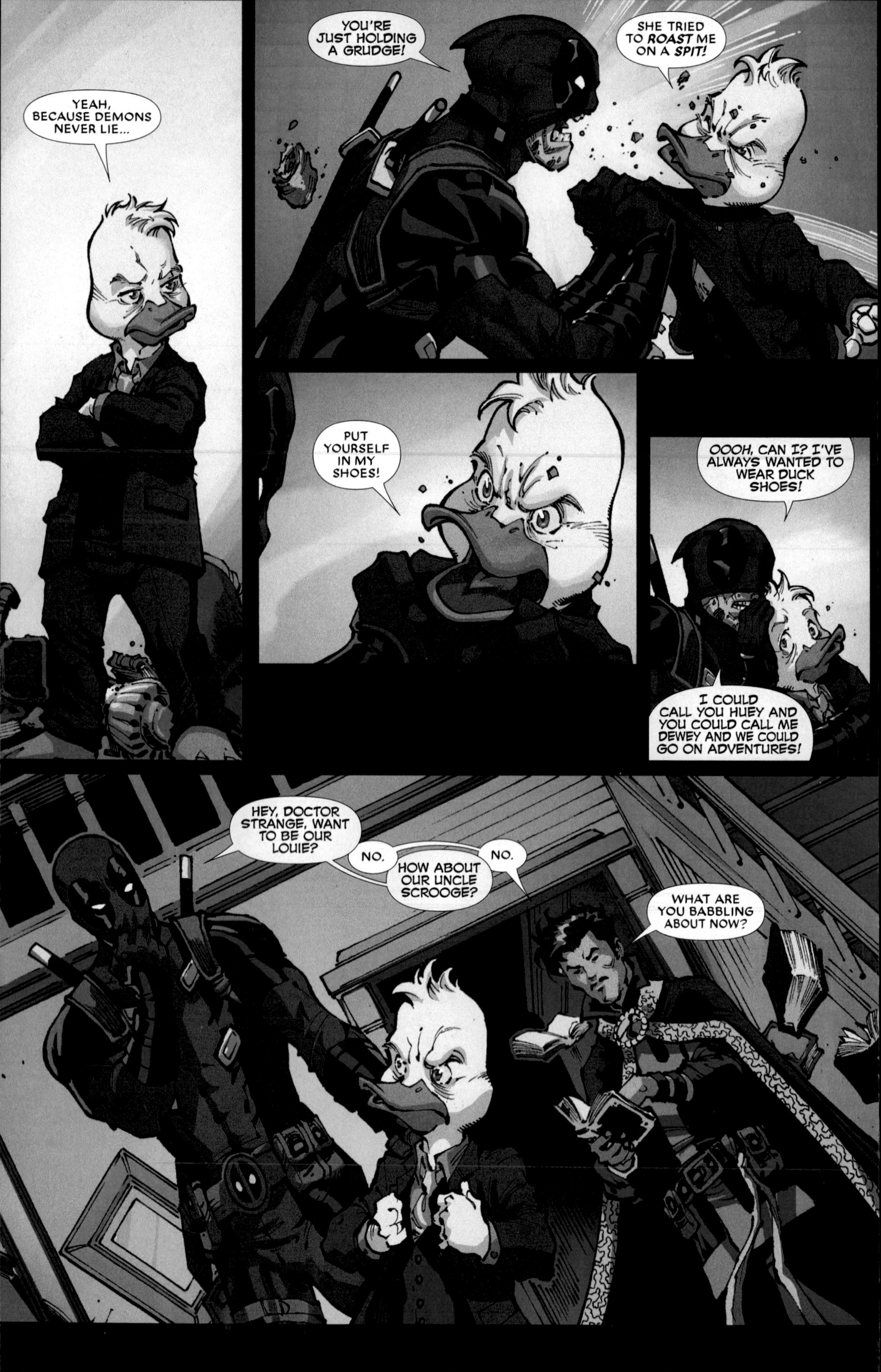
YEAH, BECAUSE DEMONS NEVER LIE...
YOU'RE JUST HOLDING A GRUDGE!
SHE TRIED TO ROAST ME ON A SPIT!
PUT YOURSELF IN MY SHOES!
OOOH, CAN I? I'VE ALWAYS WANTED TO WEAR DUCK SHOES!
I COULD CALL YOU HUEY AND YOU COULD CALL ME DEWEY AND WE COULD GO ON ADVENTURES!
HEY, DOCTOR STRANGE, WANT TO BE OUR LOUIE?
NO.
HOW ABOUT OUR UNCLE SCROOGE?
NO.
WHAT ARE YOU BABBLING ABOUT NOW?

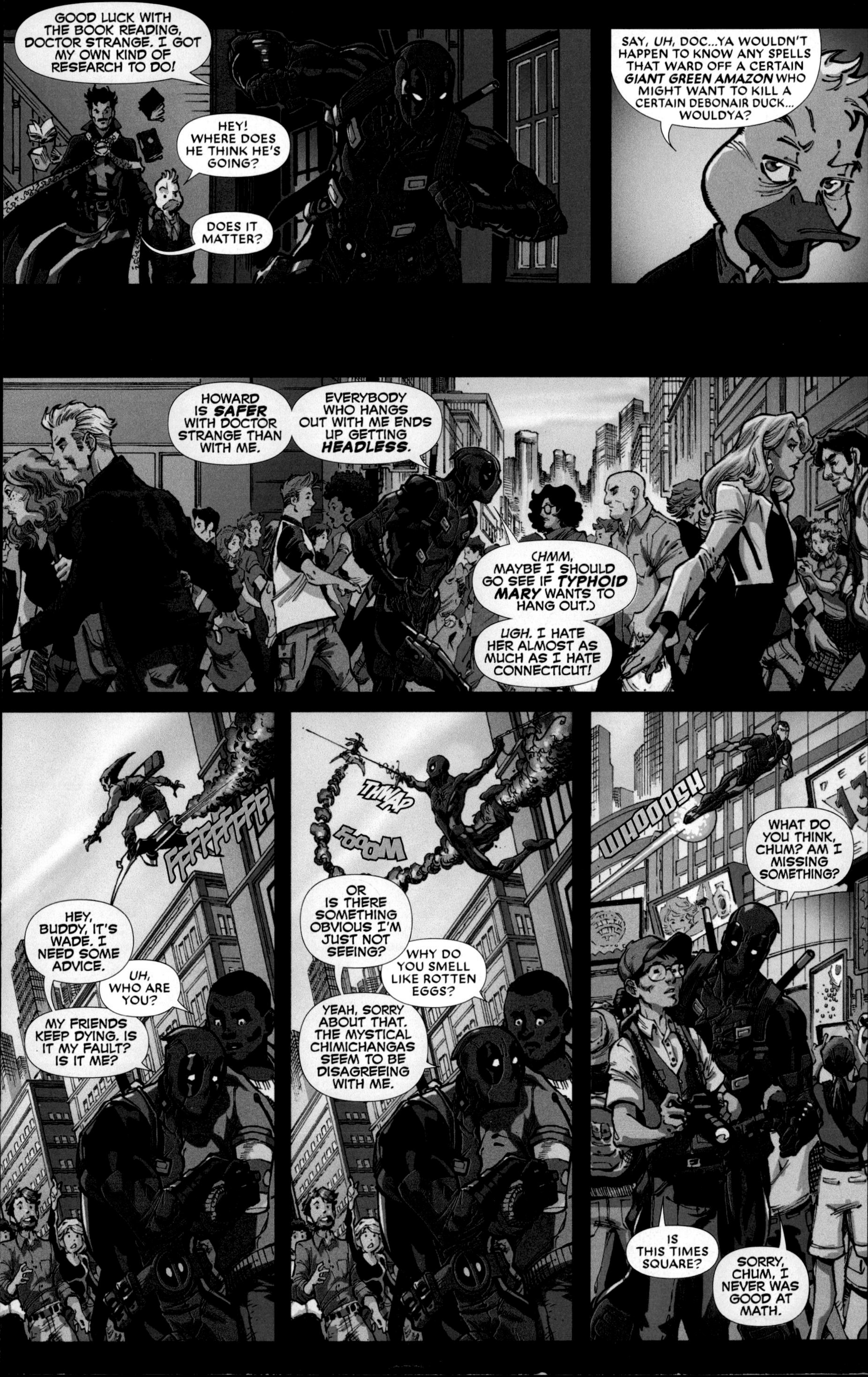
GOOD LUCK WITH THE BOOK READING, DOCTOR STRANGE. I GOT MY OWN KIND OF RESEARCH TO DO!
HEY! WHERE DOES HE THINK HE'S GOING?
DOES IT MATTER?
SAY, UH, DOC...YA WOULDN'T HAPPEN TO KNOW ANY SPELLS THAT WARD OFF A CERTAIN GIANT GREEN AMAZON WHO MIGHT WANT TO KILL A CERTAIN DEBONAIR DUCK... WOULDYA?
HOWARD IS SAFER WITH DOCTOR STRANGE THAN WITH ME.
EVERYBODY WHO HANGS OUT WITH ME ENDS UP GETTING HEADLESS.
(HMM, MAYBE I SHOULD GO SEE IF TYPHOID MARY WANTS TO HANG OUT.)
UGH. I HATE HER ALMOST AS MUCH AS I HATE CONNECTICUT!
FFFFFFFFP
HEY, BUDDY, IT'S WADE. I NEED SOME ADVICE.
UH, WHO ARE YOU?
MY FRIENDS KEEP DYING. IS IT MY FAULT? IS IT ME?
THWAP
FOOOM
OR IS THERE SOMETHING OBVIOUS I'M JUST NOT SEEING?
WHY DO YOU SMELL LIKE ROTTEN EGGS?
YEAH, SORRY ABOUT THAT. THE MYSTICAL CHIMICHANGAS SEEM TO BE DISAGREEING WITH ME.
WHOOOOSH
WHAT DO YOU THINK, CHUM? AM I MISSING SOMETHING?
IS THIS TIMES SQUARE?
SORRY, CHUM, I NEVER WAS GOOD AT MATH.

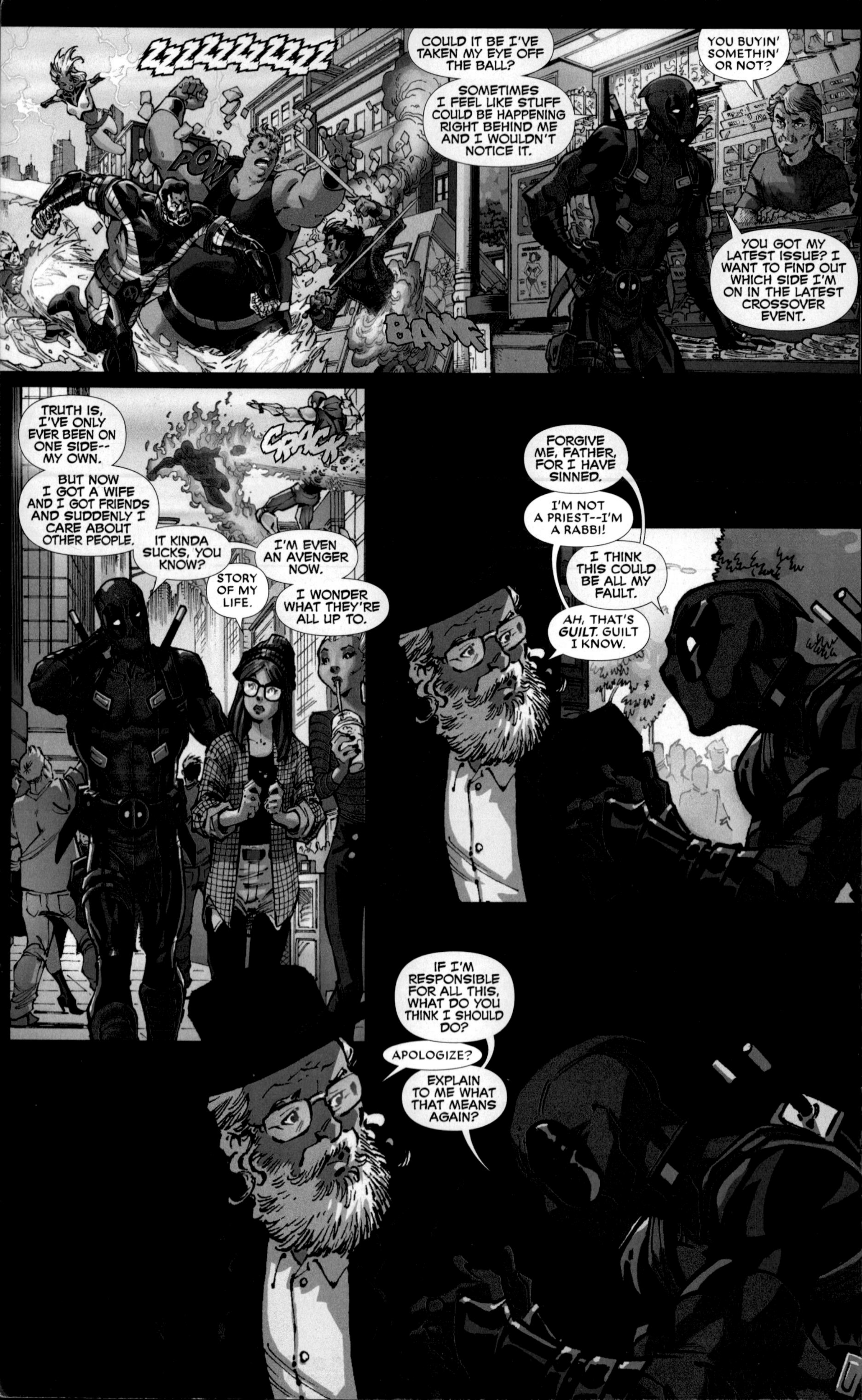
ZZZZZZZZZZZ
POW
BAMF
COULD IT BE I'VE TAKEN MY EYE OFF THE BALL?
SOMETIMES I FEEL LIKE STUFF COULD BE HAPPENING RIGHT BEHIND ME AND I WOULDN'T NOTICE IT.
YOU BUYIN' SOMETHIN' OR NOT?
YOU GOT MY LATEST ISSUE? I WANT TO FIND OUT WHICH SIDE I'M ON IN THE LATEST CROSSOVER EVENT.
CRACK
TRUTH IS, I'VE ONLY EVER BEEN ON ONE SIDE--MY OWN.
BUT NOW I GOT A WIFE AND I GOT FRIENDS AND SUDDENLY I CARE ABOUT OTHER PEOPLE.
IT KINDA SUCKS, YOU KNOW?
STORY OF MY LIFE.
I'M EVEN AN AVENGER NOW.
I WONDER WHAT THEY'RE ALL UP TO.
FORGIVE ME, FATHER, FOR I HAVE SINNED.
I'M NOT A PRIEST--I'M A RABBI!
I THINK THIS COULD BE ALL MY FAULT.
AH, THAT'S GUILT. GUILT I KNOW.
IF I'M RESPONSIBLE FOR ALL THIS, WHAT DO YOU THINK I SHOULD DO?
APOLOGIZE?
EXPLAIN TO ME WHAT THAT MEANS AGAIN?

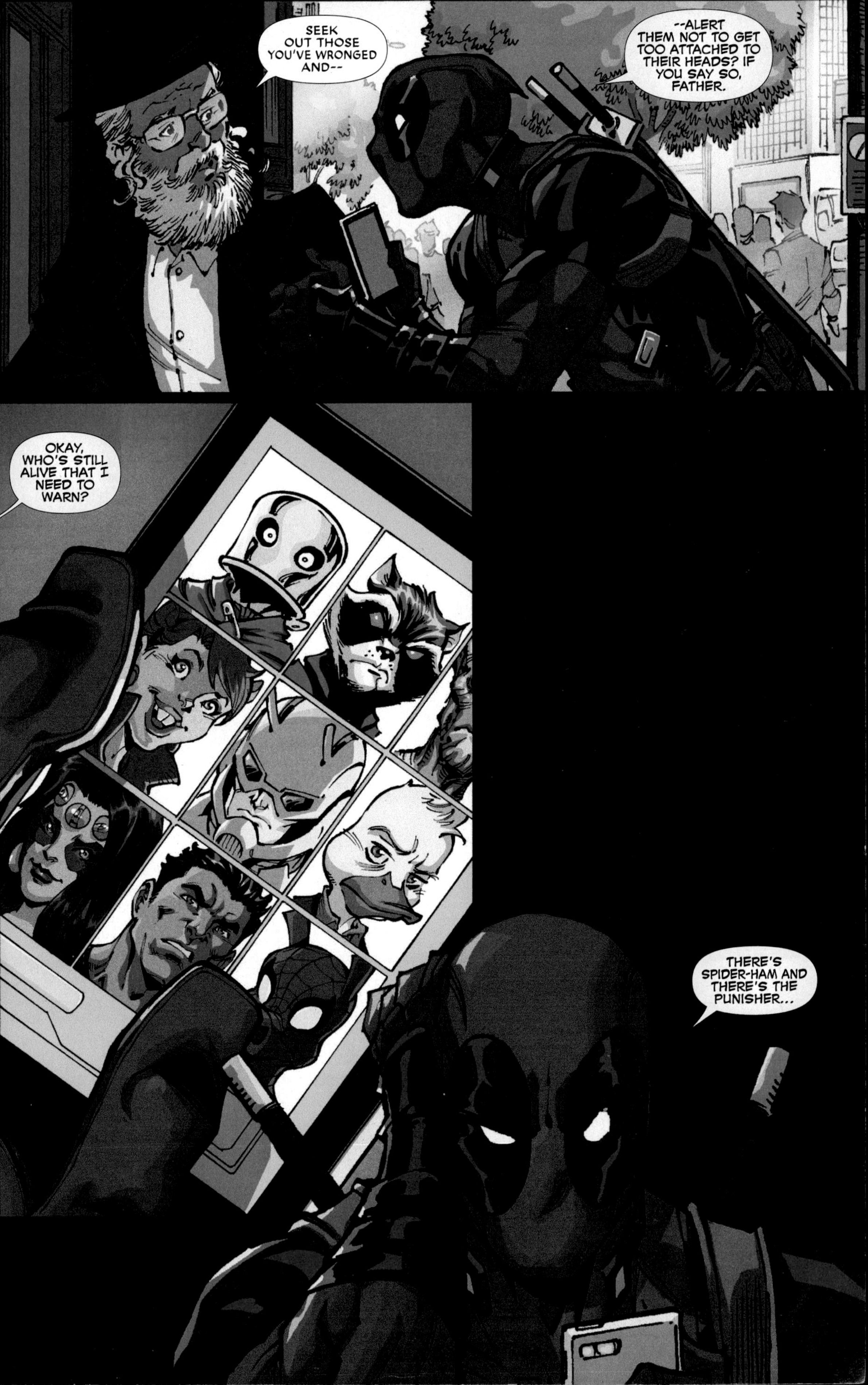
SEEK OUT THOSE YOU'VE WRONGED AND--
--ALERT THEM NOT TO GET TOO ATTACHED TO THEIR HEADS? IF YOU SAY SO, FATHER.
OKAY, WHO'S STILL ALIVE THAT I NEED TO WARN?
THERE'S SPIDER-HAM AND THERE'S THE PUNISHER...

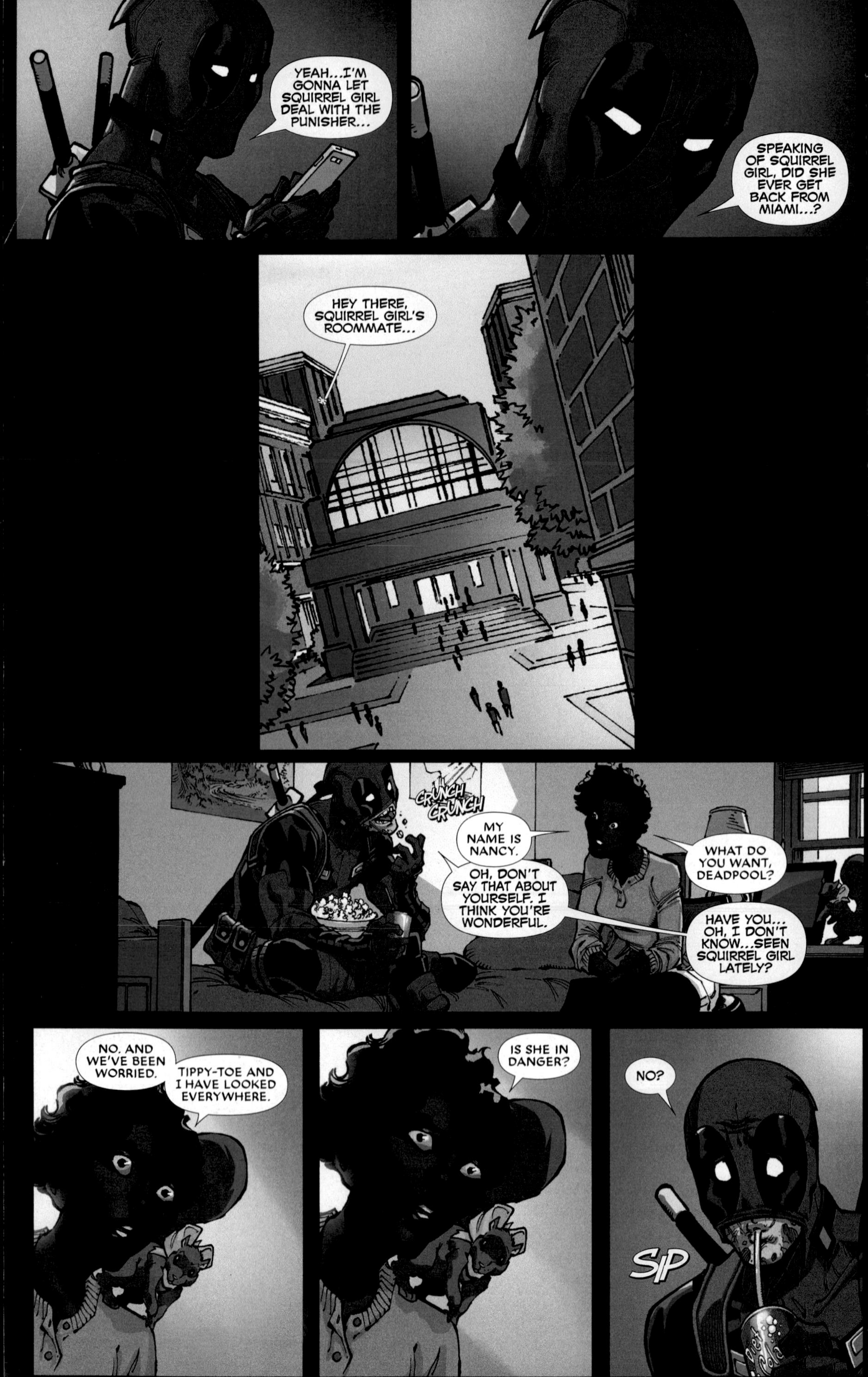
YEAH...I'M GONNA LET SQUIRREL GIRL DEAL WITH THE PUNISHER...
SPEAKING OF SQUIRREL GIRL, DID SHE EVER GET BACK FROM MIAMI...?
HEY THERE, SQUIRREL GIRL'S ROOMMATE...
CRUNCH CRUNCH
MY NAME IS NANCY.
OH, DON'T SAY THAT ABOUT YOURSELF. I THINK YOU'RE WONDERFUL.
WHAT DO YOU WANT, DEADPOOL?
HAVE YOU... OH, I DON'T KNOW...SEEN SQUIRREL GIRL LATELY?
NO. AND WE'VE BEEN WORRIED.
TIPPY-TOE AND I HAVE LOOKED EVERYWHERE.
IS SHE IN DANGER?
NO?
SIP

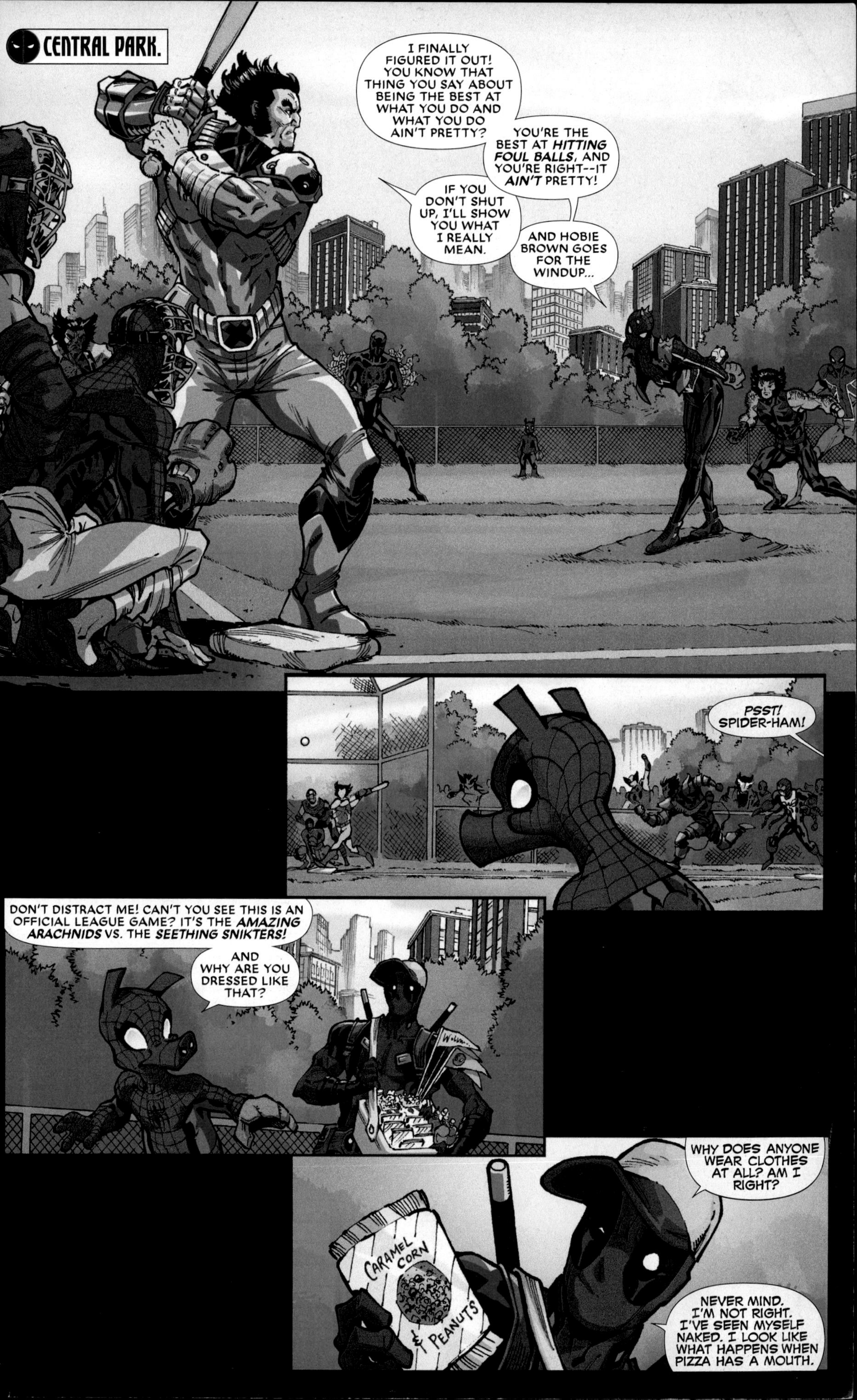
CENTRAL PARK.
I FINALLY FIGURED IT OUT! YOU KNOW THAT THING YOU SAY ABOUT BEING THE BEST AT WHAT YOU DO AND WHAT YOU DO AIN'T PRETTY?
YOU'RE THE BEST AT HITTING FOUL BALLS, AND YOU'RE RIGHT--IT AIN'T PRETTY!
IF YOU DON'T SHUT UP, I'LL SHOW YOU WHAT I REALLY MEAN.
AND HOBIE BROWN GOES FOR THE WINDUP...
PSST! SPIDER-HAM!
DON'T DISTRACT ME! CAN'T YOU SEE THIS IS AN OFFICIAL LEAGUE GAME? IT'S THE AMAZING ARACHNIDS VS. THE SEETHING SNIKTERS!
AND WHY ARE YOU DRESSED LIKE THAT?
WHY DOES ANYONE WEAR CLOTHES AT ALL? AM I RIGHT?
CARAMEL CORN & PEANUTS
NEVER MIND. I'M NOT RIGHT. I'VE SEEN MYSELF NAKED. I LOOK LIKE WHAT HAPPENS WHEN PIZZA HAS A MOUTH.

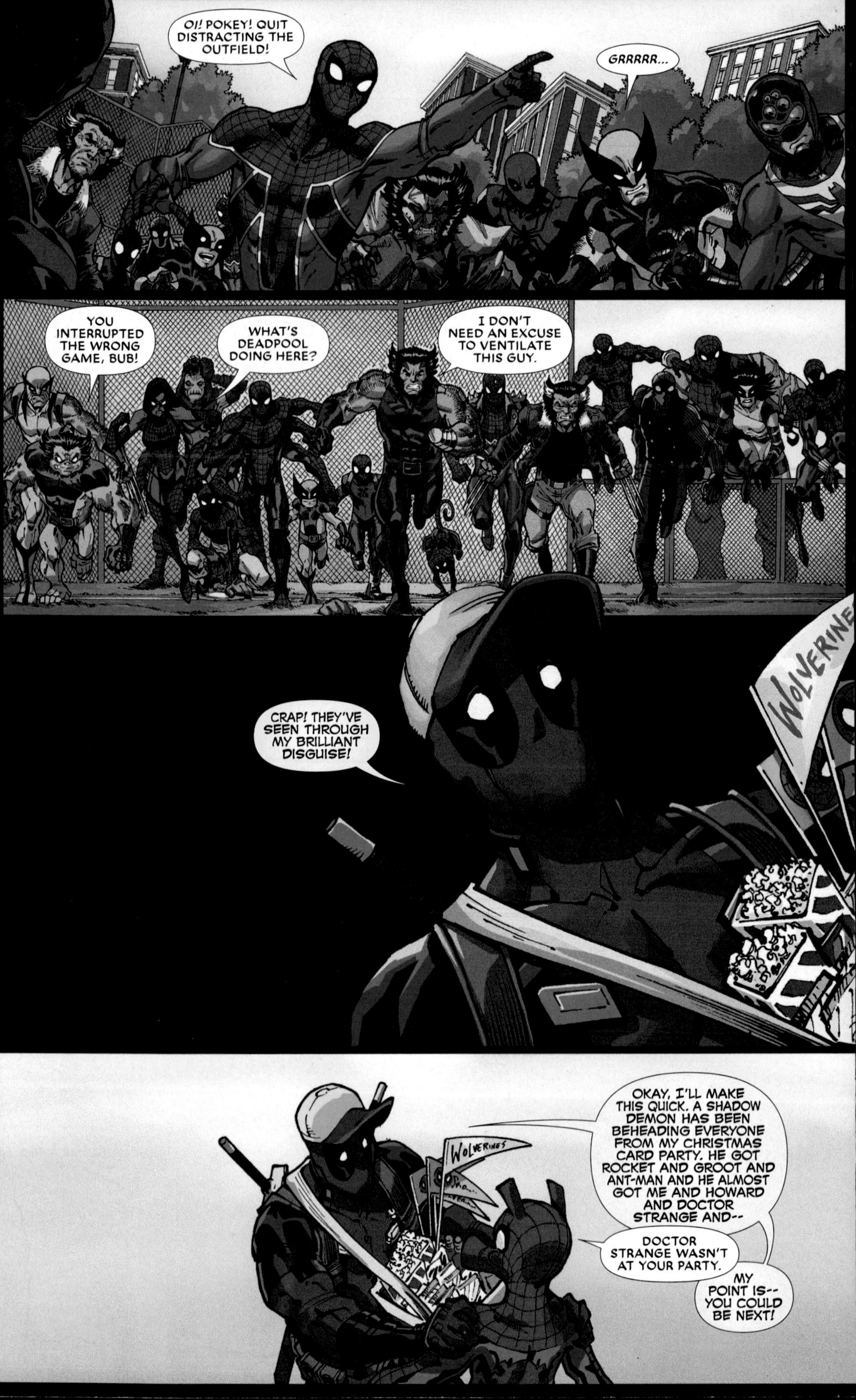
OI! POKEY! QUIT DISTRACTING THE OUTFIELD!
GRRRRR...
YOU INTERRUPTED THE WRONG GAME, BUB!
WHAT'S DEADPOOL DOING HERE?
I DON'T NEED AN EXCUSE TO VENTILATE THIS GUY.
CRAP! THEY'VE SEEN THROUGH MY BRILLIANT DISGUISE!
WOLVERINES
OKAY, I'LL MAKE THIS QUICK. A SHADOW DEMON HAS BEEN BEHEADING EVERYONE FROM MY CHRISTMAS CARD PARTY. HE GOT ROCKET AND GROOT AND ANT-MAN AND HE ALMOST GOT ME AND HOWARD AND DOCTOR STRANGE AND--
DOCTOR STRANGE WASN'T AT YOUR PARTY.
MY POINT IS-- YOU COULD BE NEXT!

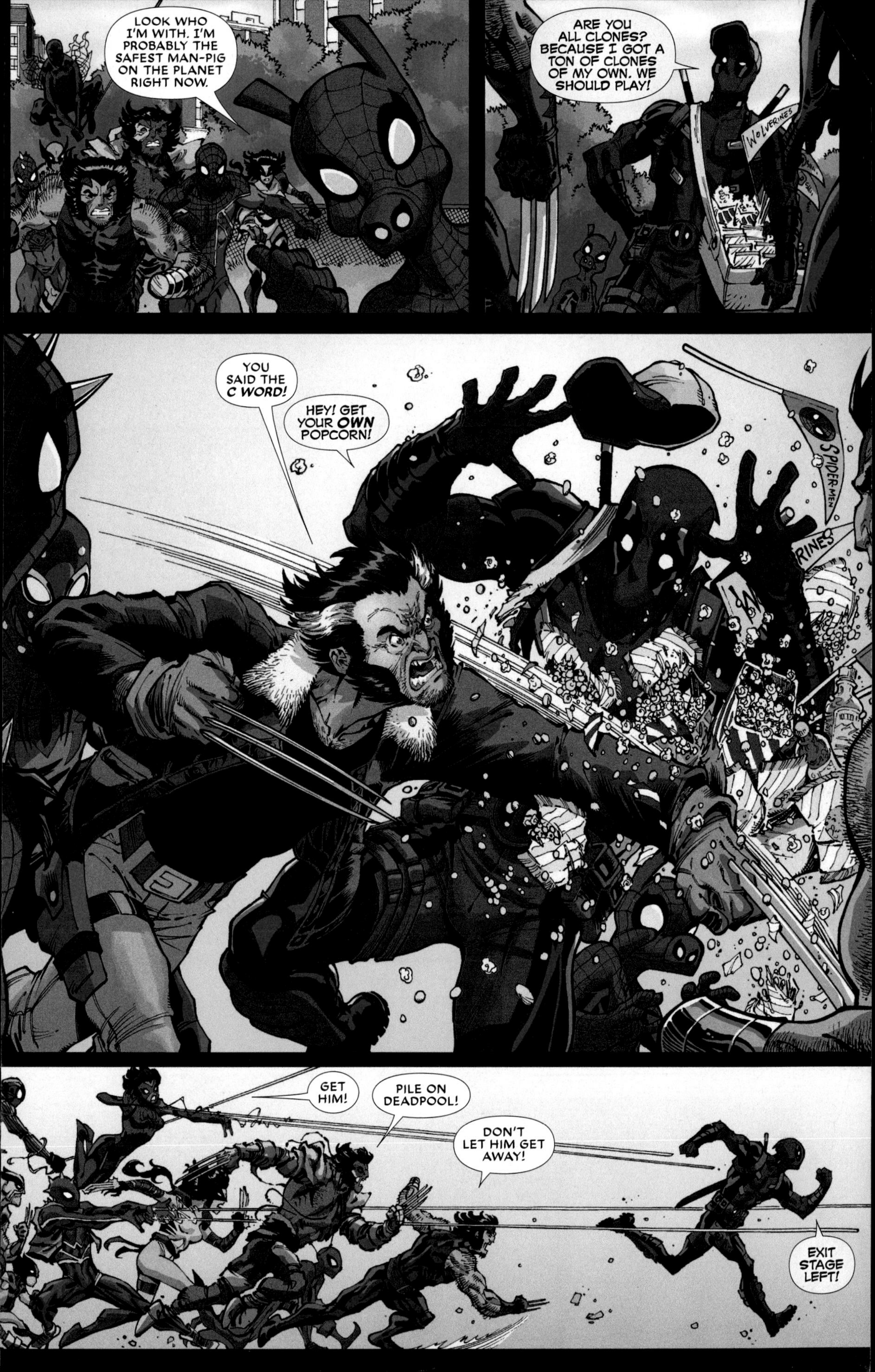
LOOK WHO I'M WITH. I'M PROBABLY THE SAFEST MAN-PIG ON THE PLANET RIGHT NOW.
ARE YOU ALL CLONES? BECAUSE I GOT A TON OF CLONES OF MY OWN. WE SHOULD PLAY!
WOLVERINES
YOU SAID THE C WORD!
HEY! GET YOUR OWN POPCORN!
SPIDER-MEN
GET HIM!
PILE ON DEADPOOL!
DON'T LET HIM GET AWAY!
EXIT STAGE LEFT!

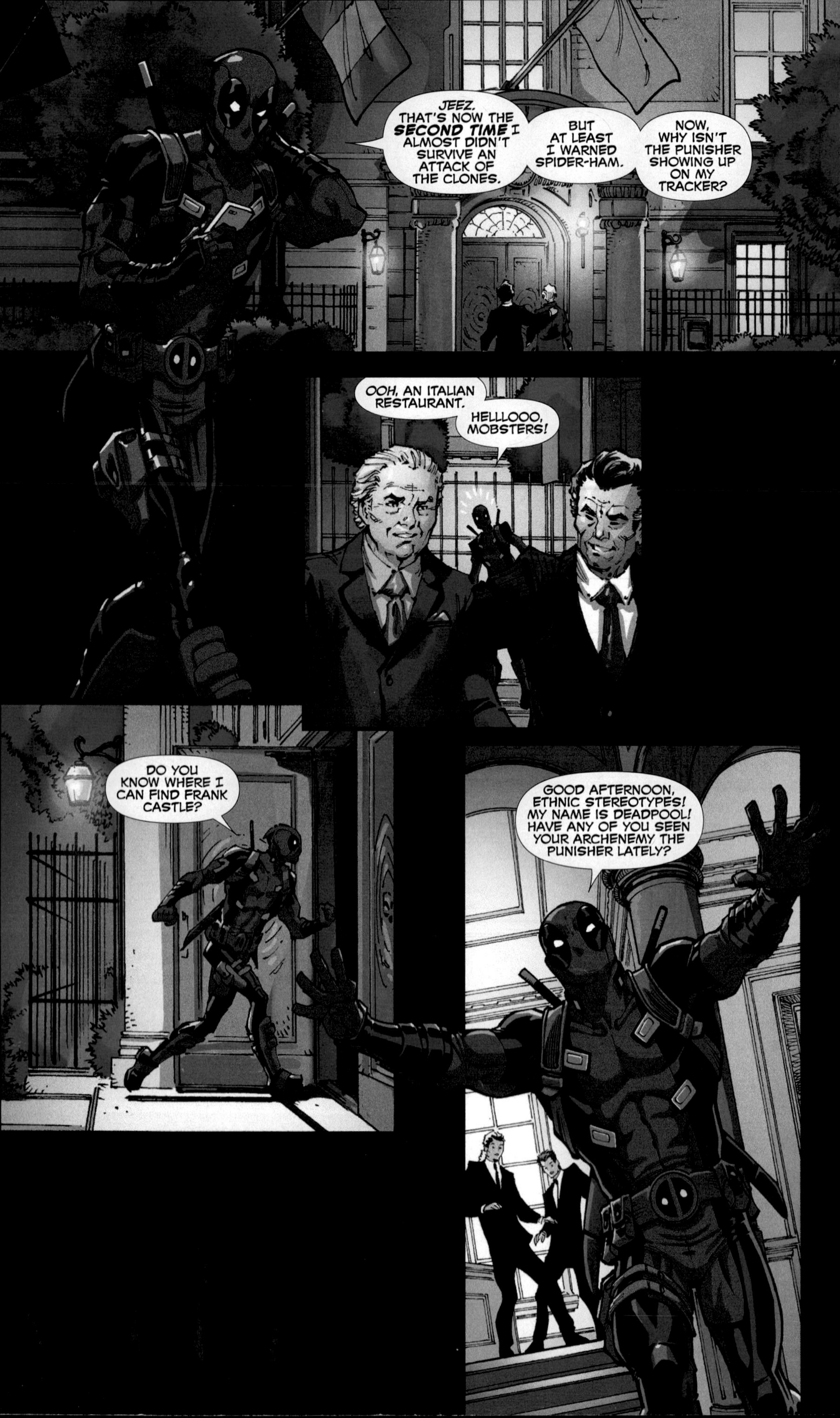
JEEZ. THAT'S NOW THE SECOND TIME I ALMOST DIDN'T SURVIVE AN ATTACK OF THE CLONES.
BUT AT LEAST I WARNED SPIDER-HAM.
NOW, WHY ISN'T THE PUNISHER SHOWING UP ON MY TRACKER?
OOH, AN ITALIAN RESTAURANT.
HELLLOOO, MOBSTERS!
DO YOU KNOW WHERE I CAN FIND FRANK CASTLE?
GOOD AFTERNOON, ETHNIC STEREOTYPES! MY NAME IS DEADPOOL! HAVE ANY OF YOU SEEN YOUR ARCHENEMY THE PUNISHER LATELY?

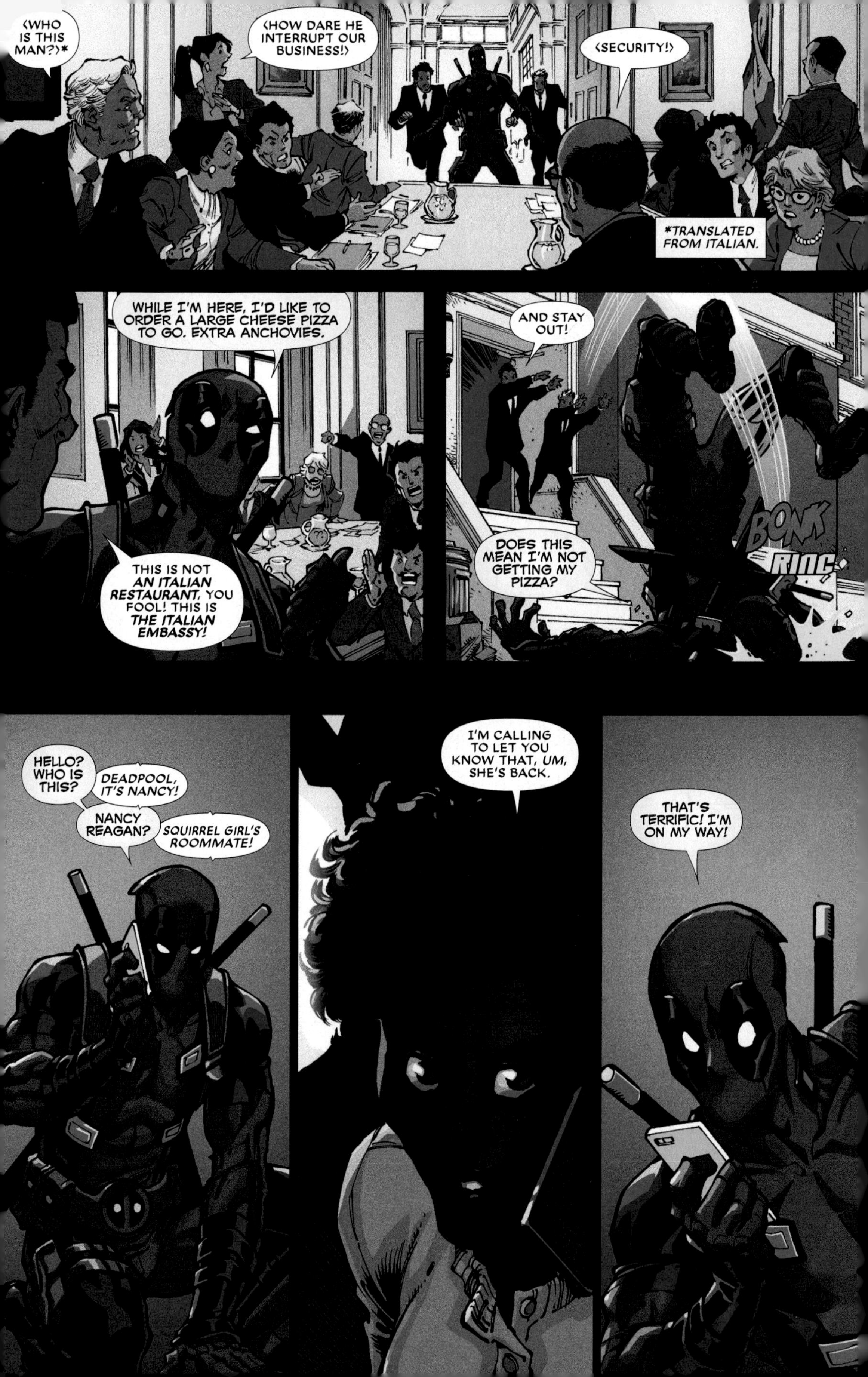
‹WHO IS THIS MAN?›*
‹HOW DARE HE INTERRUPT OUR BUSINESS!›
‹SECURITY!›
*TRANSLATED FROM ITALIAN.
WHILE I'M HERE, I'D LIKE TO ORDER A LARGE CHEESE PIZZA TO GO. EXTRA ANCHOVIES.
THIS IS NOT AN ITALIAN RESTAURANT, YOU FOOL! THIS IS THE ITALIAN EMBASSY!
AND STAY OUT!
DOES THIS MEAN I'M NOT GETTING MY PIZZA?
BONK
RING
HELLO? WHO IS THIS?
DEADPOOL, IT'S NANCY!
NANCY REAGAN?
SQUIRREL GIRL'S ROOMMATE!
I'M CALLING TO LET YOU KNOW THAT, UM, SHE'S BACK.
THAT'S TERRIFIC! I'M ON MY WAY!

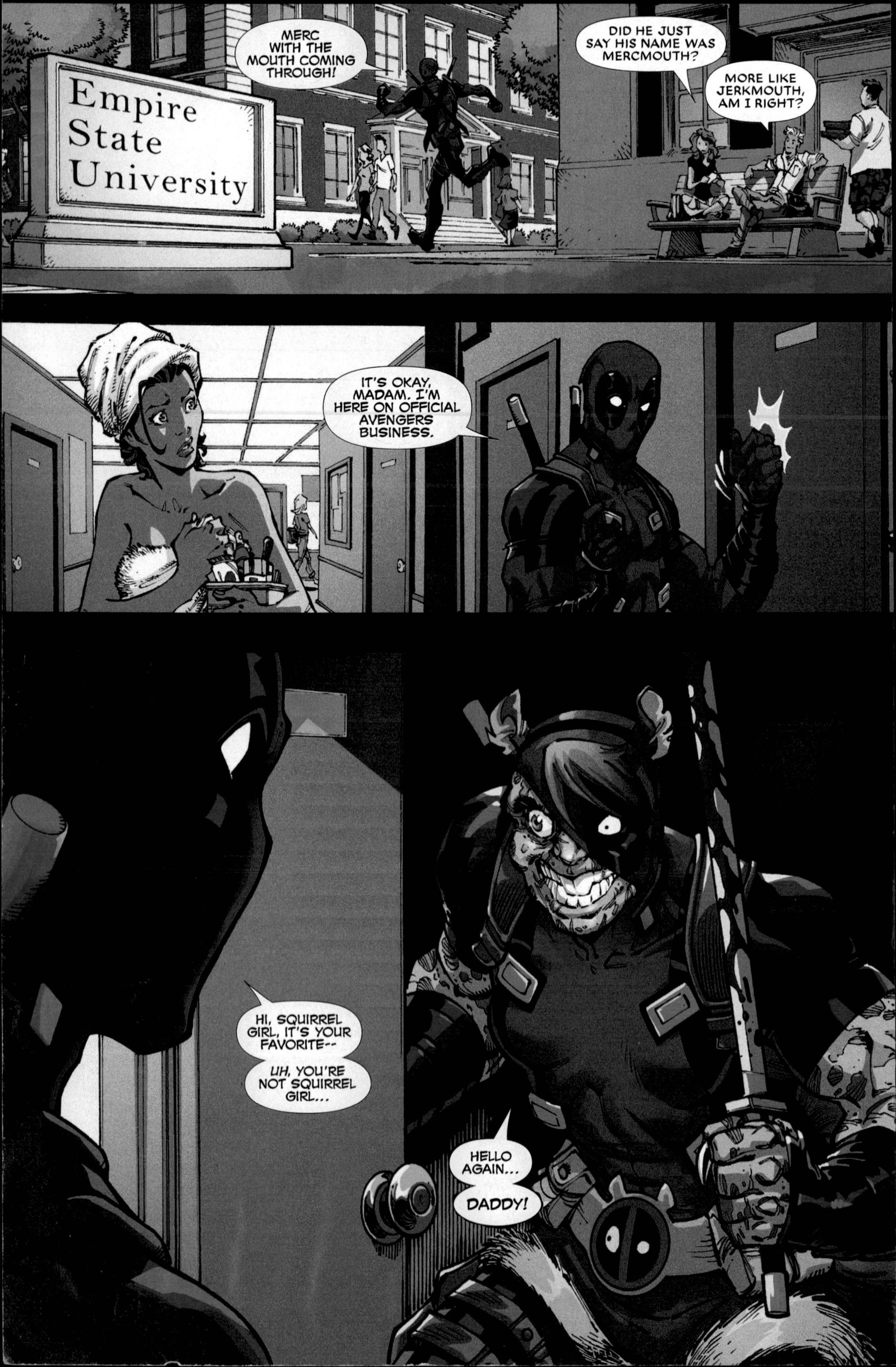
Empire State University
MERC WITH THE MOUTH COMING THROUGH!
DID HE JUST SAY HIS NAME WAS MERCMOUTH?
MORE LIKE JERKMOUTH, AM I RIGHT?
IT'S OKAY, MADAM. I'M HERE ON OFFICIAL AVENGERS BUSINESS.
HI, SQUIRREL GIRL, IT'S YOUR FAVORITE--
UH, YOU'RE NOT SQUIRREL GIRL...
HELLO AGAIN...
DADDY!

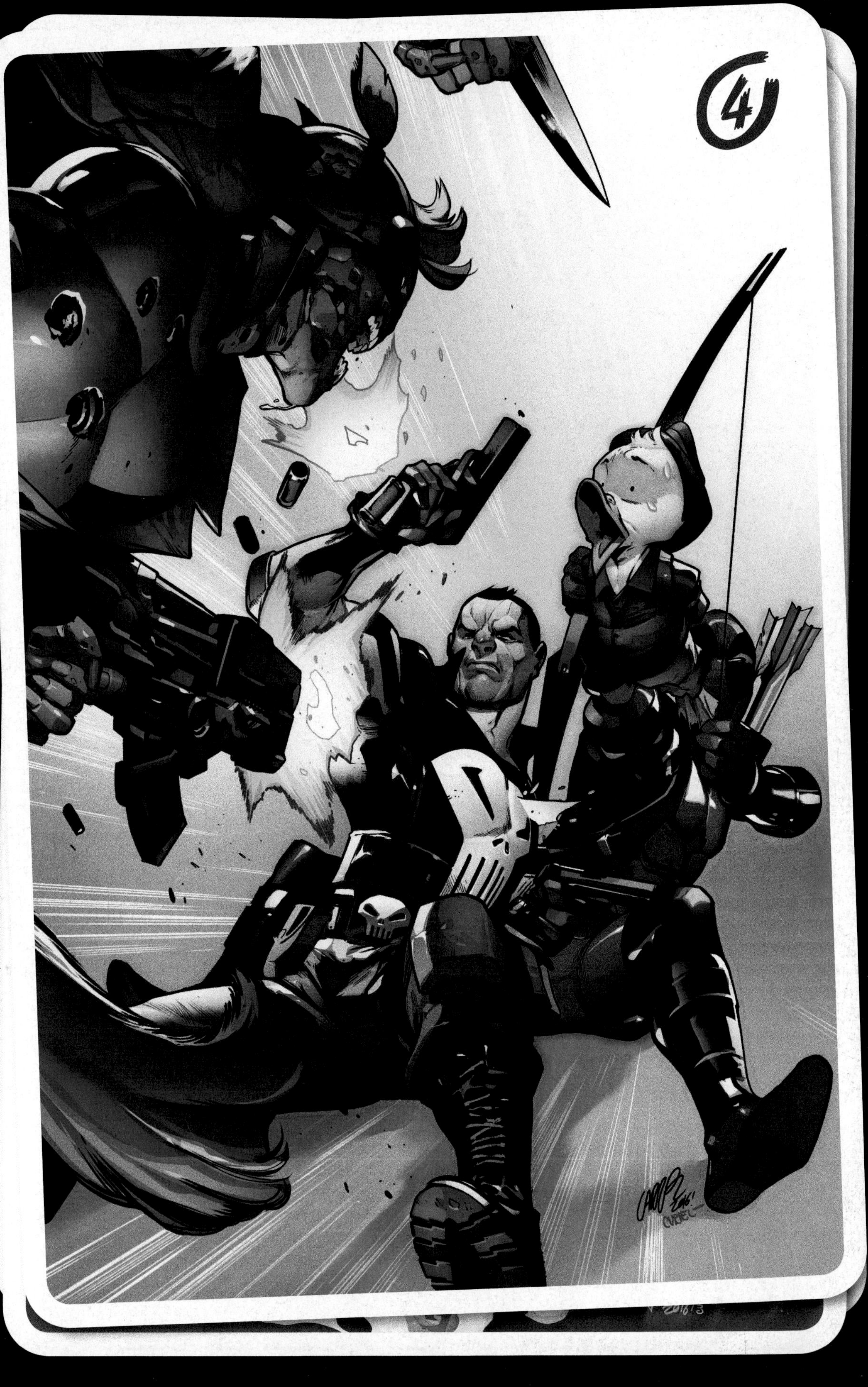
4

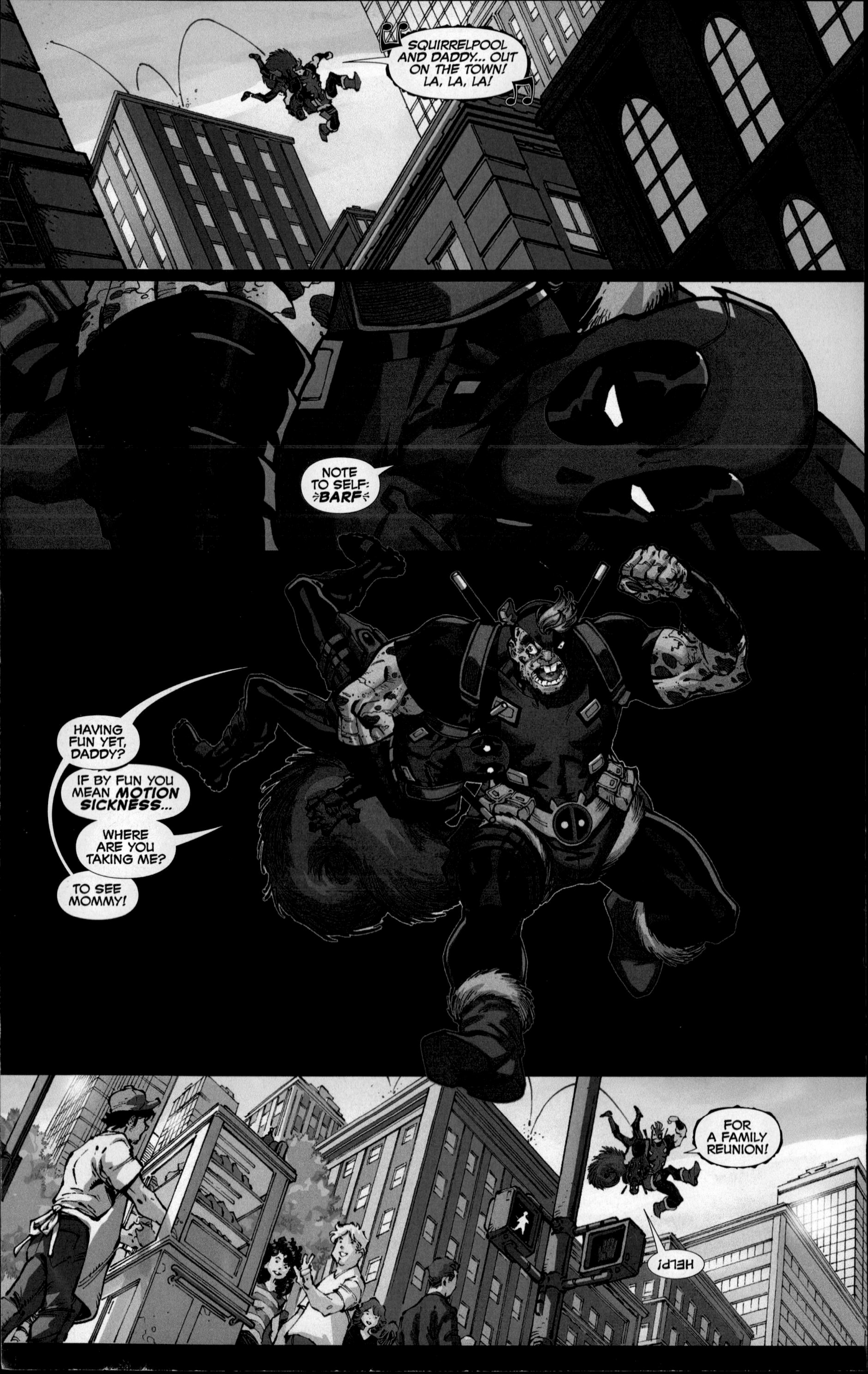
SQUIRRELPOOL AND DADDY... OUT ON THE TOWN! LA, LA, LA!
NOTE TO SELF: BARF
HAVING FUN YET, DADDY?
IF BY FUN YOU MEAN MOTION SICKNESS...
WHERE ARE YOU TAKING ME?
TO SEE MOMMY!
FOR A FAMILY REUNION!
HELP!

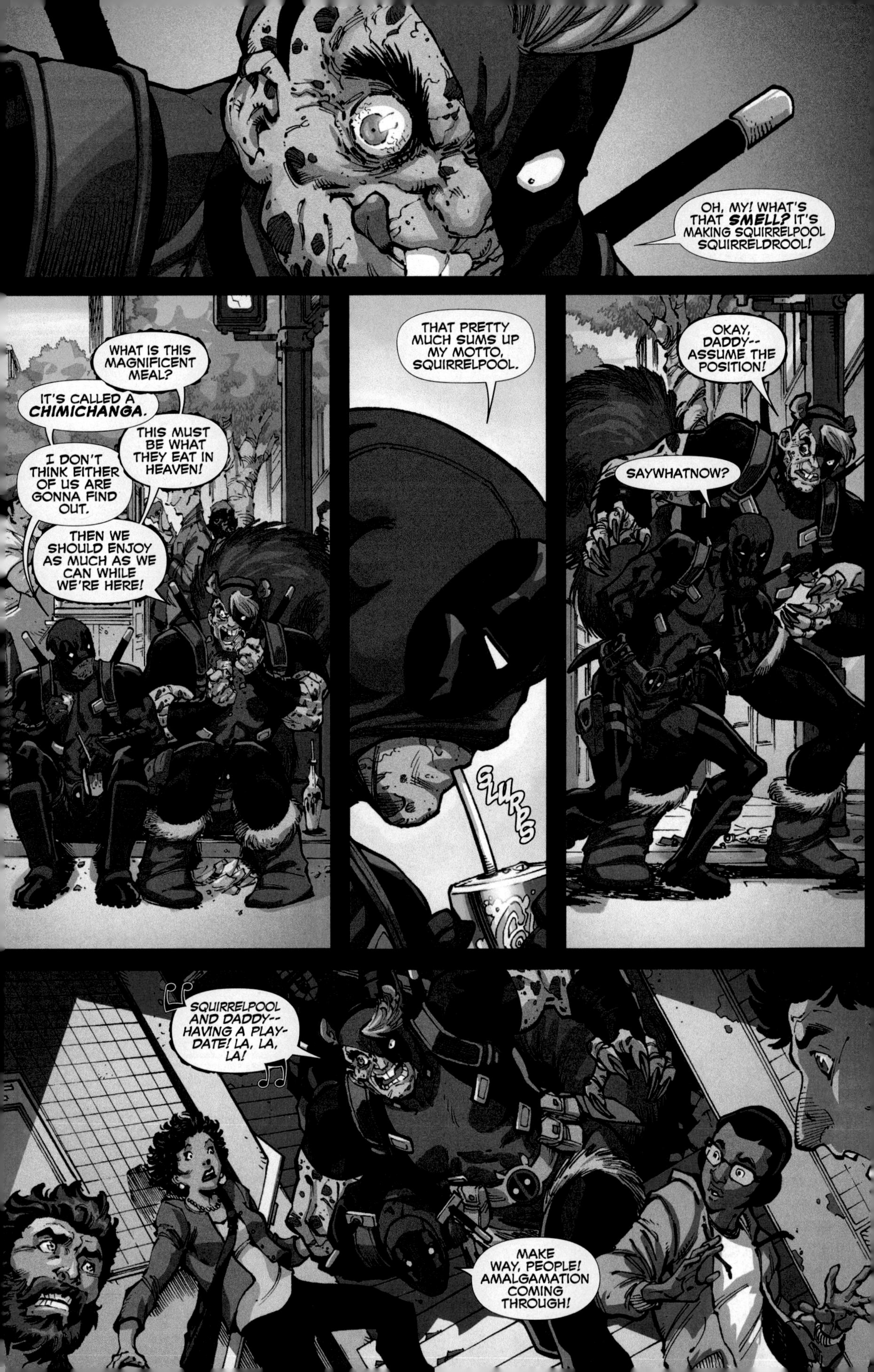
OH, MY! WHAT'S THAT **SMELL?** IT'S MAKING SQUIRRELPOOL SQUIRRELDROOL!
WHAT IS THIS MAGNIFICENT MEAL?
IT'S CALLED A **CHIMICHANGA**.
THIS MUST BE WHAT THEY EAT IN HEAVEN!
I DON'T THINK EITHER OF US ARE GONNA FIND OUT.
THEN WE SHOULD ENJOY AS MUCH AS WE CAN WHILE WE'RE HERE!
THAT PRETTY MUCH SUMS UP MY MOTTO, SQUIRRELPOOL.
SLURPS
OKAY, DADDY-- ASSUME THE POSITION!
SAYWHATNOW?
SQUIRRELPOOL AND DADDY-- HAVING A PLAY-DATE! LA, LA, LA!
MAKE WAY, PEOPLE! AMALGAMATION COMING THROUGH!

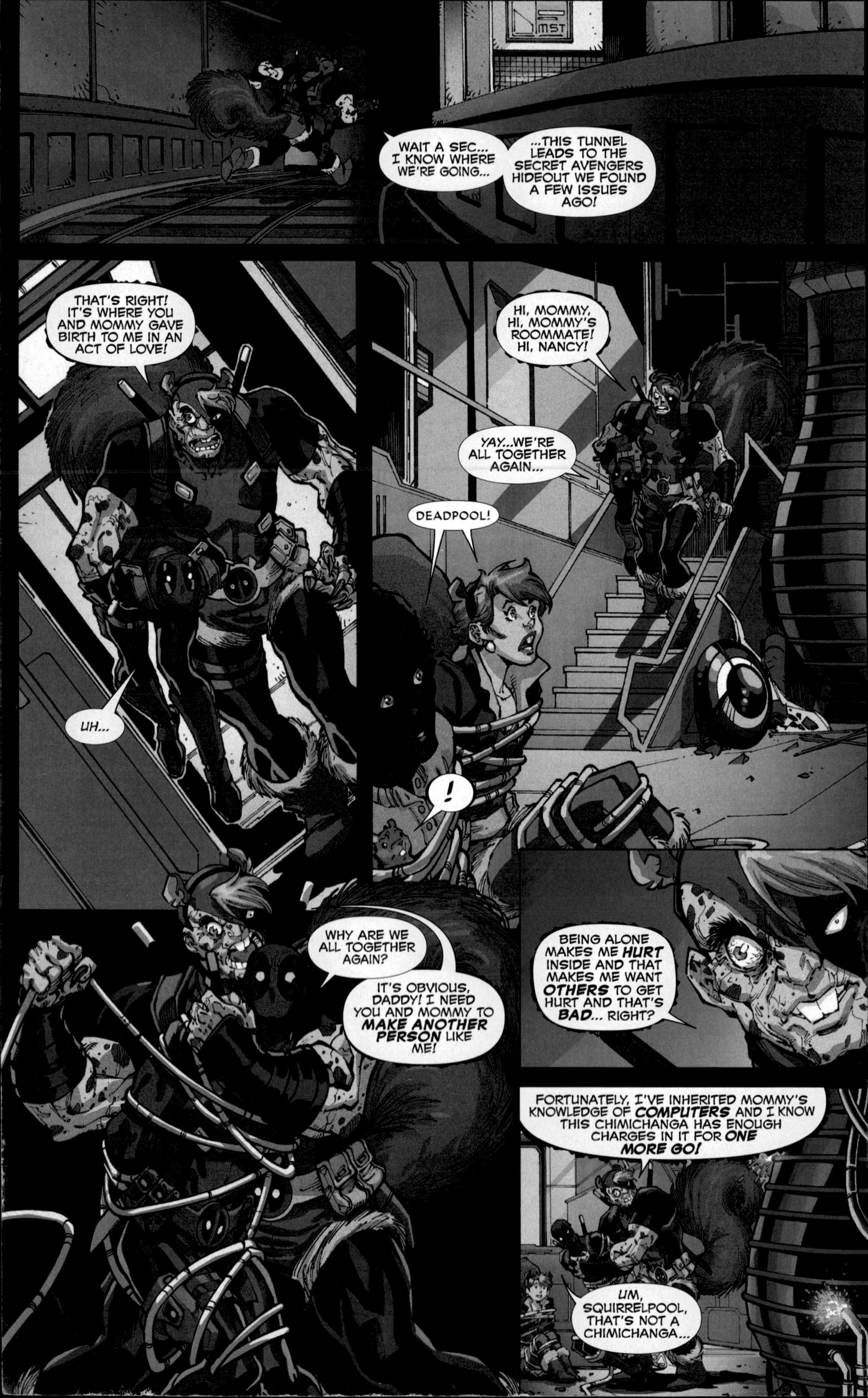

MST
WAIT A SEC... I KNOW WHERE WE'RE GOING...
...THIS TUNNEL LEADS TO THE SECRET AVENGERS HIDEOUT WE FOUND A FEW ISSUES AGO!
THAT'S RIGHT! IT'S WHERE YOU AND MOMMY GAVE BIRTH TO ME IN AN ACT OF LOVE!
UH...
HI, MOMMY, HI, MOMMY'S ROOMMATE! HI, NANCY!
YAY...WE'RE ALL TOGETHER AGAIN...
DEADPOOL!
!
WHY ARE WE ALL TOGETHER AGAIN?
IT'S OBVIOUS, DADDY! I NEED YOU AND MOMMY TO MAKE ANOTHER PERSON LIKE ME!
BEING ALONE MAKES ME HURT INSIDE AND THAT MAKES ME WANT OTHERS TO GET HURT AND THAT'S BAD... RIGHT?
FORTUNATELY, I'VE INHERITED MOMMY'S KNOWLEDGE OF COMPUTERS AND I KNOW THIS CHIMICHANGA HAS ENOUGH CHARGES IN IT FOR ONE MORE GO!
UM, SQUIRRELPOOL, THAT'S NOT A CHIMICHANGA...

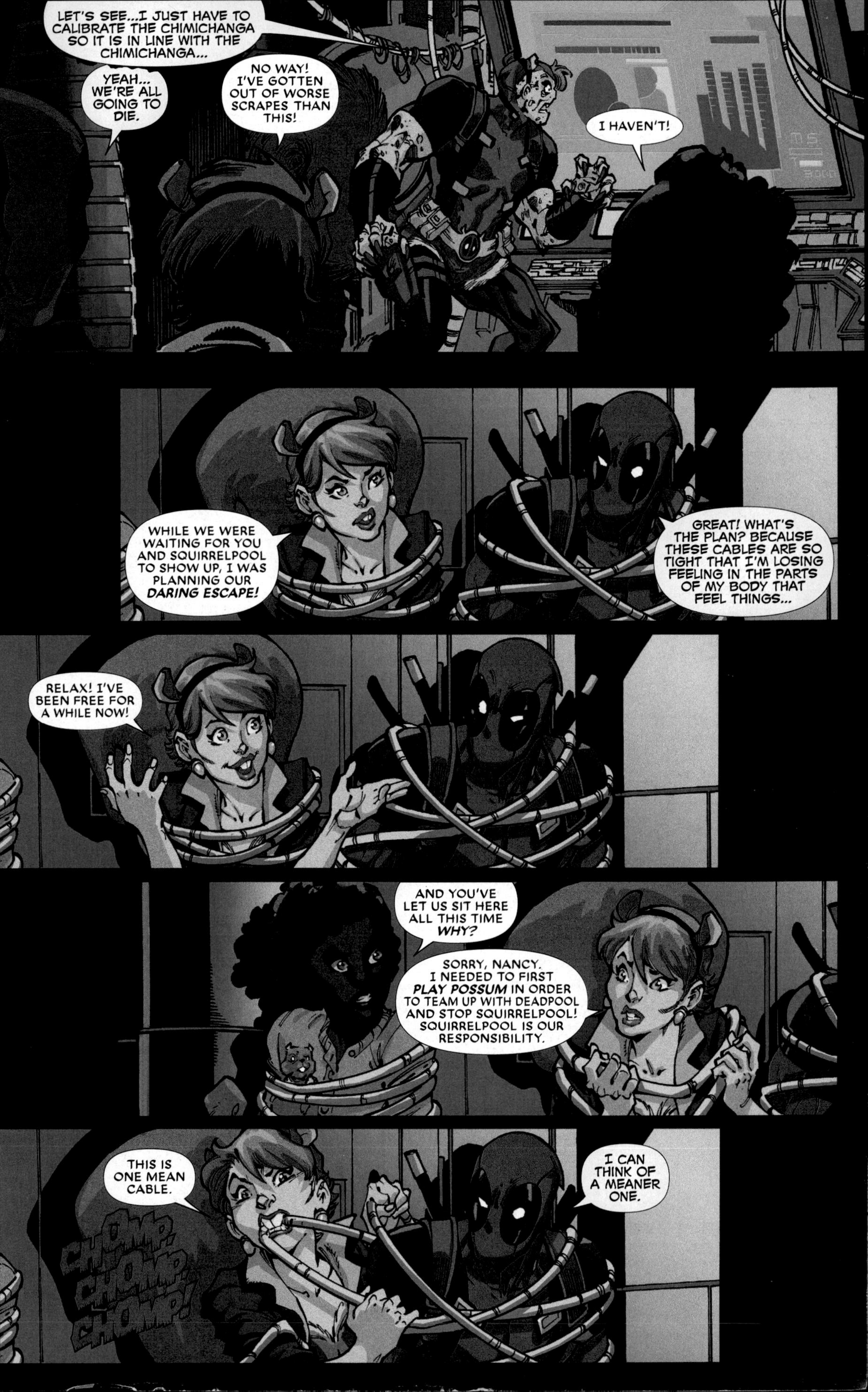

LET'S SEE...I JUST HAVE TO CALIBRATE THE CHIMICHANGA SO IT IS IN LINE WITH THE CHIMICHANGA...
YEAH... WE'RE ALL GOING TO DIE.
NO WAY! I'VE GOTTEN OUT OF WORSE SCRAPES THAN THIS!
I HAVEN'T!
WHILE WE WERE WAITING FOR YOU AND SQUIRRELPOOL TO SHOW UP, I WAS PLANNING OUR DARING ESCAPE!
GREAT! WHAT'S THE PLAN? BECAUSE THESE CABLES ARE SO TIGHT THAT I'M LOSING FEELING IN THE PARTS OF MY BODY THAT FEEL THINGS...
RELAX! I'VE BEEN FREE FOR A WHILE NOW!
AND YOU'VE LET US SIT HERE ALL THIS TIME WHY?
SORRY, NANCY. I NEEDED TO FIRST PLAY POSSUM IN ORDER TO TEAM UP WITH DEADPOOL AND STOP SQUIRRELPOOL! SQUIRRELPOOL IS OUR RESPONSIBILITY.
THIS IS ONE MEAN CABLE.
I CAN THINK OF A MEANER ONE.
CHOMP! CHOMP! CHOMP!

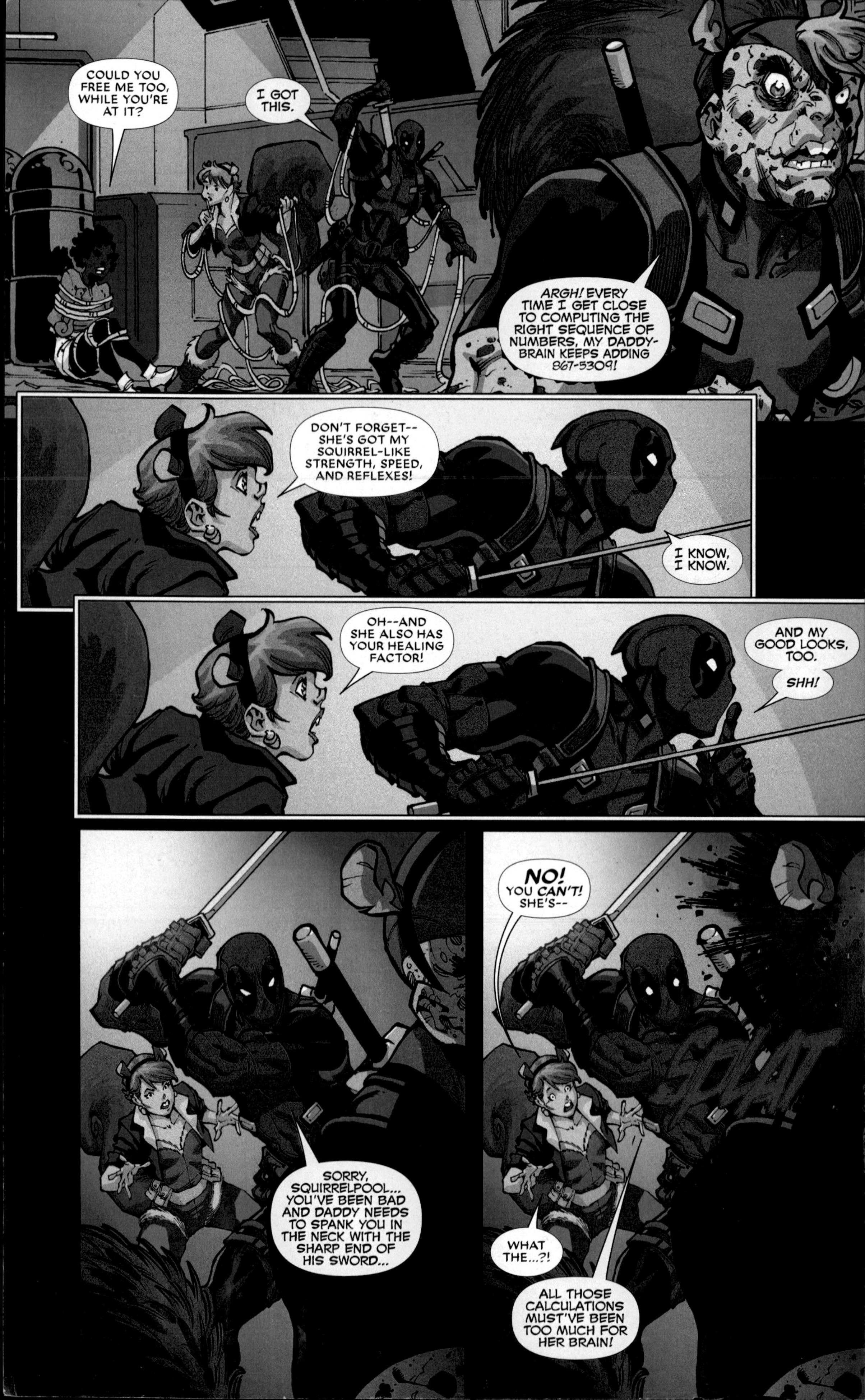
COULD YOU FREE ME TOO, WHILE YOU'RE AT IT?
I GOT THIS.
ARGH! EVERY TIME I GET CLOSE TO COMPUTING THE RIGHT SEQUENCE OF NUMBERS, MY DADDY-BRAIN KEEPS ADDING 867-5309!
DON'T FORGET-- SHE'S GOT MY SQUIRREL-LIKE STRENGTH, SPEED, AND REFLEXES!
I KNOW, I KNOW.
OH--AND SHE ALSO HAS YOUR HEALING FACTOR!
AND MY GOOD LOOKS, TOO.
SHH!
SORRY, SQUIRRELPOOL... YOU'VE BEEN BAD AND DADDY NEEDS TO SPANK YOU IN THE NECK WITH THE SHARP END OF HIS SWORD...
NO! YOU CAN'T! SHE'S--
WHAT THE...?!
ALL THOSE CALCULATIONS MUST'VE BEEN TOO MUCH FOR HER BRAIN!

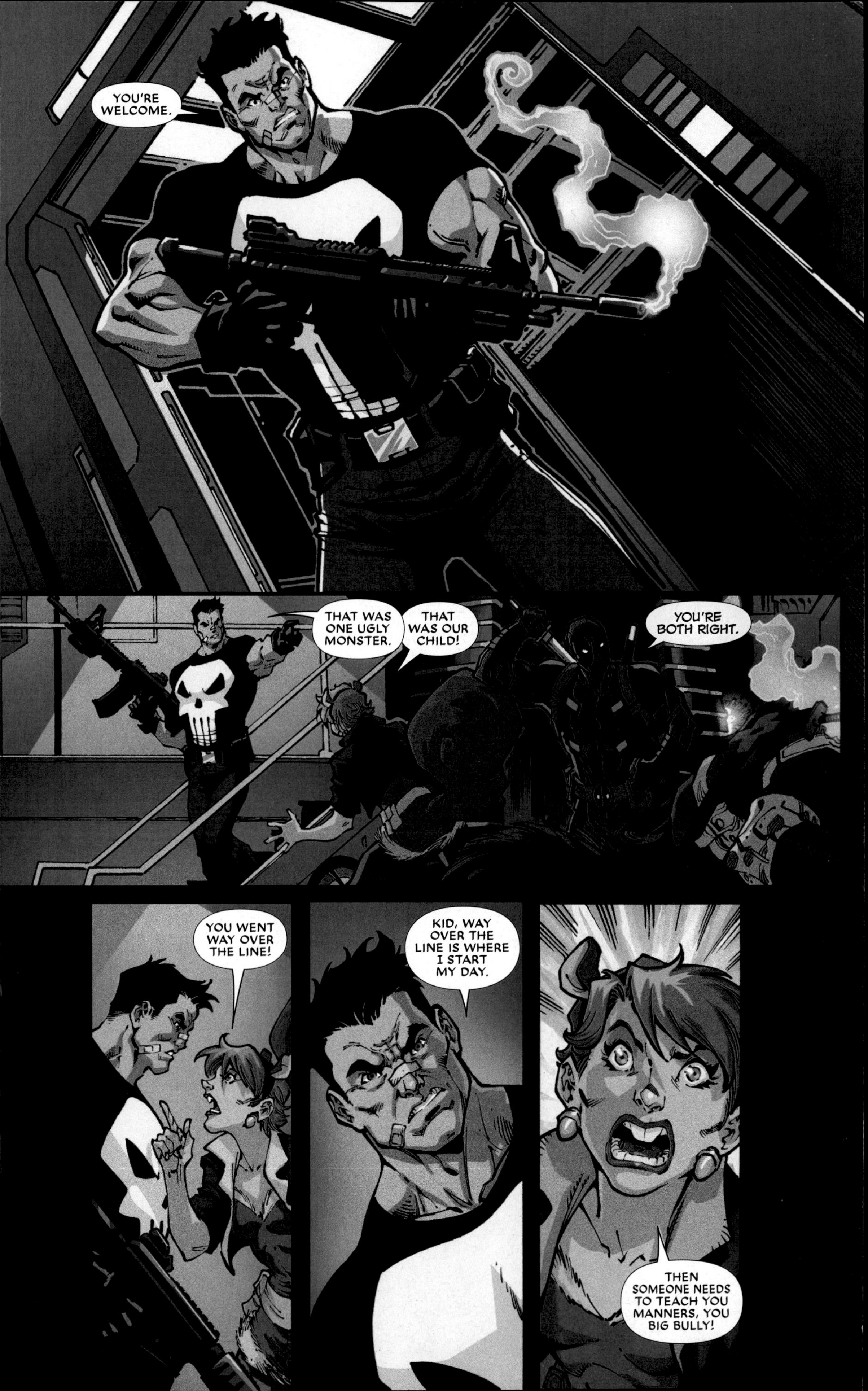
YOU'RE WELCOME.
THAT WAS ONE UGLY MONSTER.
THAT WAS OUR CHILD!
YOU'RE BOTH RIGHT.
YOU WENT WAY OVER THE LINE!
KID, WAY OVER THE LINE IS WHERE I START MY DAY.
THEN SOMEONE NEEDS TO TEACH YOU MANNERS, YOU BIG BULLY!

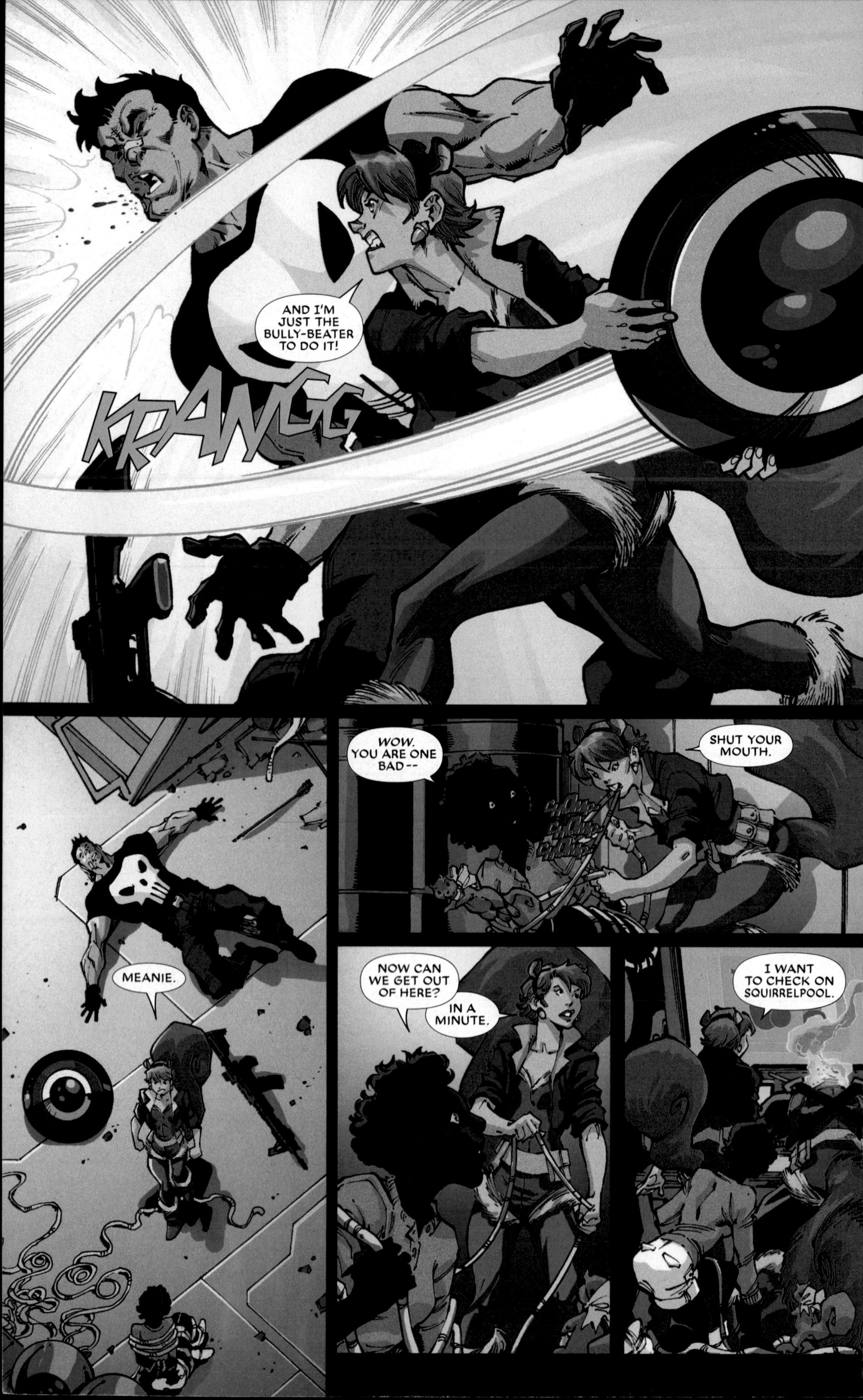
AND I'M JUST THE BULLY-BEATER TO DO IT!
KRANGG
WOW. YOU ARE ONE BAD--
SHUT YOUR MOUTH.
MEANIE.
NOW CAN WE GET OUT OF HERE?
IN A MINUTE.
I WANT TO CHECK ON SQUIRRELPOOL.

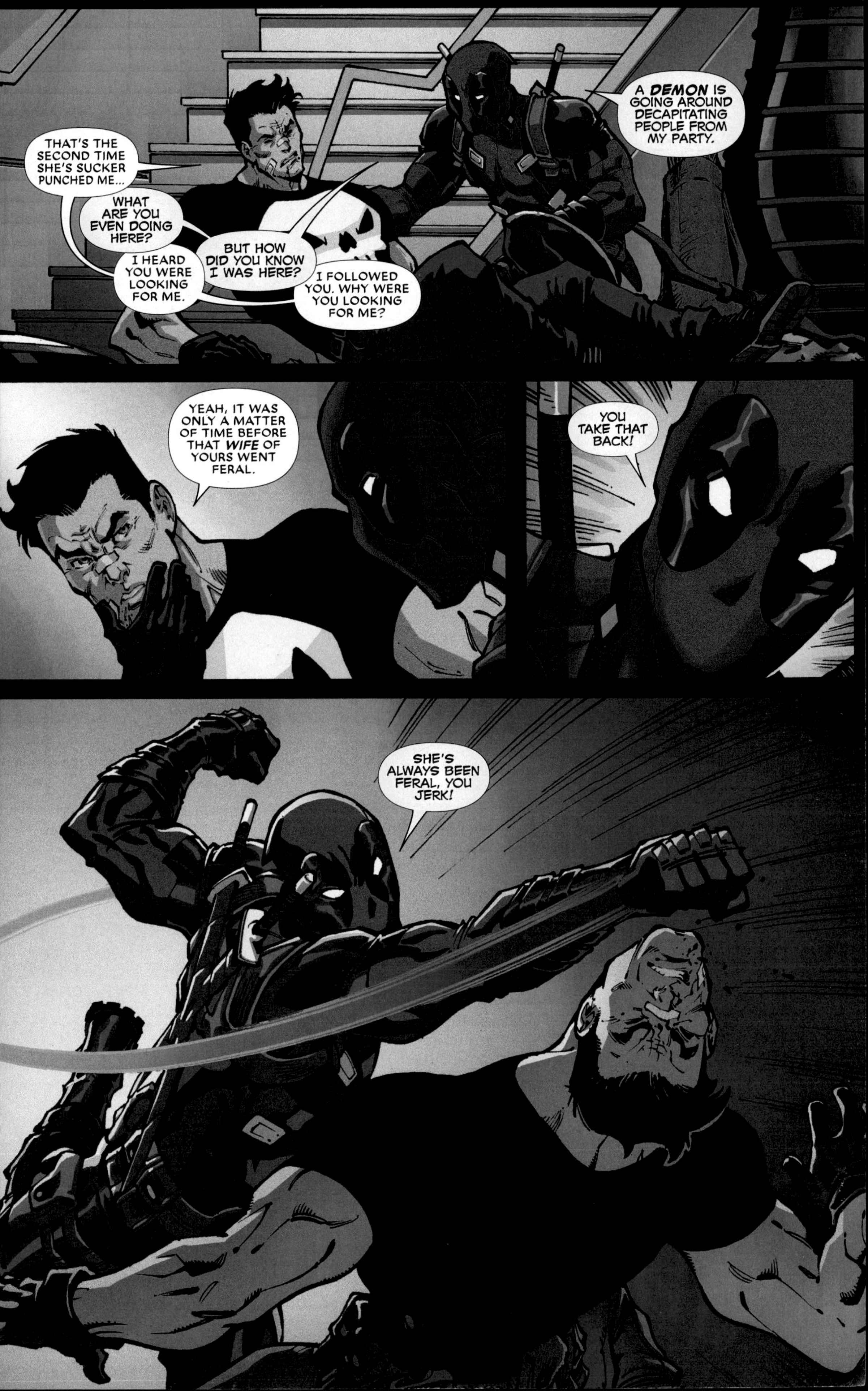
A DEMON IS GOING AROUND DECAPITATING PEOPLE FROM MY PARTY.
THAT'S THE SECOND TIME SHE'S SUCKER PUNCHED ME...
WHAT ARE YOU EVEN DOING HERE?
I HEARD YOU WERE LOOKING FOR ME.
BUT HOW DID YOU KNOW I WAS HERE?
I FOLLOWED YOU. WHY WERE YOU LOOKING FOR ME?
YEAH, IT WAS ONLY A MATTER OF TIME BEFORE THAT WIFE OF YOURS WENT FERAL.
YOU TAKE THAT BACK!
SHE'S ALWAYS BEEN FERAL, YOU JERK!

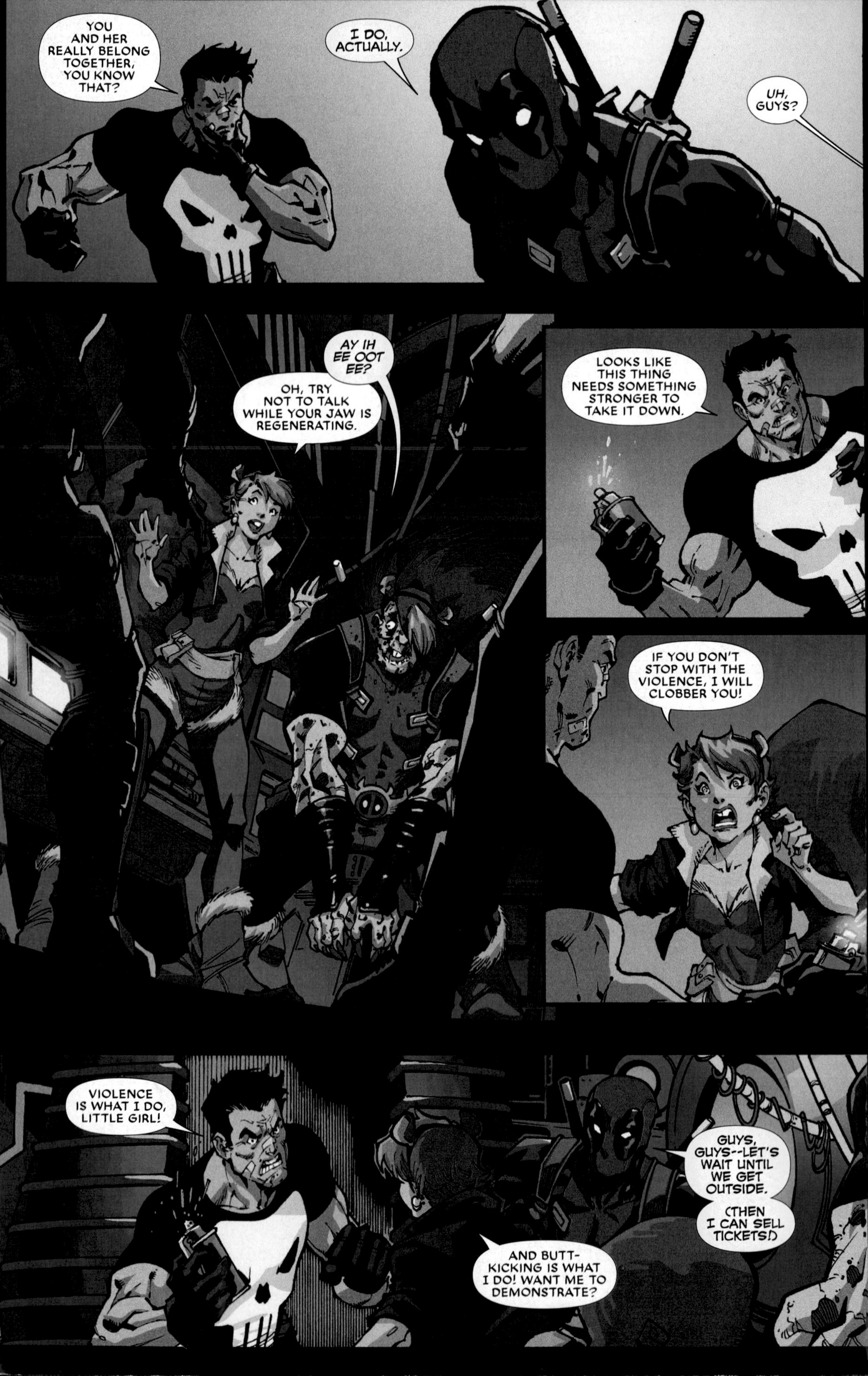
YOU AND HER REALLY BELONG TOGETHER, YOU KNOW THAT?
I DO, ACTUALLY.
UH, GUYS?
AY IH EE OOT EE?
OH, TRY NOT TO TALK WHILE YOUR JAW IS REGENERATING.
LOOKS LIKE THIS THING NEEDS SOMETHING STRONGER TO TAKE IT DOWN.
IF YOU DON'T STOP WITH THE VIOLENCE, I WILL CLOBBER YOU!
VIOLENCE IS WHAT I DO, LITTLE GIRL!
AND BUTT-KICKING IS WHAT I DO! WANT ME TO DEMONSTRATE?
GUYS, GUYS--LET'S WAIT UNTIL WE GET OUTSIDE.
(THEN I CAN SELL TICKETS!)

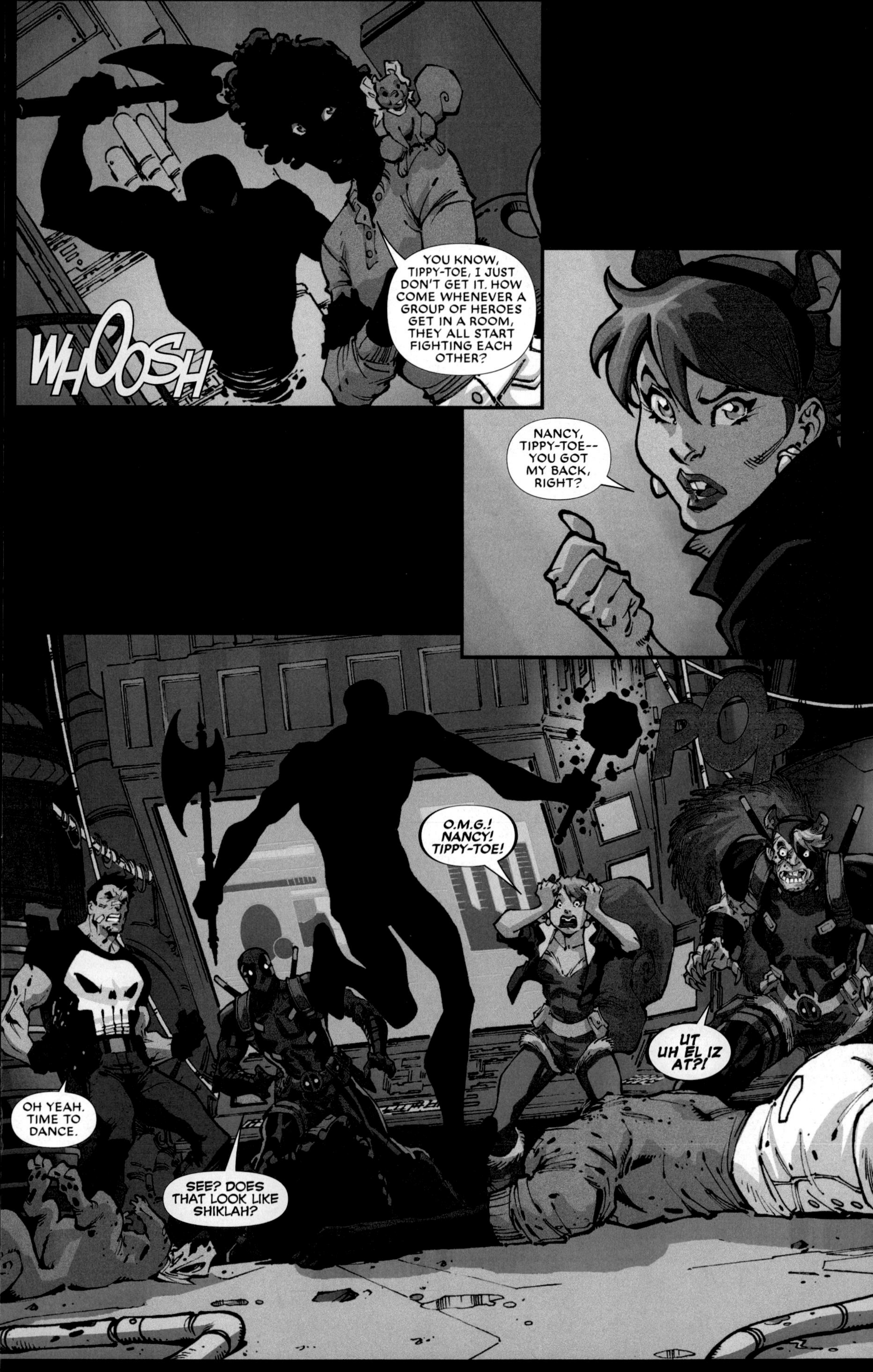
YOU KNOW, TIPPY-TOE, I JUST DON'T GET IT. HOW COME WHENEVER A GROUP OF HEROES GET IN A ROOM, THEY ALL START FIGHTING EACH OTHER?
WHOOSH
NANCY, TIPPY-TOE-- YOU GOT MY BACK, RIGHT?
O.M.G.! NANCY! TIPPY-TOE!
UT UH EL IZ AT?!
OH YEAH. TIME TO DANCE.
SEE? DOES THAT LOOK LIKE SHIKLAH?

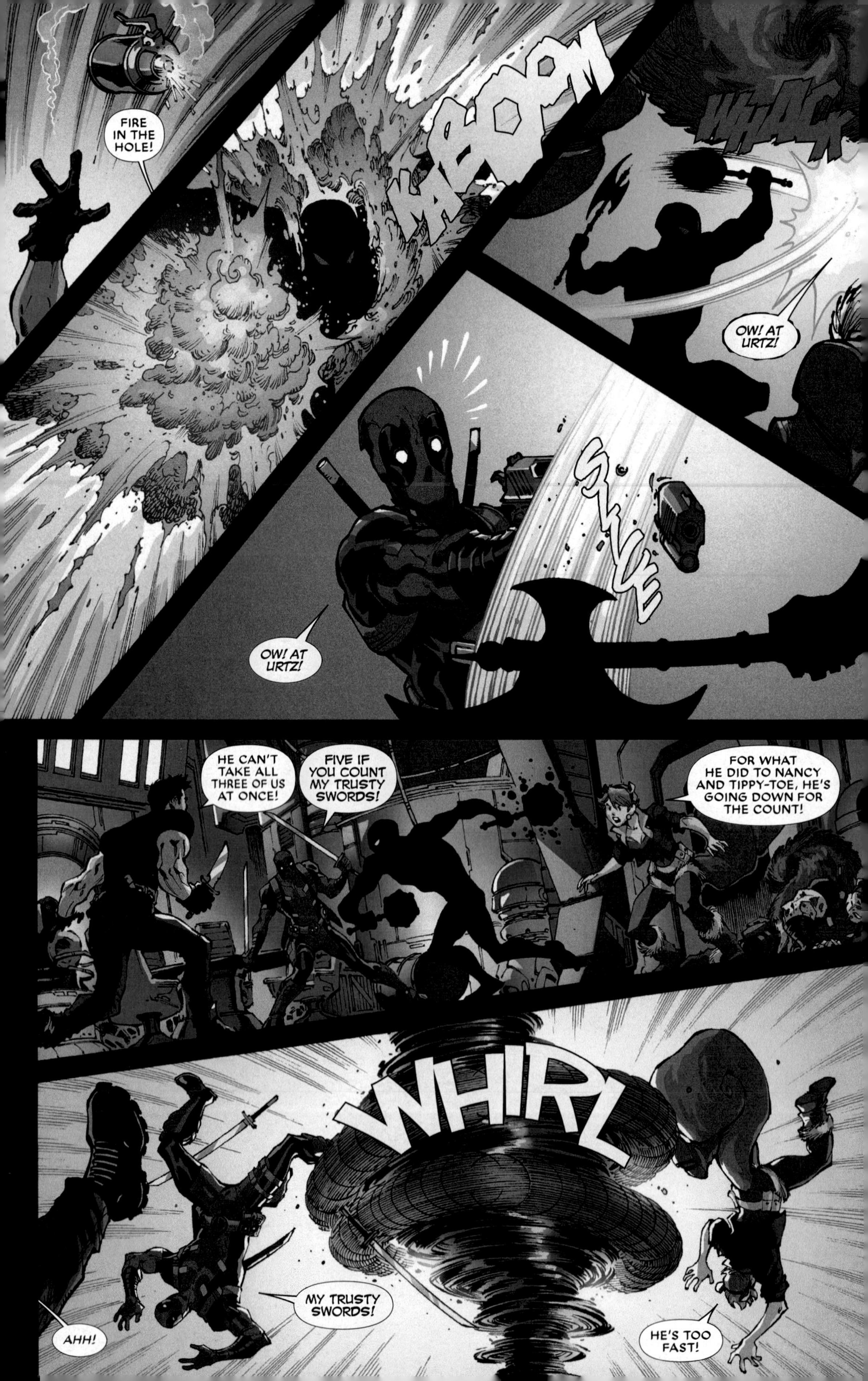
FIRE IN THE HOLE!
KA-BOOM
WHACK
OW! AT URTZ!
SCHWING
OW! AT URTZ!
HE CAN'T TAKE ALL THREE OF US AT ONCE!
FIVE IF YOU COUNT MY TRUSTY SWORDS!
FOR WHAT HE DID TO NANCY AND TIPPY-TOE, HE'S GOING DOWN FOR THE COUNT!
WHIRL
MY TRUSTY SWORDS!
AHH!
HE'S TOO FAST!

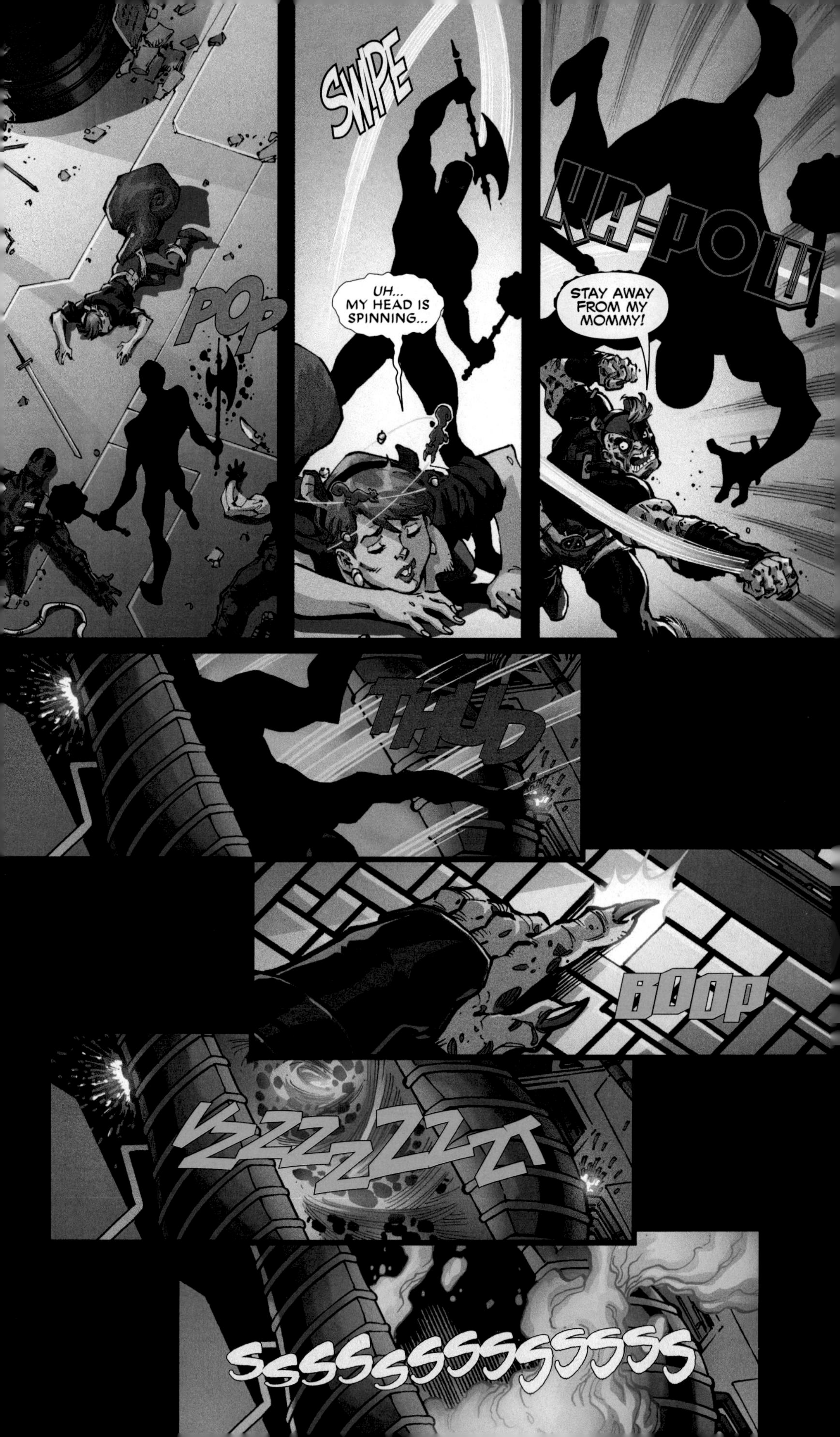
POP
SWIPE
UH... MY HEAD IS SPINNING...
KA-POW
STAY AWAY FROM MY MOMMY!
THUD
BOOP
VZZZZZZT
SSSSSSSSSSSSSS

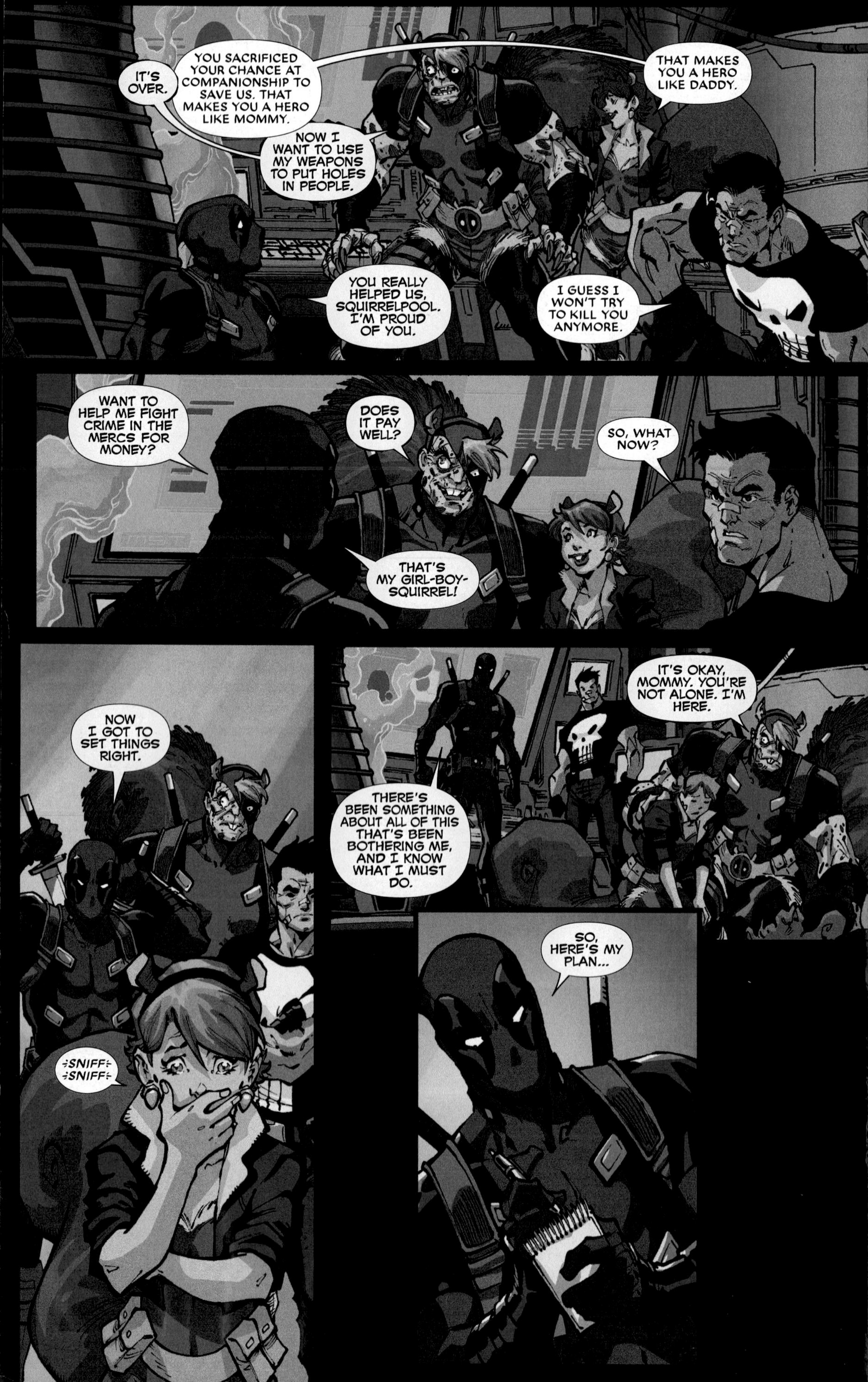
IT'S OVER.
YOU SACRIFICED YOUR CHANCE AT COMPANIONSHIP TO SAVE US. THAT MAKES YOU A HERO LIKE MOMMY.
THAT MAKES YOU A HERO LIKE DADDY.
NOW I WANT TO USE MY WEAPONS TO PUT HOLES IN PEOPLE.
YOU REALLY HELPED US, SQUIRRELPOOL. I'M PROUD OF YOU.
I GUESS I WON'T TRY TO KILL YOU ANYMORE.
WANT TO HELP ME FIGHT CRIME IN THE MERCS FOR MONEY?
DOES IT PAY WELL?
SO, WHAT NOW?
THAT'S MY GIRL-BOY-SQUIRREL!
NOW I GOT TO SET THINGS RIGHT.
SNIFF SNIFF
IT'S OKAY, MOMMY. YOU'RE NOT ALONE. I'M HERE.
THERE'S BEEN SOMETHING ABOUT ALL OF THIS THAT'S BEEN BOTHERING ME, AND I KNOW WHAT I MUST DO.
SO, HERE'S MY PLAN...

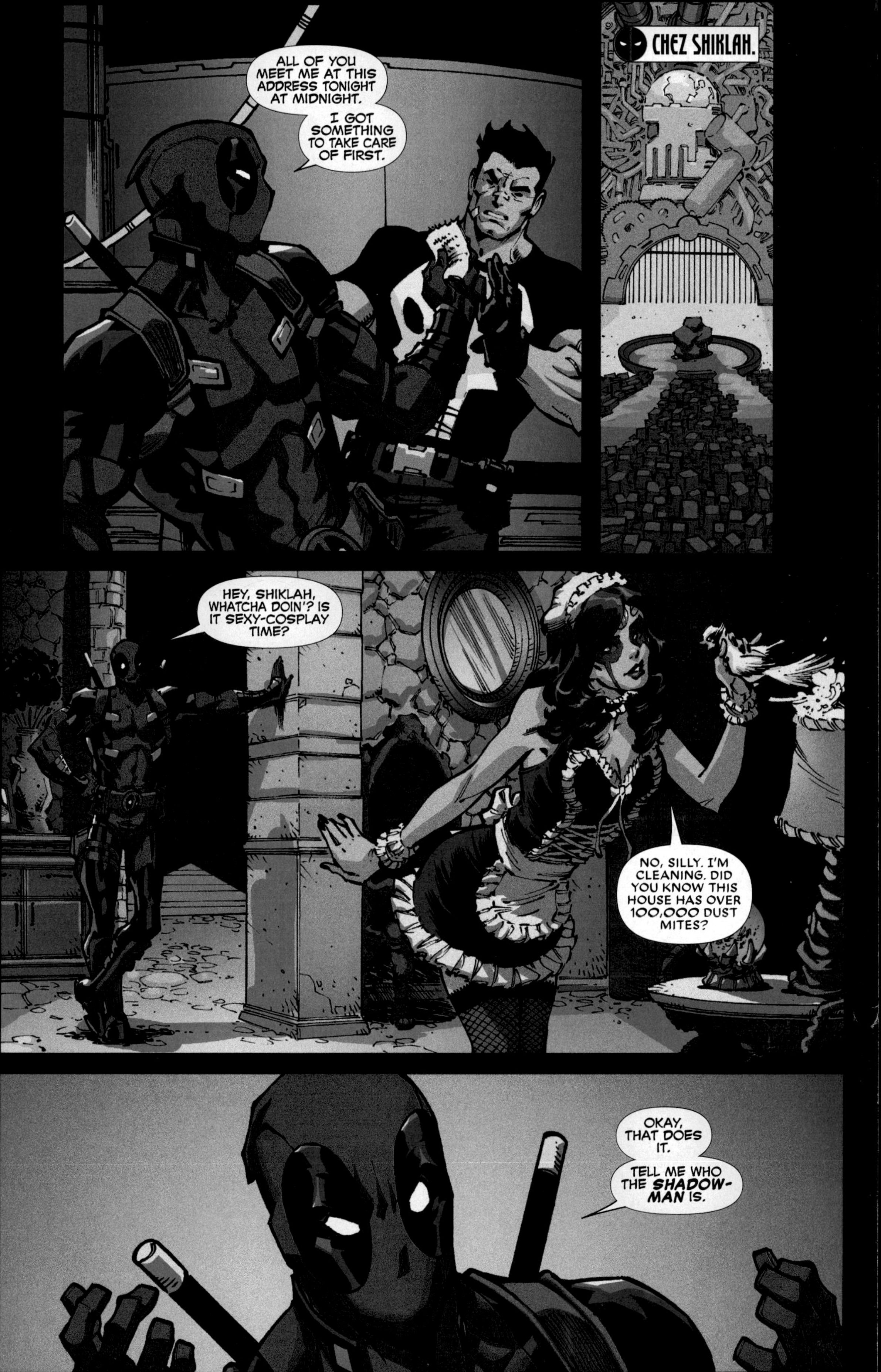

CHEZ SHIKLAH.
ALL OF YOU MEET ME AT THIS ADDRESS TONIGHT AT MIDNIGHT.
I GOT SOMETHING TO TAKE CARE OF FIRST.
HEY, SHIKLAH, WHATCHA DOIN'? IS IT SEXY-COSPLAY TIME?
NO, SILLY. I'M CLEANING. DID YOU KNOW THIS HOUSE HAS OVER 100,000 DUST MITES?
OKAY, THAT DOES IT.
TELL ME WHO THE SHADOW-MAN IS.

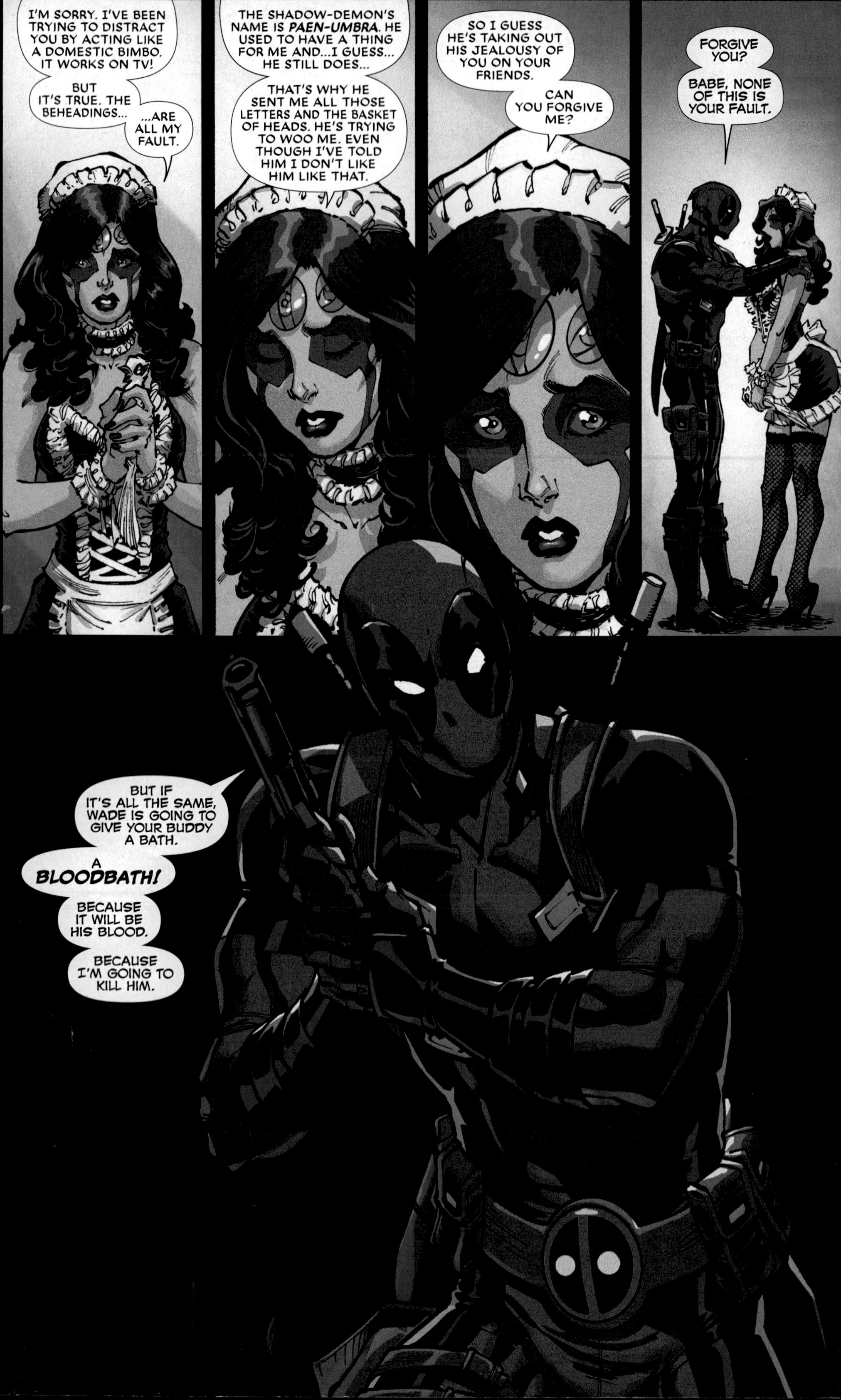

I'M SORRY. I'VE BEEN TRYING TO DISTRACT YOU BY ACTING LIKE A DOMESTIC BIMBO. IT WORKS ON TV!
BUT IT'S TRUE. THE BEHEADINGS...
...ARE ALL MY FAULT.
THE SHADOW-DEMON'S NAME IS PAEN-UMBRA. HE USED TO HAVE A THING FOR ME AND...I GUESS... HE STILL DOES...
THAT'S WHY HE SENT ME ALL THOSE LETTERS AND THE BASKET OF HEADS. HE'S TRYING TO WOO ME. EVEN THOUGH I'VE TOLD HIM I DON'T LIKE HIM LIKE THAT.
SO I GUESS HE'S TAKING OUT HIS JEALOUSY OF YOU ON YOUR FRIENDS.
CAN YOU FORGIVE ME?
FORGIVE YOU?
BABE, NONE OF THIS IS YOUR FAULT.
BUT IF IT'S ALL THE SAME, WADE IS GOING TO GIVE YOUR BUDDY A BATH.
A BLOODBATH!
BECAUSE IT WILL BE HIS BLOOD.
BECAUSE I'M GOING TO KILL HIM.

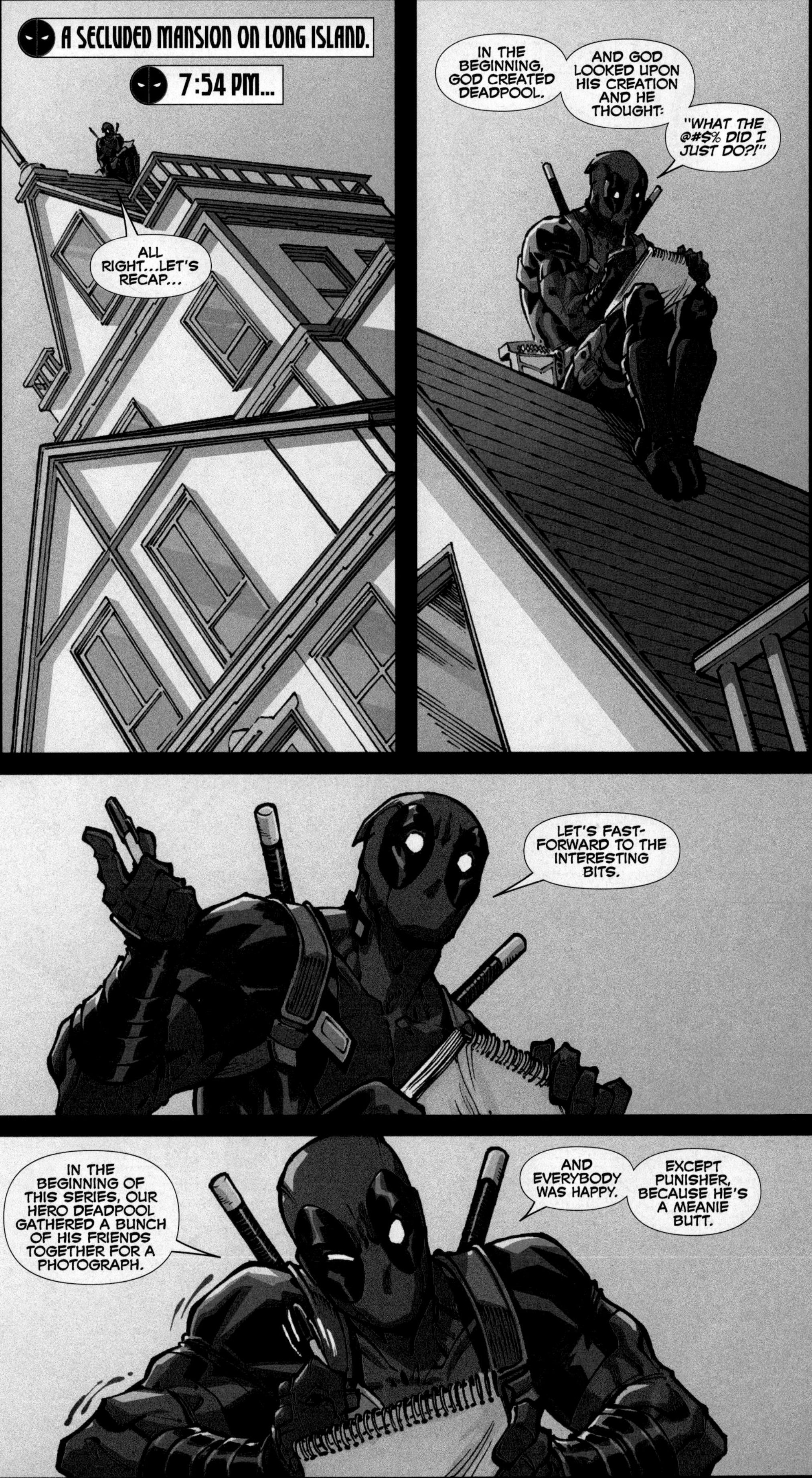
A SECLUDED MANSION ON LONG ISLAND.
7:54 PM...
ALL RIGHT...LET'S RECAP...
IN THE BEGINNING, GOD CREATED DEADPOOL.
AND GOD LOOKED UPON HIS CREATION AND HE THOUGHT:
"WHAT THE @#$% DID I JUST DO?!"
LET'S FAST-FORWARD TO THE INTERESTING BITS.
IN THE BEGINNING OF THIS SERIES, OUR HERO DEADPOOL GATHERED A BUNCH OF HIS FRIENDS TOGETHER FOR A PHOTOGRAPH.
AND EVERYBODY WAS HAPPY.
EXCEPT PUNISHER, BECAUSE HE'S A MEANIE BUTT.

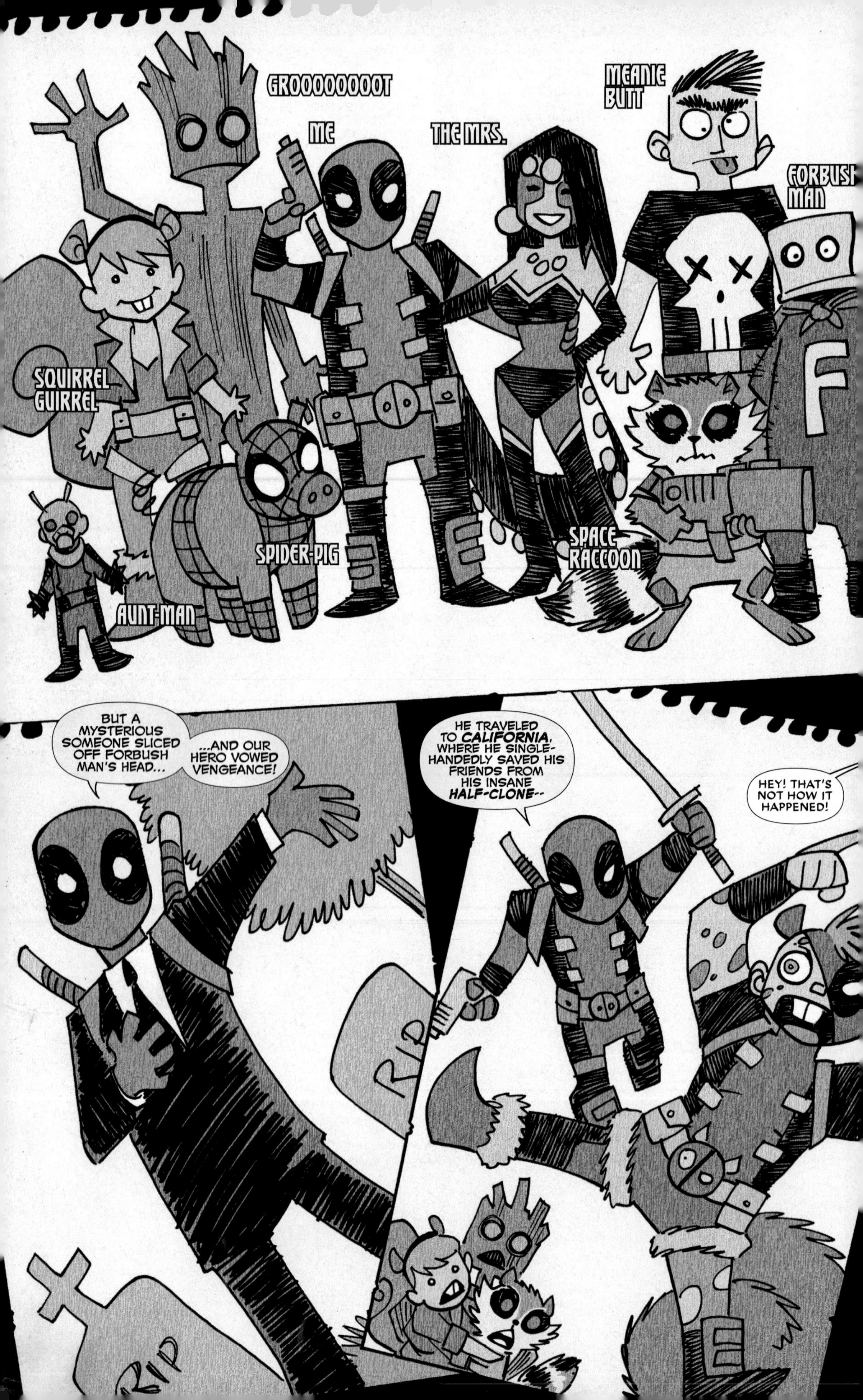
GROOOOOOOOOT
ME
THE MRS.
MEANIE BUTT
FORBUSH MAN
SQUIRREL GUIRREL
SPIDER-PIG
SPACE RACCOON
AUNT-MAN
BUT A MYSTERIOUS SOMEONE SLICED OFF FORBUSH MAN'S HEAD...
...AND OUR HERO VOWED VENGEANCE!
RIP
RIP
RIP
HE TRAVELED TO CALIFORNIA, WHERE HE SINGLE-HANDEDLY SAVED HIS FRIENDS FROM HIS INSANE HALF-CLONE--
HEY! THAT'S NOT HOW IT HAPPENED!

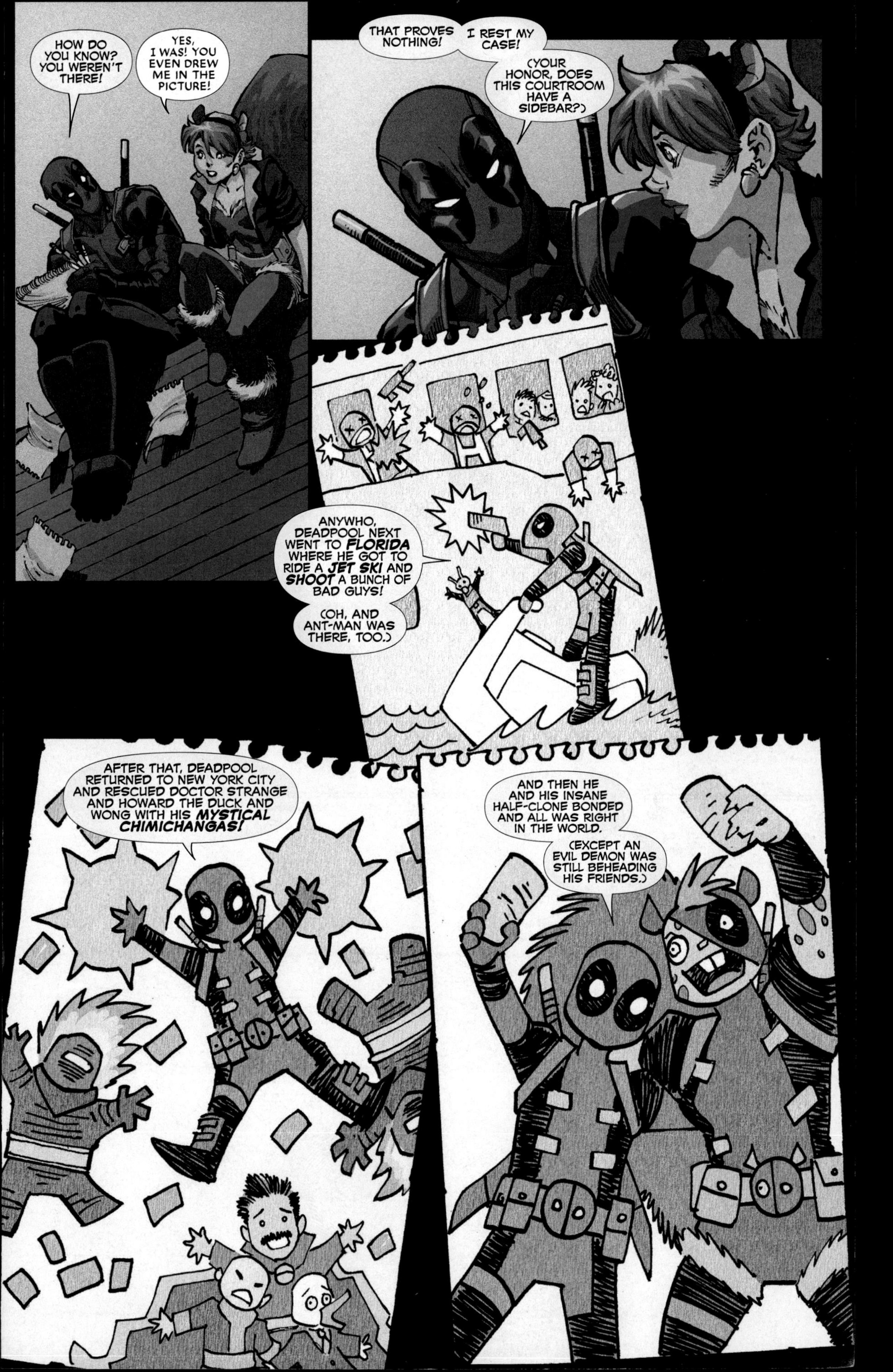
HOW DO YOU KNOW? YOU WEREN'T THERE!
YES, I WAS! YOU EVEN DREW ME IN THE PICTURE!
THAT PROVES NOTHING!
I REST MY CASE!
(YOUR HONOR, DOES THIS COURTROOM HAVE A SIDEBAR?)
ANYWHO, DEADPOOL NEXT WENT TO FLORIDA WHERE HE GOT TO RIDE A JET SKI AND SHOOT A BUNCH OF BAD GUYS!
(OH, AND ANT-MAN WAS THERE, TOO.)
AFTER THAT, DEADPOOL RETURNED TO NEW YORK CITY AND RESCUED DOCTOR STRANGE AND HOWARD THE DUCK AND WONG WITH HIS MYSTICAL CHIMICHANGAS!
AND THEN HE AND HIS INSANE HALF-CLONE BONDED AND ALL WAS RIGHT IN THE WORLD.
(EXCEPT AN EVIL DEMON WAS STILL BEHEADING HIS FRIENDS.)

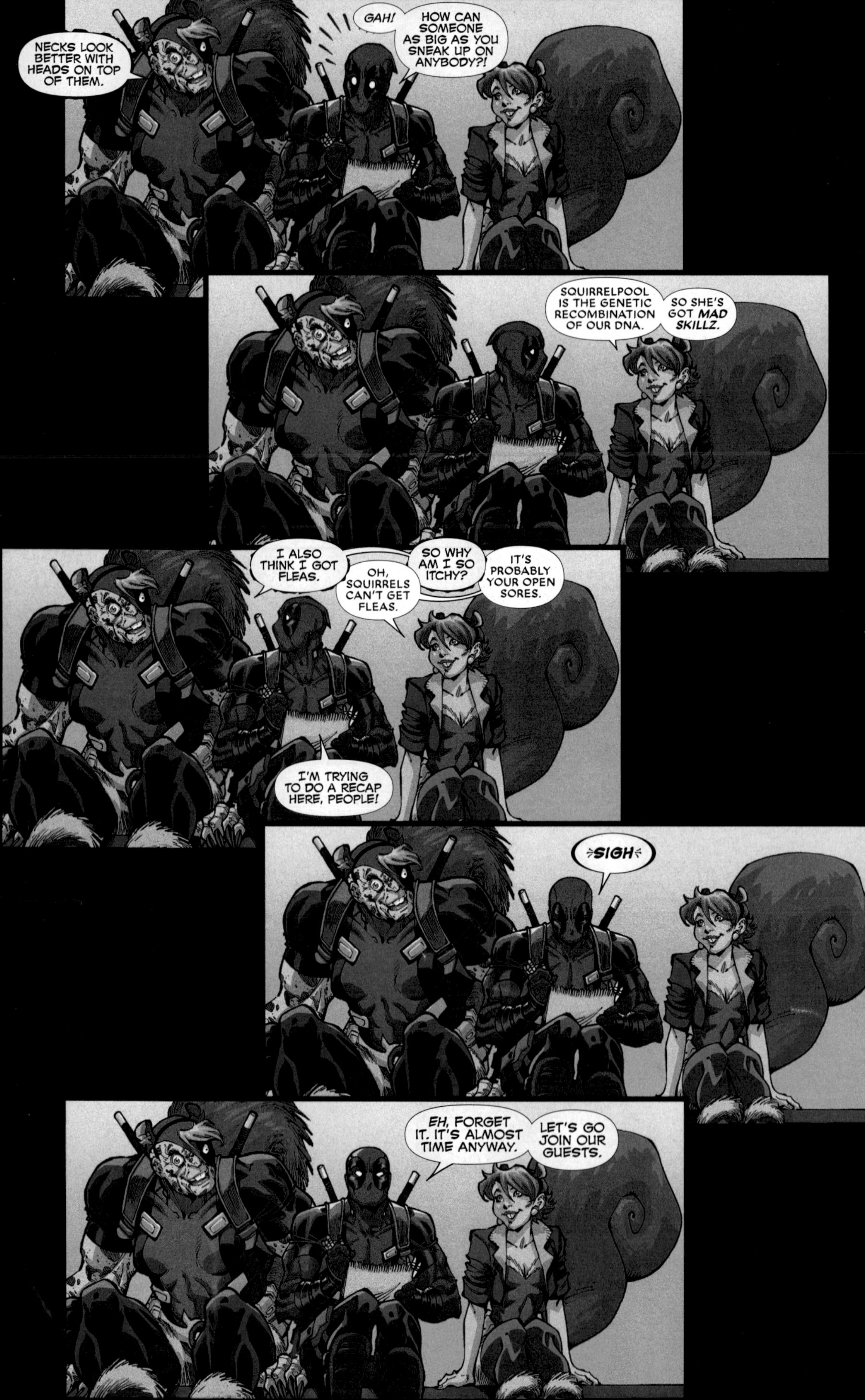
NECKS LOOK BETTER WITH HEADS ON TOP OF THEM.
GAH!
HOW CAN SOMEONE AS BIG AS YOU SNEAK UP ON ANYBODY?!
SQUIRRELPOOL IS THE GENETIC RECOMBINATION OF OUR DNA.
SO SHE'S GOT MAD SKILLZ.
I ALSO THINK I GOT FLEAS.
OH, SQUIRRELS CAN'T GET FLEAS.
SO WHY AM I SO ITCHY?
IT'S PROBABLY YOUR OPEN SORES.
I'M TRYING TO DO A RECAP HERE, PEOPLE!
SIGH
EH, FORGET IT. IT'S ALMOST TIME ANYWAY.
LET'S GO JOIN OUR GUESTS.

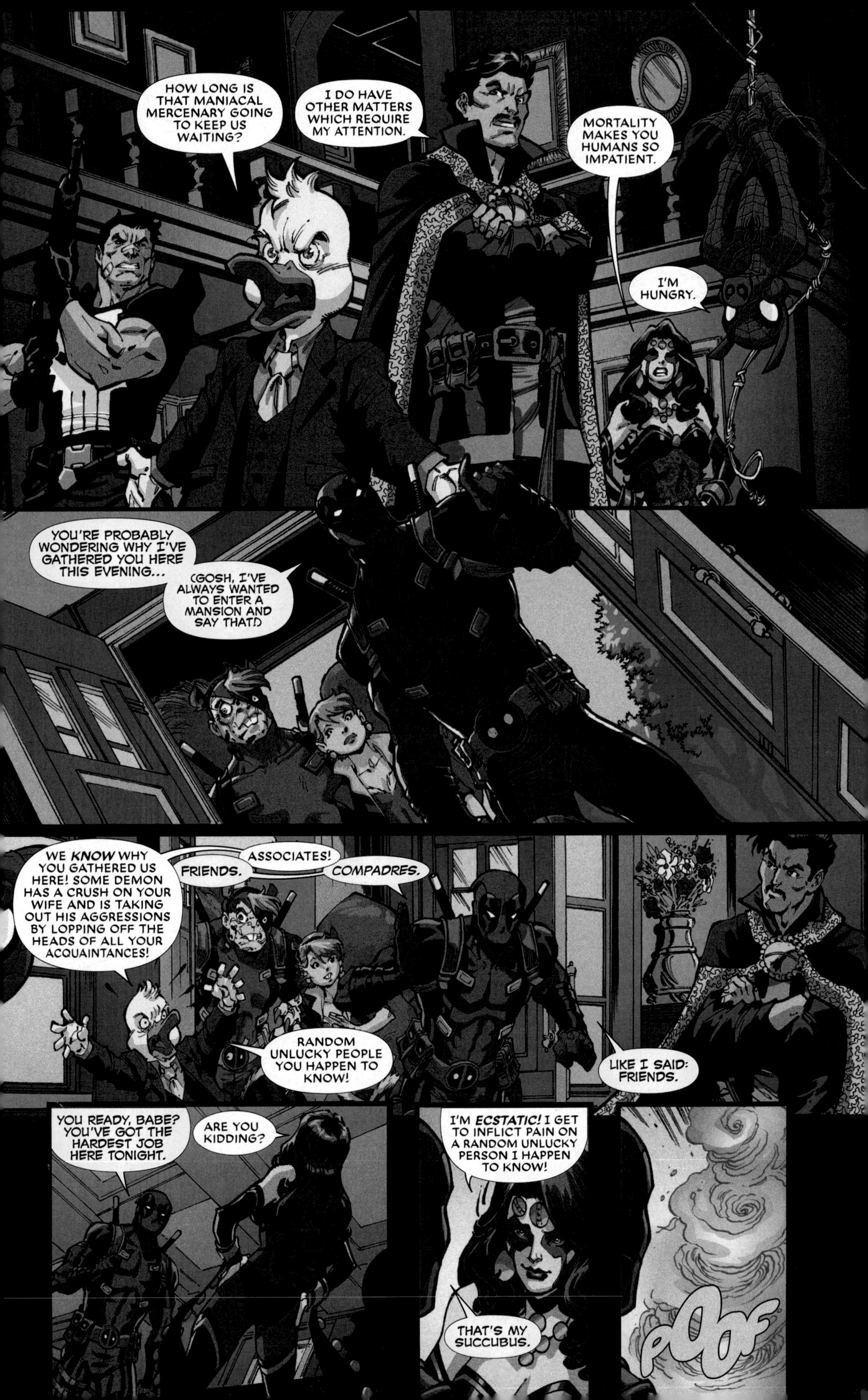
HOW LONG IS THAT MANIACAL MERCENARY GOING TO KEEP US WAITING?
I DO HAVE OTHER MATTERS WHICH REQUIRE MY ATTENTION.
MORTALITY MAKES YOU HUMANS SO IMPATIENT.
I'M HUNGRY.
YOU'RE PROBABLY WONDERING WHY I'VE GATHERED YOU HERE THIS EVENING...
(GOSH, I'VE ALWAYS WANTED TO ENTER A MANSION AND SAY THAT!)
WE KNOW WHY YOU GATHERED US HERE! SOME DEMON HAS A CRUSH ON YOUR WIFE AND IS TAKING OUT HIS AGGRESSIONS BY LOPPING OFF THE HEADS OF ALL YOUR ACQUAINTANCES!
FRIENDS.
ASSOCIATES!
COMPADRES.
RANDOM UNLUCKY PEOPLE YOU HAPPEN TO KNOW!
LIKE I SAID: FRIENDS.
YOU READY, BABE? YOU'VE GOT THE HARDEST JOB HERE TONIGHT.
ARE YOU KIDDING?
I'M ECSTATIC! I GET TO INFLICT PAIN ON A RANDOM UNLUCKY PERSON I HAPPEN TO KNOW!
THAT'S MY SUCCUBUS.
POOF

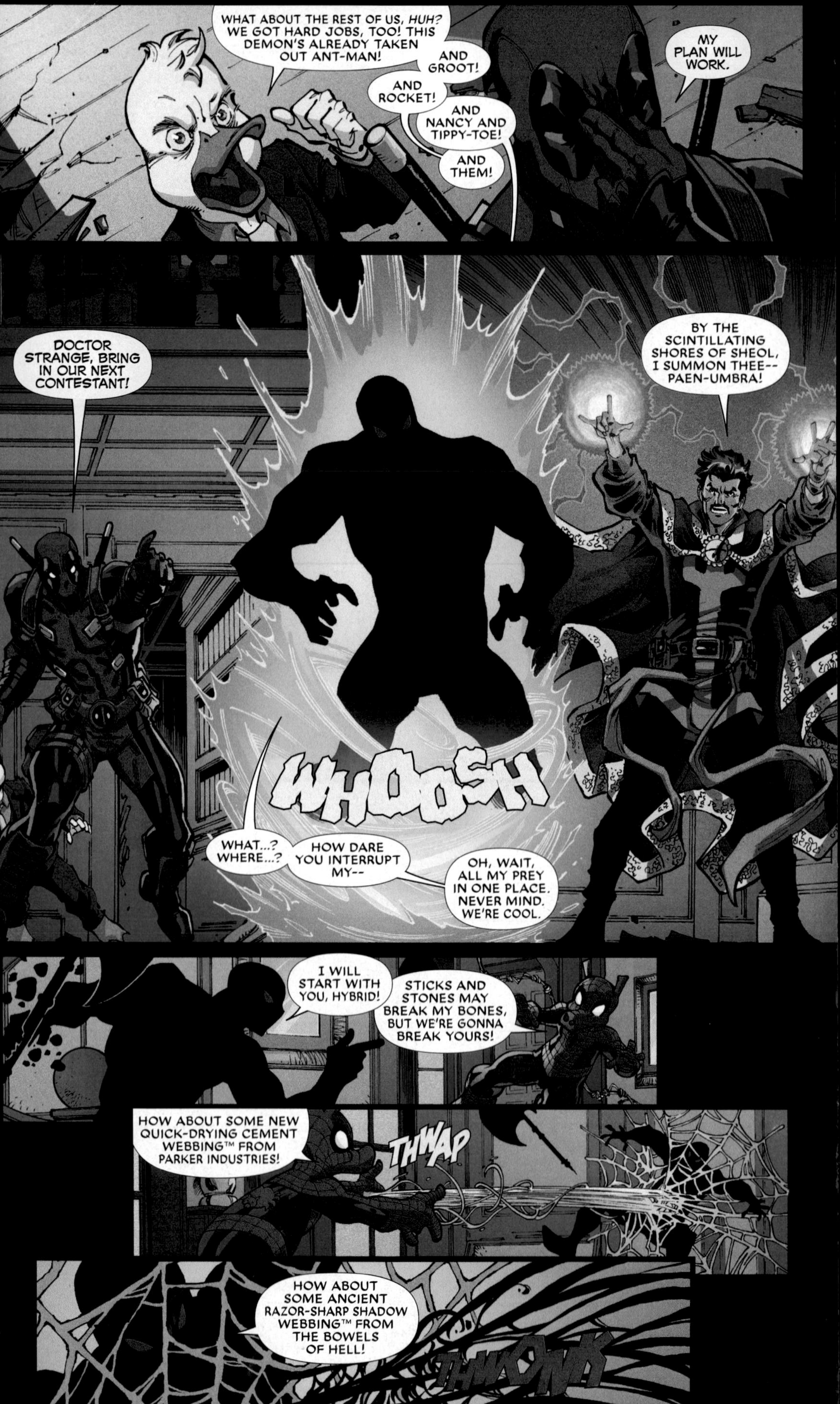
WHAT ABOUT THE REST OF US, HUH? WE GOT HARD JOBS, TOO! THIS DEMON'S ALREADY TAKEN OUT ANT-MAN!
AND GROOT!
AND ROCKET!
AND NANCY AND TIPPY-TOE!
AND THEM!
MY PLAN WILL WORK.
DOCTOR STRANGE, BRING IN OUR NEXT CONTESTANT!
BY THE SCINTILLATING SHORES OF SHEOL, I SUMMON THEE-- PAEN-UMBRA!
WHOOSH
WHAT...? WHERE...?
HOW DARE YOU INTERRUPT MY--
OH, WAIT, ALL MY PREY IN ONE PLACE. NEVER MIND. WE'RE COOL.
I WILL START WITH YOU, HYBRID!
STICKS AND STONES MAY BREAK MY BONES, BUT WE'RE GONNA BREAK YOURS!
HOW ABOUT SOME NEW QUICK-DRYING CEMENT WEBBING™ FROM PARKER INDUSTRIES!
THWAP
HOW ABOUT SOME ANCIENT RAZOR-SHARP SHADOW WEBBING™ FROM THE BOWELS OF HELL!
THWONK

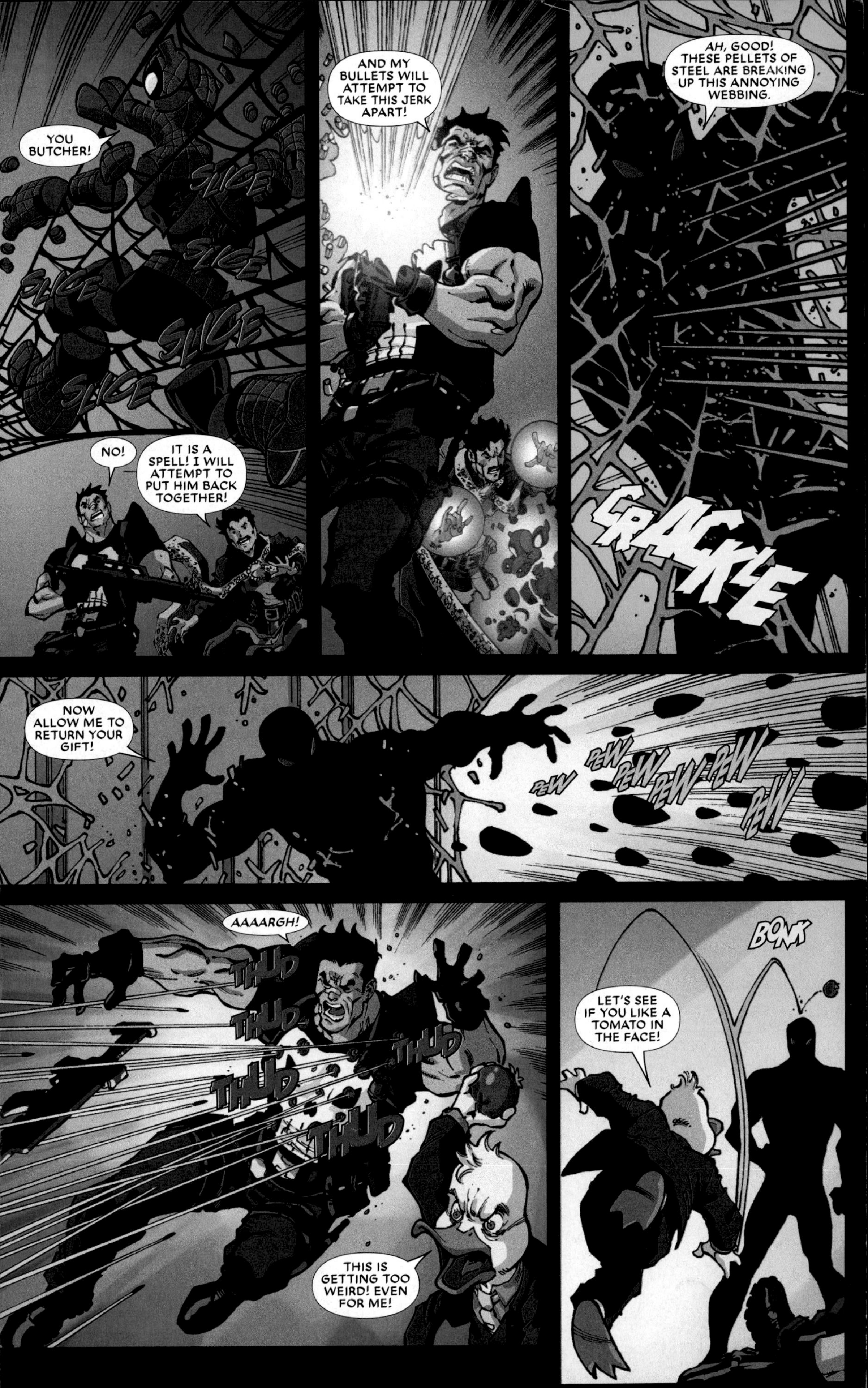
YOU BUTCHER!
SLICE
SLICE
SLICE
SLICE
SLICE
NO!
IT IS A SPELL! I WILL ATTEMPT TO PUT HIM BACK TOGETHER!
AND MY BULLETS WILL ATTEMPT TO TAKE THIS JERK APART!
AH, GOOD! THESE PELLETS OF STEEL ARE BREAKING UP THIS ANNOYING WEBBING.
CRACKLE
NOW ALLOW ME TO RETURN YOUR GIFT!
PEW PEW PEW PEW PEW PEW
AAAARGH!
THUD
THUD
THUD
THUD
THUD
THIS IS GETTING TOO WEIRD! EVEN FOR ME!
BONK
LET'S SEE IF YOU LIKE A TOMATO IN THE FACE!

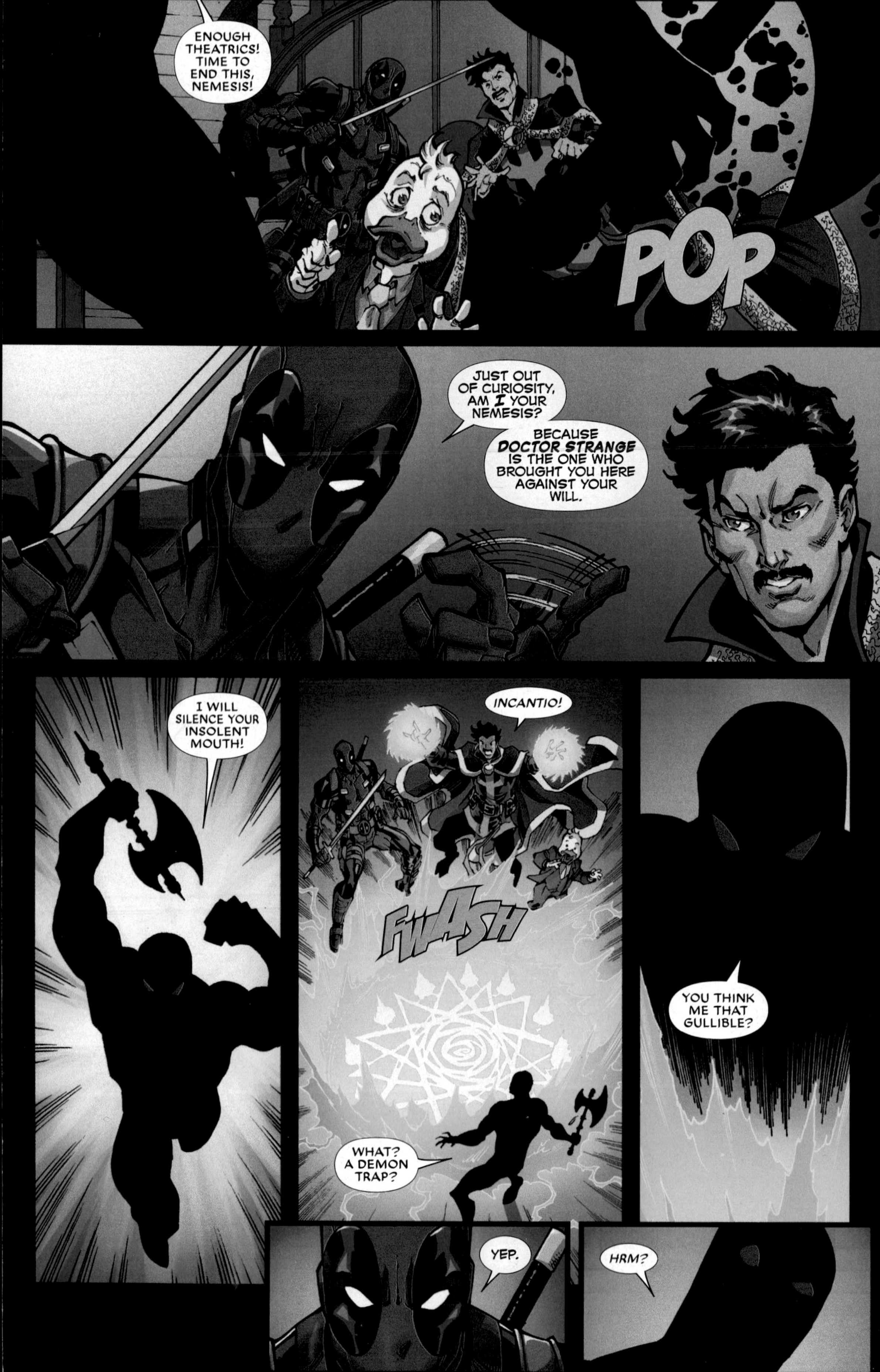
ENOUGH THEATRICS! TIME TO END THIS, NEMESIS!
POP
JUST OUT OF CURIOSITY, AM I YOUR NEMESIS?
BECAUSE DOCTOR STRANGE IS THE ONE WHO BROUGHT YOU HERE AGAINST YOUR WILL.
I WILL SILENCE YOUR INSOLENT MOUTH!
INCANTIO!
FWASH
WHAT? A DEMON TRAP?
YOU THINK ME THAT GULLIBLE?
YEP.
HRM?

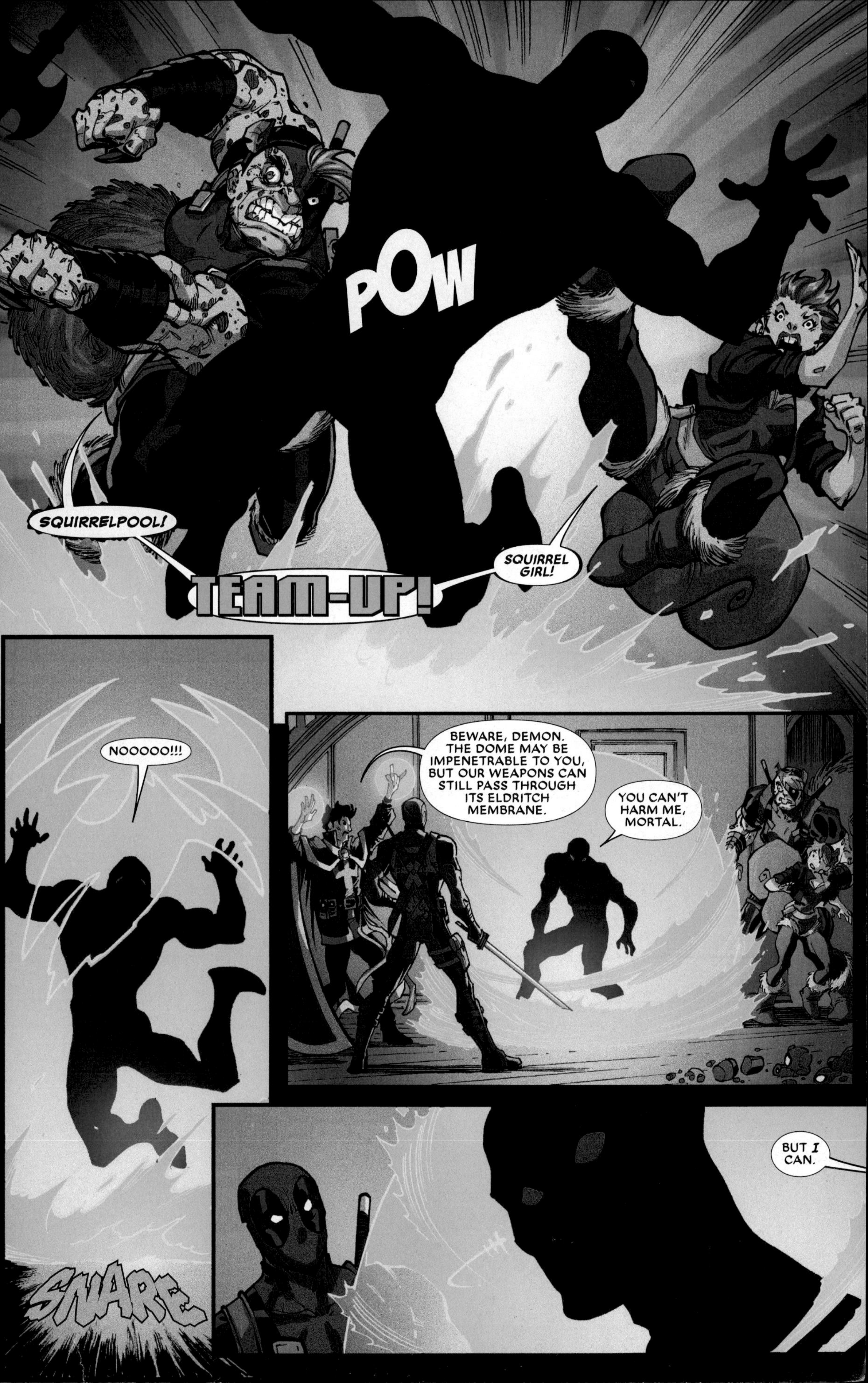
POW
SQUIRRELPOOL!
TEAM-UP!
SQUIRREL GIRL!
NOOOOO!!!
BEWARE, DEMON. THE DOME MAY BE IMPENETRABLE TO YOU, BUT OUR WEAPONS CAN STILL PASS THROUGH ITS ELDRITCH MEMBRANE.
YOU CAN'T HARM ME, MORTAL.
SNARE
BUT I CAN.

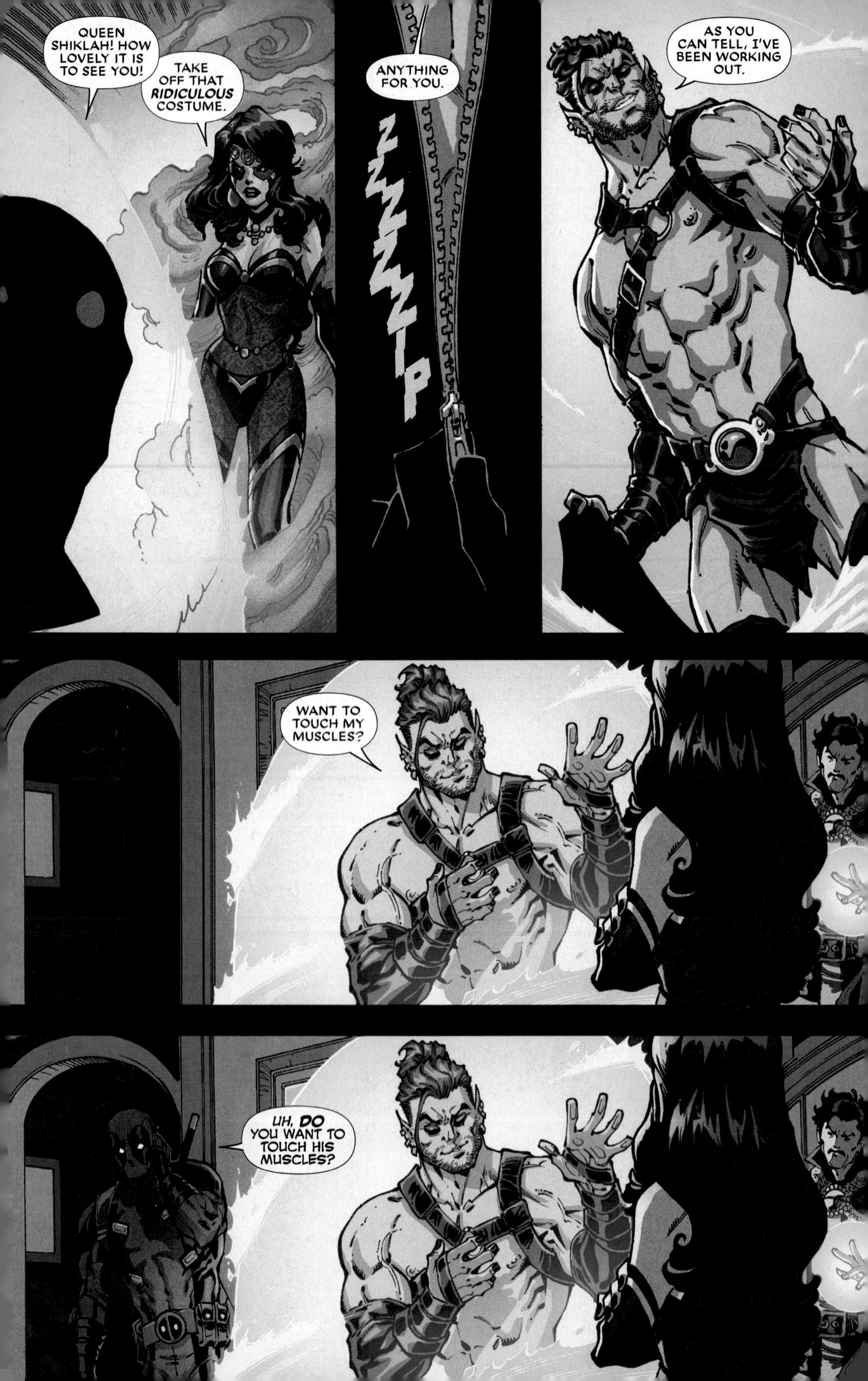
QUEEN SHIKLAH! HOW LOVELY IT IS TO SEE YOU!
TAKE OFF THAT *RIDICULOUS* COSTUME.
ANYTHING FOR YOU.
ZZZZZIP
AS YOU CAN TELL, I'VE BEEN WORKING OUT.
WANT TO TOUCH MY MUSCLES?
UH, ***DO*** YOU WANT TO TOUCH HIS MUSCLES?

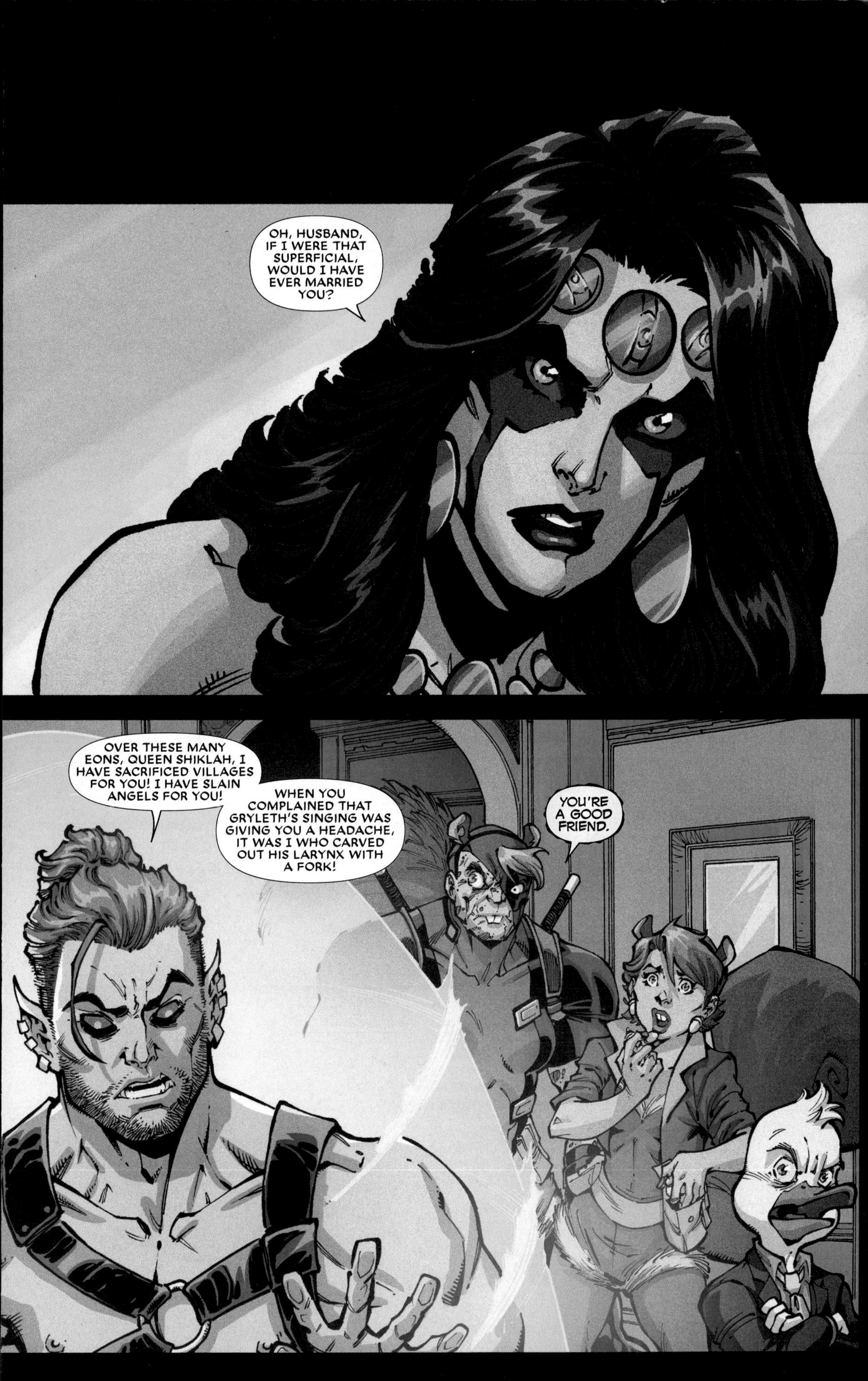
OH, HUSBAND, IF I WERE THAT SUPERFICIAL, WOULD I HAVE EVER MARRIED YOU?
OVER THESE MANY EONS, QUEEN SHIKLAH, I HAVE SACRIFICED VILLAGES FOR YOU! I HAVE SLAIN ANGELS FOR YOU!
WHEN YOU COMPLAINED THAT GRYLETH'S SINGING WAS GIVING YOU A HEADACHE, IT WAS I WHO CARVED OUT HIS LARYNX WITH A FORK!
YOU'RE A GOOD FRIEND.

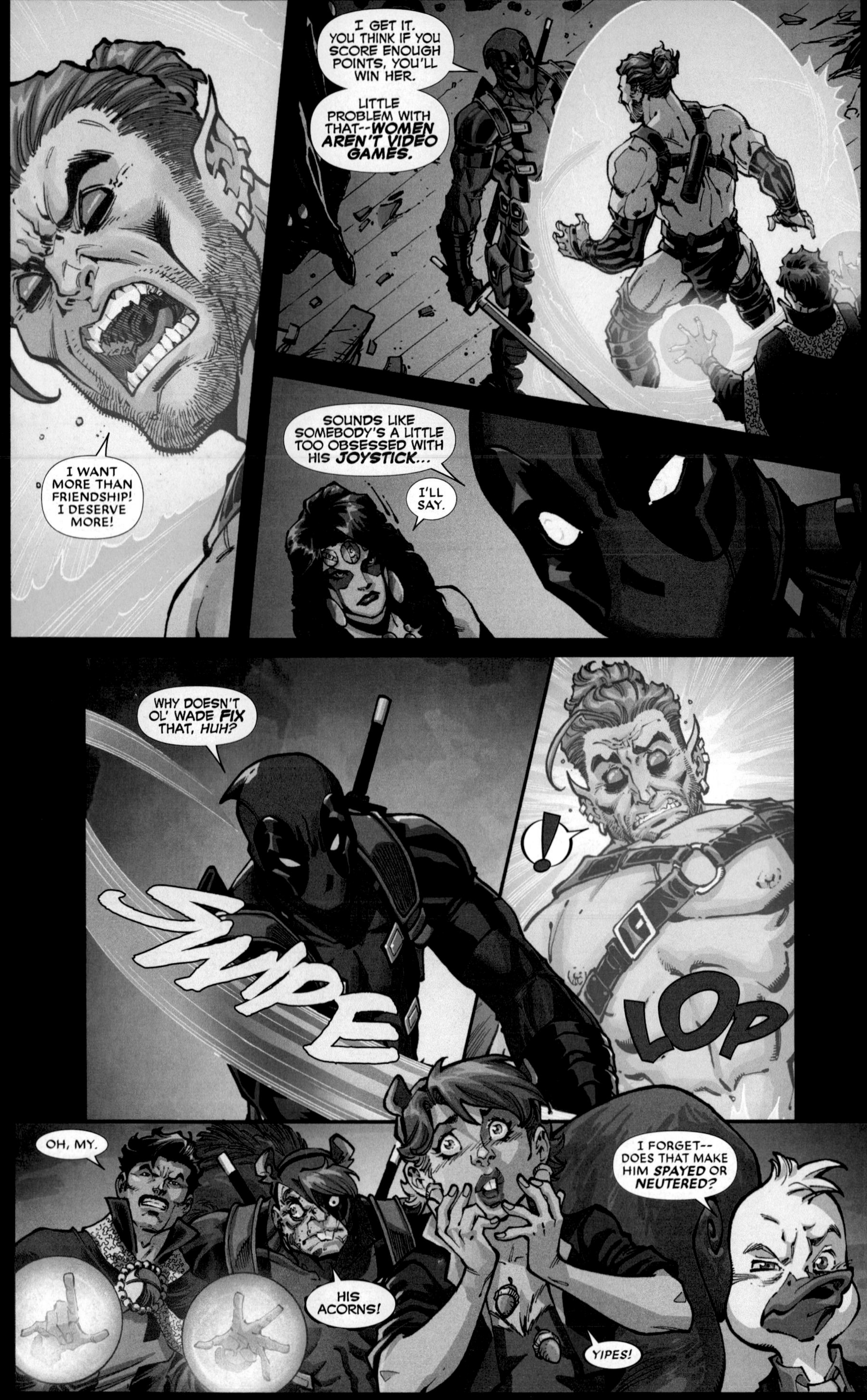
I GET IT. YOU THINK IF YOU SCORE ENOUGH POINTS, YOU'LL WIN HER.
LITTLE PROBLEM WITH THAT--**WOMEN AREN'T VIDEO GAMES.**
I WANT MORE THAN FRIENDSHIP! I DESERVE MORE!
SOUNDS LIKE SOMEBODY'S A LITTLE TOO OBSESSED WITH HIS ***JOYSTICK...***
I'LL SAY.
WHY DOESN'T OL' WADE **FIX** THAT, *HUH?*
SWIPE
!
LOP
OH, MY.
HIS ACORNS!
I FORGET--DOES THAT MAKE HIM ***SPAYED*** OR ***NEUTERED?***
YIPES!

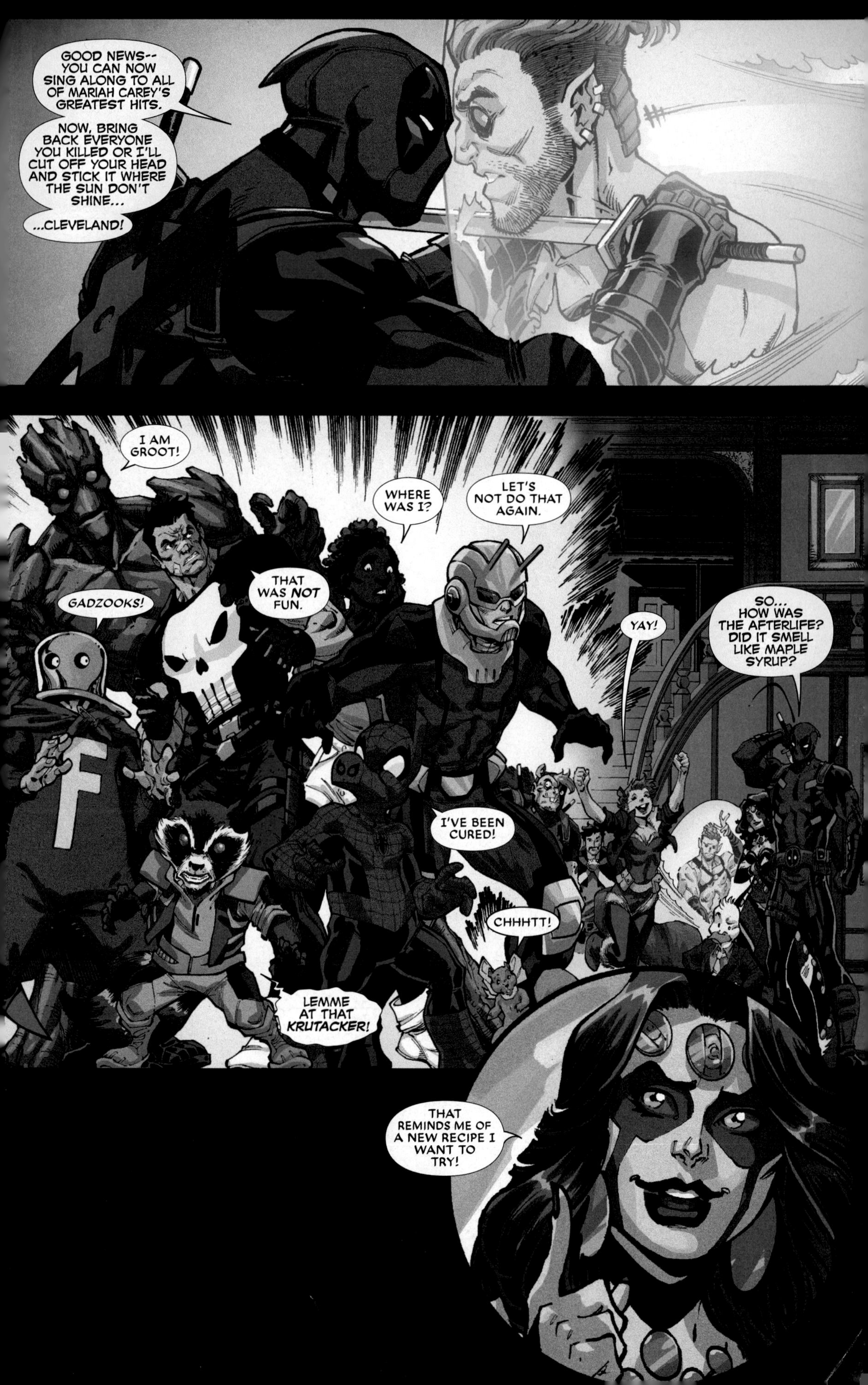
GOOD NEWS-- YOU CAN NOW SING ALONG TO ALL OF MARIAH CAREY'S GREATEST HITS.
NOW, BRING BACK EVERYONE YOU KILLED OR I'LL CUT OFF YOUR HEAD AND STICK IT WHERE THE SUN DON'T SHINE...
...CLEVELAND!
I AM GROOT!
GADZOOKS!
THAT WAS **NOT** FUN.
WHERE WAS I?
LET'S NOT DO THAT AGAIN.
YAY!
SO... HOW WAS THE AFTERLIFE? DID IT SMELL LIKE MAPLE SYRUP?
I'VE BEEN CURED!
CHHHTT!
LEMME AT THAT ***KRUTACKER!***
THAT REMINDS ME OF A NEW RECIPE I WANT TO TRY!

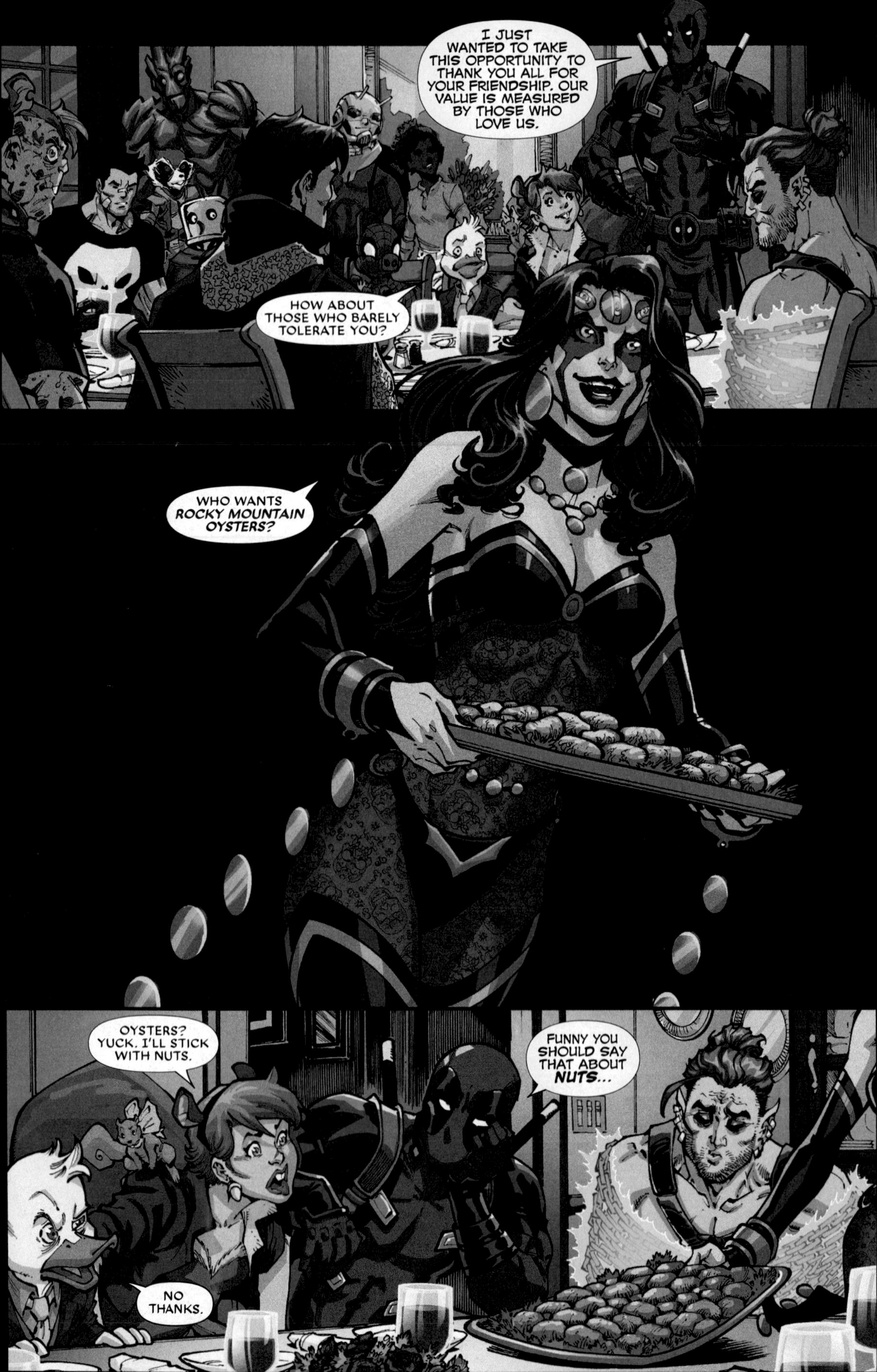
I JUST WANTED TO TAKE THIS OPPORTUNITY TO THANK YOU ALL FOR YOUR FRIENDSHIP. OUR VALUE IS MEASURED BY THOSE WHO LOVE US.
HOW ABOUT THOSE WHO BARELY TOLERATE YOU?
WHO WANTS *ROCKY MOUNTAIN OYSTERS?*
OYSTERS? YUCK. I'LL STICK WITH NUTS.
FUNNY YOU SHOULD SAY THAT ABOUT ***NUTS...***
NO THANKS.

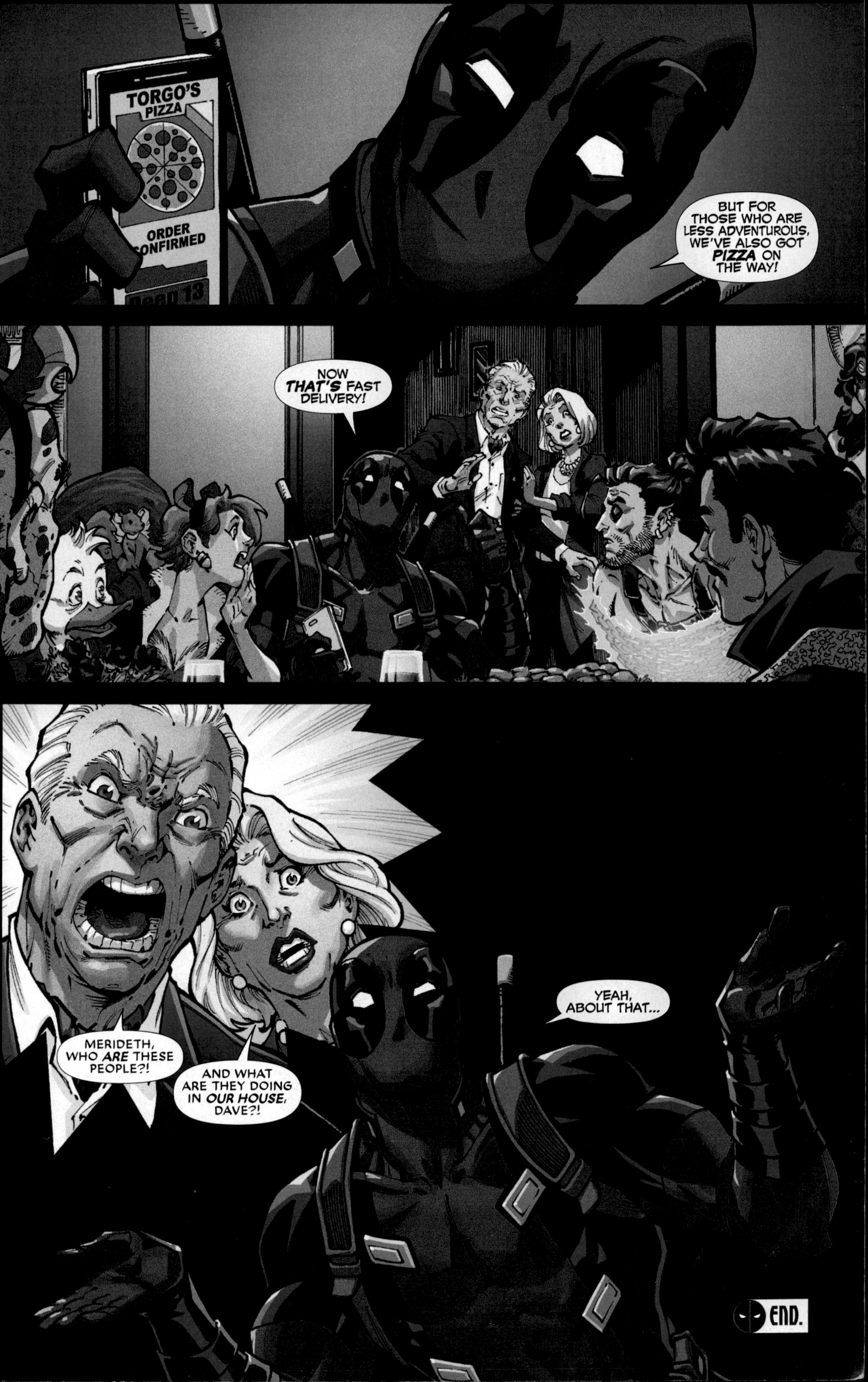
TORGO'S
PIZZA
ORDER
CONFIRMED
BUT FOR THOSE WHO ARE LESS ADVENTUROUS, WE'VE ALSO GOT **PIZZA** ON THE WAY!
NOW ***THAT'S*** FAST DELIVERY!
MERIDETH, WHO ***ARE*** THESE PEOPLE?!
AND WHAT ARE THEY DOING IN ***OUR HOUSE***, DAVE?!
YEAH, ABOUT THAT...
END.

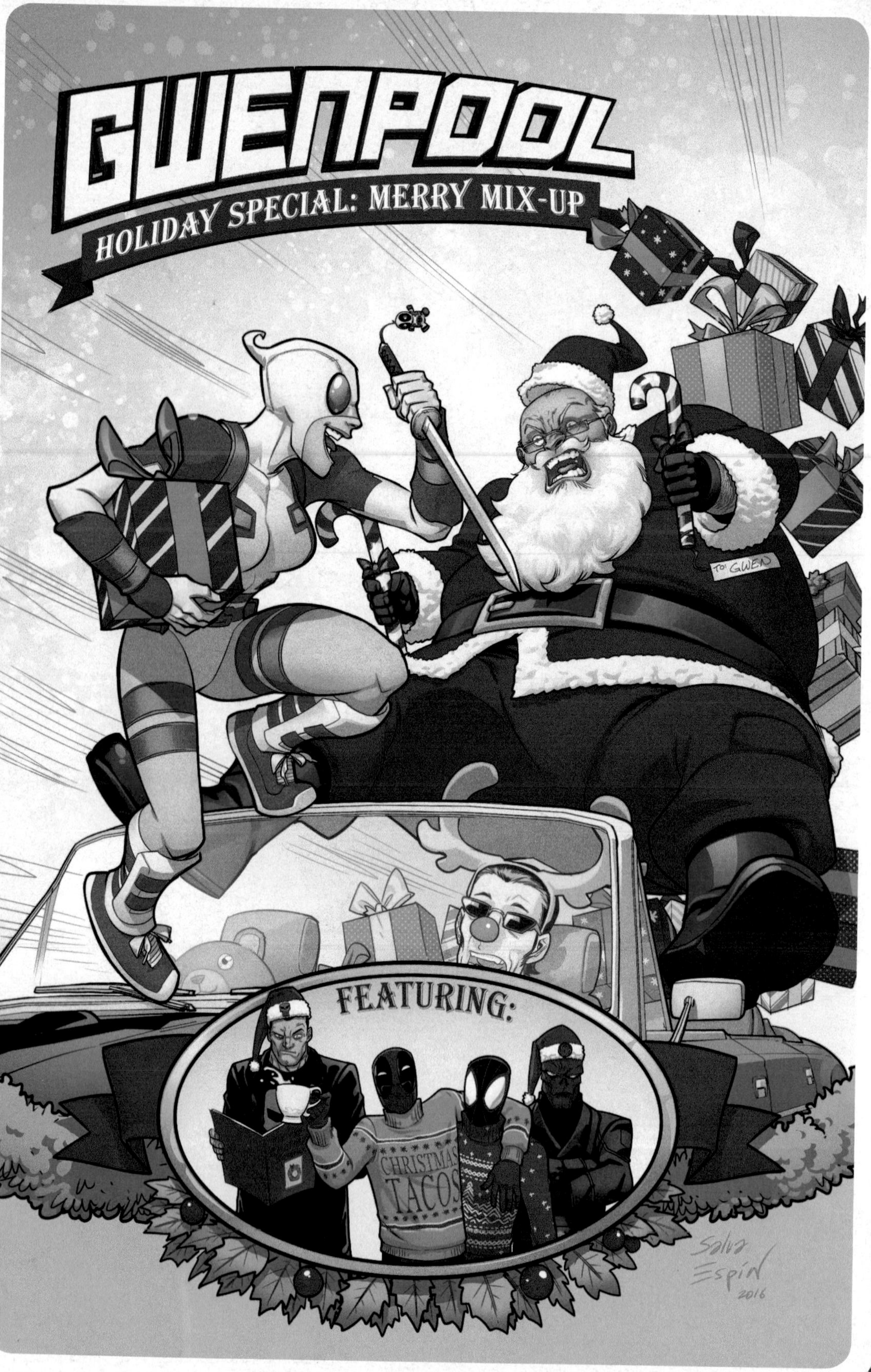
GWENPOOL
HOLIDAY SPECIAL: MERRY MIX-UP
TO: GWEN
FEATURING:
CHRISTMAS TACOS
Salva Espín 2016

Avenger...Assassin...Superstar...Smelly person...Possibly the world's most skilled mercenary, definitely the world's most annoying, Wade Wilson was chosen for a top-secret government program that gave him a healing factor allowing him to heal from any wound. Somehow, despite making his money as a gun for hire, Wade has become one of the most beloved "heroes" in the world. Call him the Merc with the Mouth...call him the Regeneratin' Degenerate...call him...

DEADPOOL

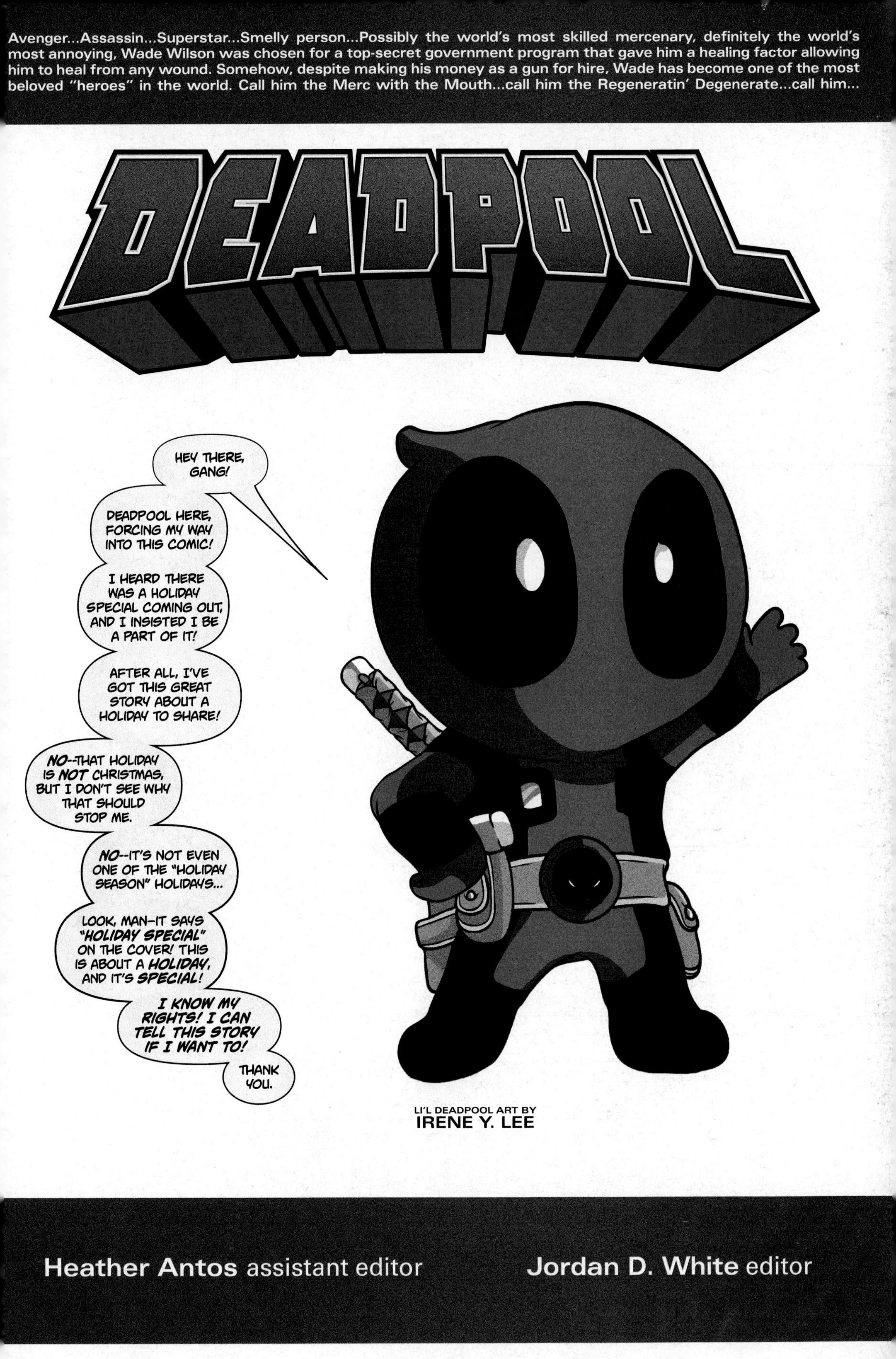

HEY THERE, GANG!
DEADPOOL HERE, FORCING MY WAY INTO THIS COMIC!
I HEARD THERE WAS A HOLIDAY SPECIAL COMING OUT, AND I INSISTED I BE A PART OF IT!
AFTER ALL, I'VE GOT THIS GREAT STORY ABOUT A HOLIDAY TO SHARE!
NO--THAT HOLIDAY IS NOT CHRISTMAS, BUT I DON'T SEE WHY THAT SHOULD STOP ME.
NO--IT'S NOT EVEN ONE OF THE "HOLIDAY SEASON" HOLIDAYS...
LOOK, MAN--IT SAYS "HOLIDAY SPECIAL" ON THE COVER! THIS IS ABOUT A HOLIDAY, AND IT'S SPECIAL!
I KNOW MY RIGHTS! I CAN TELL THIS STORY IF I WANT TO!
THANK YOU.

LI'L DEADPOOL ART BY
IRENE Y. LEE

Heather Antos assistant editor **Jordan D. White** editor

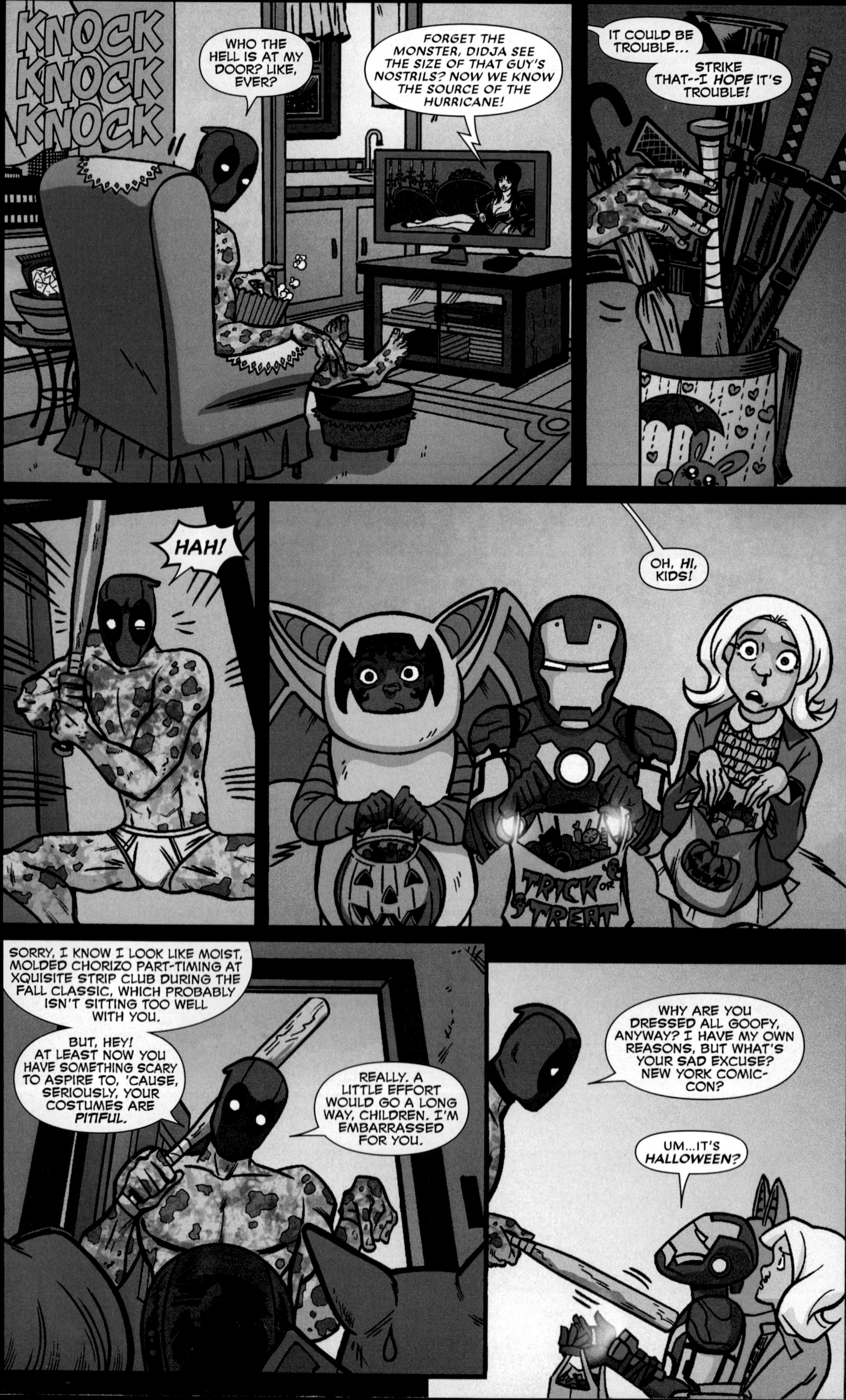
KNOCK KNOCK KNOCK
WHO THE HELL IS AT MY DOOR? LIKE, EVER?
FORGET THE MONSTER, DIDJA SEE THE SIZE OF THAT GUY'S NOSTRILS? NOW WE KNOW THE SOURCE OF THE HURRICANE!
IT COULD BE TROUBLE...
STRIKE THAT--I *HOPE* IT'S TROUBLE!
HAH!
OH, *HI*, KIDS!
TRICK OR TREAT
SORRY, I KNOW I LOOK LIKE MOIST, MOLDED CHORIZO PART-TIMING AT XQUISITE STRIP CLUB DURING THE FALL CLASSIC, WHICH PROBABLY ISN'T SITTING TOO WELL WITH YOU.
BUT, HEY! AT LEAST NOW YOU HAVE SOMETHING SCARY TO ASPIRE TO, 'CAUSE, SERIOUSLY, YOUR COSTUMES ARE *PITIFUL*.
REALLY. A LITTLE EFFORT WOULD GO A LONG WAY, CHILDREN. I'M EMBARRASSED FOR YOU.
WHY ARE YOU DRESSED ALL GOOFY, ANYWAY? I HAVE MY OWN REASONS, BUT WHAT'S YOUR SAD EXCUSE? NEW YORK COMIC-CON?
UM...IT'S *HALLOWEEN*?

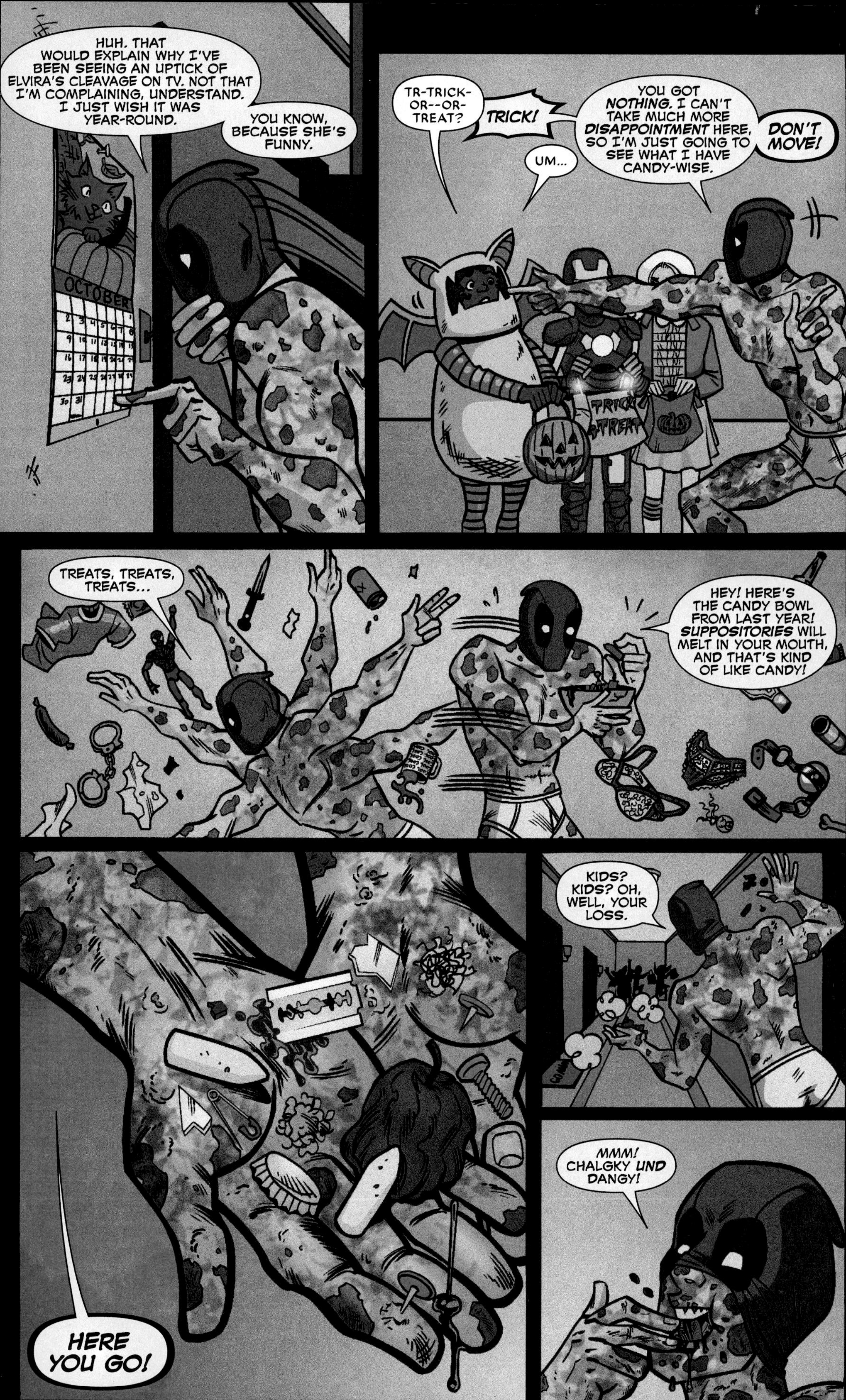
HUH. THAT WOULD EXPLAIN WHY I'VE BEEN SEEING AN UPTICK OF ELVIRA'S CLEAVAGE ON TV. NOT THAT I'M COMPLAINING, UNDERSTAND. I JUST WISH IT WAS YEAR-ROUND.
YOU KNOW, BECAUSE SHE'S FUNNY.
OCTOBER
TR-TRICK-OR--OR-TREAT?
TRICK!
UM...
YOU GOT NOTHING. I CAN'T TAKE MUCH MORE DISAPPOINTMENT HERE, SO I'M JUST GOING TO SEE WHAT I HAVE CANDY-WISE.
DON'T MOVE!
TRICK TREAT
TREATS, TREATS, TREATS...
HEY! HERE'S THE CANDY BOWL FROM LAST YEAR! SUPPOSITORIES WILL MELT IN YOUR MOUTH, AND THAT'S KIND OF LIKE CANDY!
HERE YOU GO!
KIDS? KIDS? OH, WELL, YOUR LOSS.
MMM! CHALGKY UND DANGY!

WELP, I MIGHT AS WELL GO OUT AND CELEBRATE THE MOST HOLY OF HOLIDAYS IN THE DEADPOOL UNIVERSE!

BOSS'S DAY! NO. SWEETEST DAY? ALL 'POOL'S DAY? NO... DIA DE LOS...

DEADPOOLOWEEN

STORY AND ART BY CHYNNA CLUGSTON FLORES
COLORS BY GUY MAJOR
LETTERS BY VC'S CLAYTON COWLES
SPECIAL THANKS TO RICHARD NEAL AND IAN SHAUGHNESSY!

TRICK OR TREAT!

BOOT

SHOVE

XAVIER'S SCHOOL FOR GIFTED YOUNGSTERS

...

STOMP STOMP STOMP

HA HA HA!

VWIP

WINK!

SKRITCHA SKRITCHA SKRIT

AAAAAAAA!!!

SHRIEK!

WAIL!

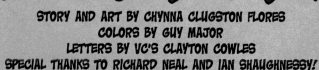

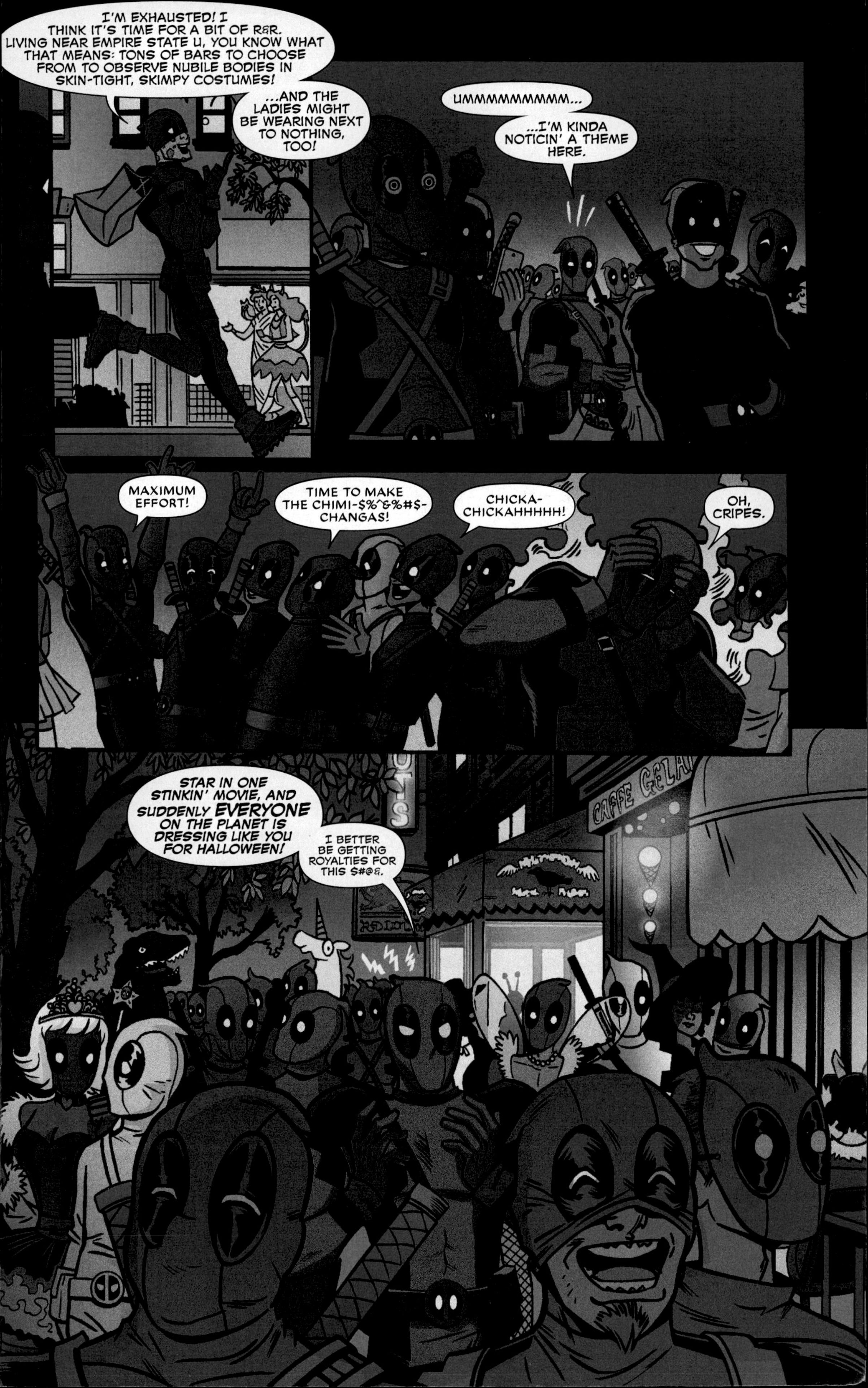
I'M EXHAUSTED! I THINK IT'S TIME FOR A BIT OF R&R. LIVING NEAR EMPIRE STATE U, YOU KNOW WHAT THAT MEANS: TONS OF BARS TO CHOOSE FROM TO OBSERVE NUBILE BODIES IN SKIN-TIGHT, SKIMPY COSTUMES!
...AND THE LADIES MIGHT BE WEARING NEXT TO NOTHING, TOO!
UMMMMMMMMM...
...I'M KINDA NOTICIN' A THEME HERE.
MAXIMUM EFFORT!
TIME TO MAKE THE CHIMI-$%^&%#$-CHANGAS!
CHICKA-CHICKAHHHHH!
OH, CRIPES.
STAR IN ONE STINKIN' MOVIE, AND SUDDENLY EVERYONE ON THE PLANET IS DRESSING LIKE YOU FOR HALLOWEEN!
I BETTER BE GETTING ROYALTIES FOR THIS $#@&.
CAFFE GELA

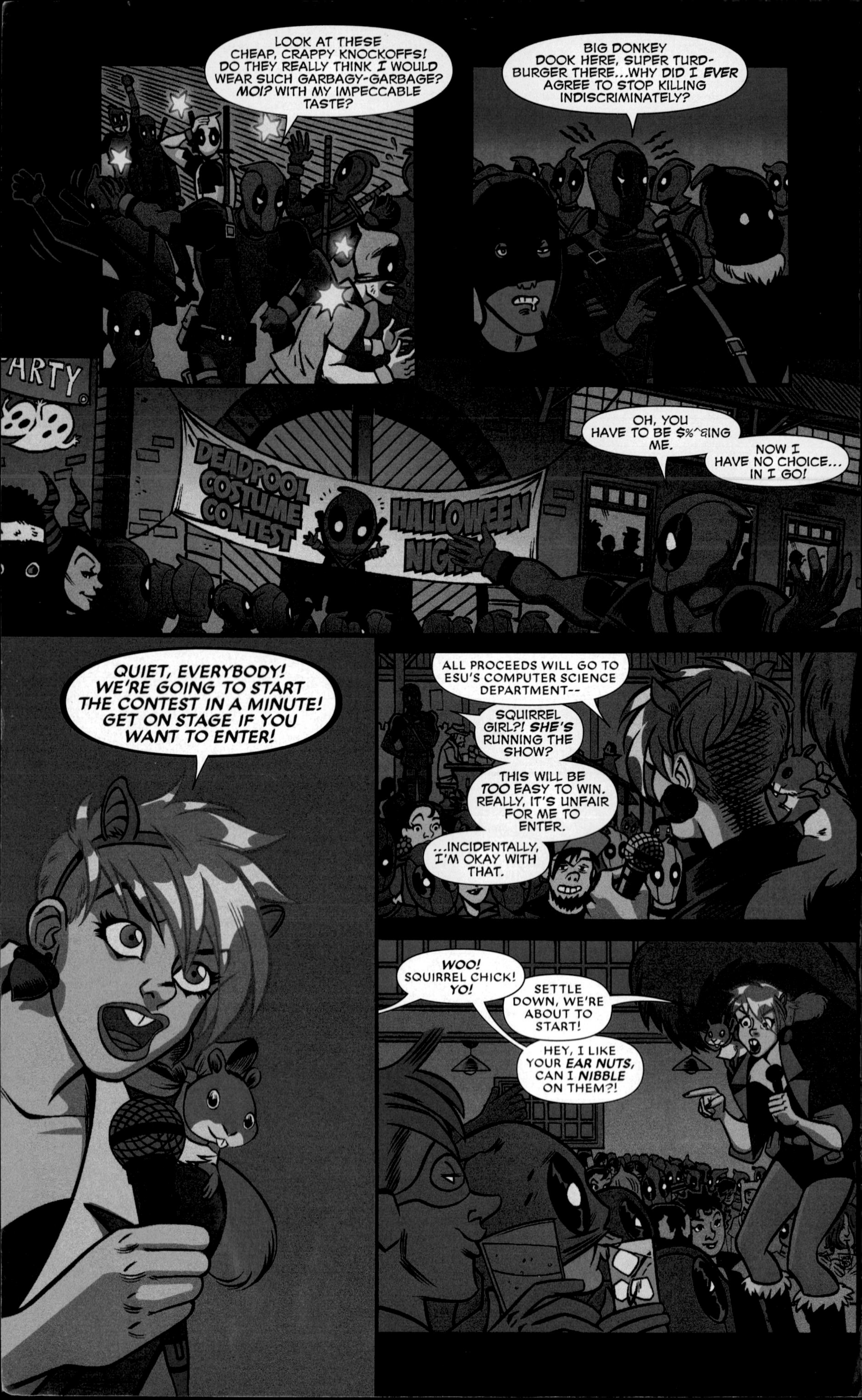
LOOK AT THESE CHEAP, CRAPPY KNOCKOFFS! DO THEY REALLY THINK *I* WOULD WEAR SUCH GARBAGY-GARBAGE? *MOI?* WITH MY IMPECCABLE TASTE?
BIG DONKEY DOOK HERE, SUPER TURD-BURGER THERE...WHY *DID* I *EVER* AGREE TO STOP KILLING INDISCRIMINATELY?
PARTY
DEADPOOL COSTUME CONTEST
HALLOWEEN NIG
OH, YOU HAVE TO BE $%^&ING ME.
NOW I HAVE NO CHOICE... IN I GO!
QUIET, EVERYBODY! WE'RE GOING TO START THE CONTEST IN A MINUTE! GET ON STAGE IF YOU WANT TO ENTER!
ALL PROCEEDS WILL GO TO ESU'S COMPUTER SCIENCE DEPARTMENT--
SQUIRREL GIRL?! *SHE'S* RUNNING THE SHOW?
THIS WILL BE *TOO* EASY TO WIN. REALLY, IT'S UNFAIR FOR ME TO ENTER.
...INCIDENTALLY, I'M OKAY WITH THAT.
WOO! SQUIRREL CHICK! *YO!*
SETTLE DOWN, WE'RE ABOUT TO START!
HEY, I LIKE YOUR *EAR NUTS*, CAN I *NIBBLE* ON THEM?!

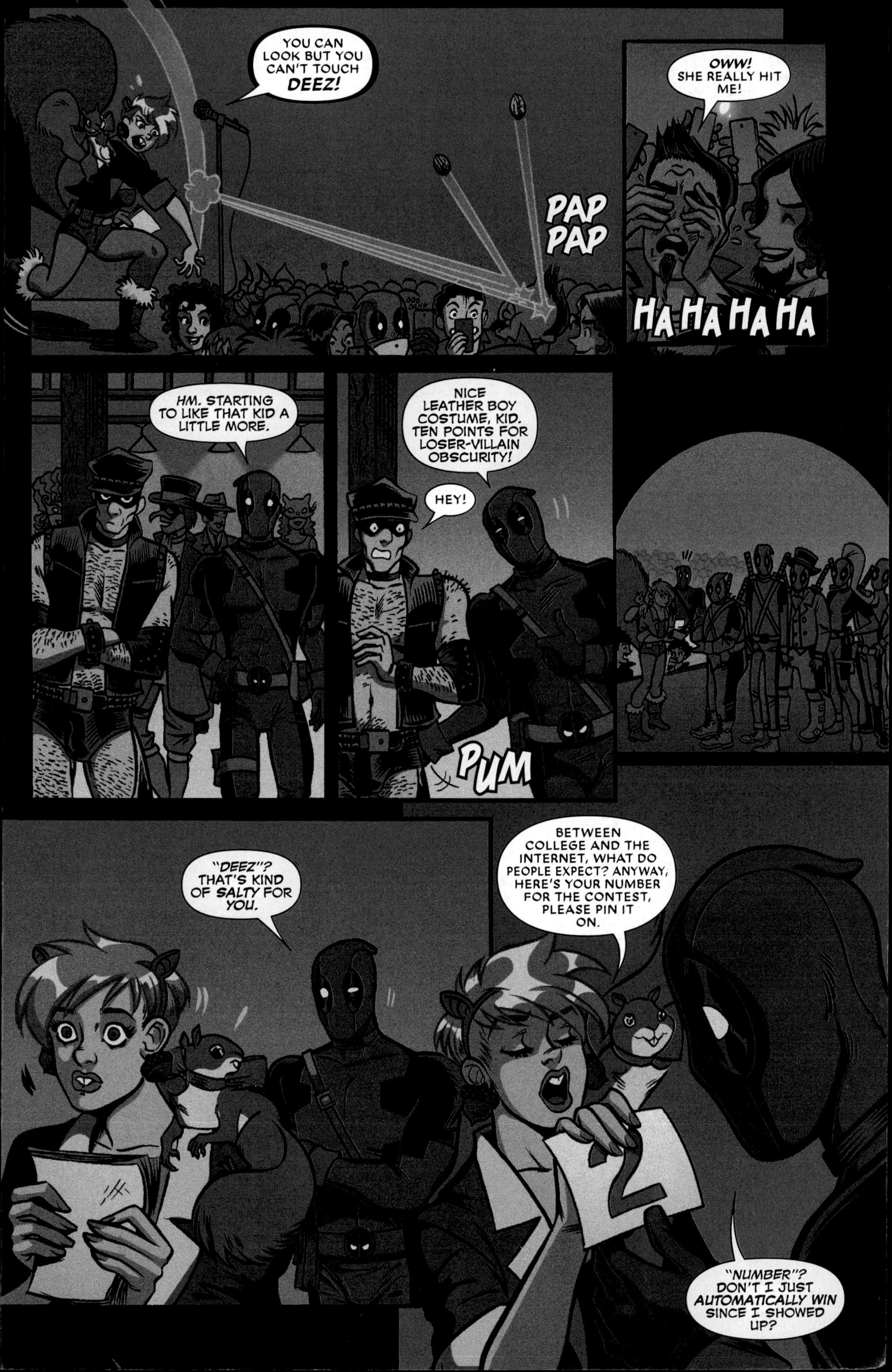
YOU CAN LOOK BUT YOU CAN'T TOUCH DEEZ!
PAP PAP
OWW! SHE REALLY HIT ME!
HA HA HA HA
HM. STARTING TO LIKE THAT KID A LITTLE MORE.
NICE LEATHER BOY COSTUME, KID. TEN POINTS FOR LOSER-VILLAIN OBSCURITY!
HEY!
PUM
"DEEZ"? THAT'S KIND OF SALTY FOR YOU.
BETWEEN COLLEGE AND THE INTERNET, WHAT DO PEOPLE EXPECT? ANYWAY, HERE'S YOUR NUMBER FOR THE CONTEST, PLEASE PIN IT ON.
"NUMBER"? DON'T I JUST AUTOMATICALLY WIN SINCE I SHOWED UP?

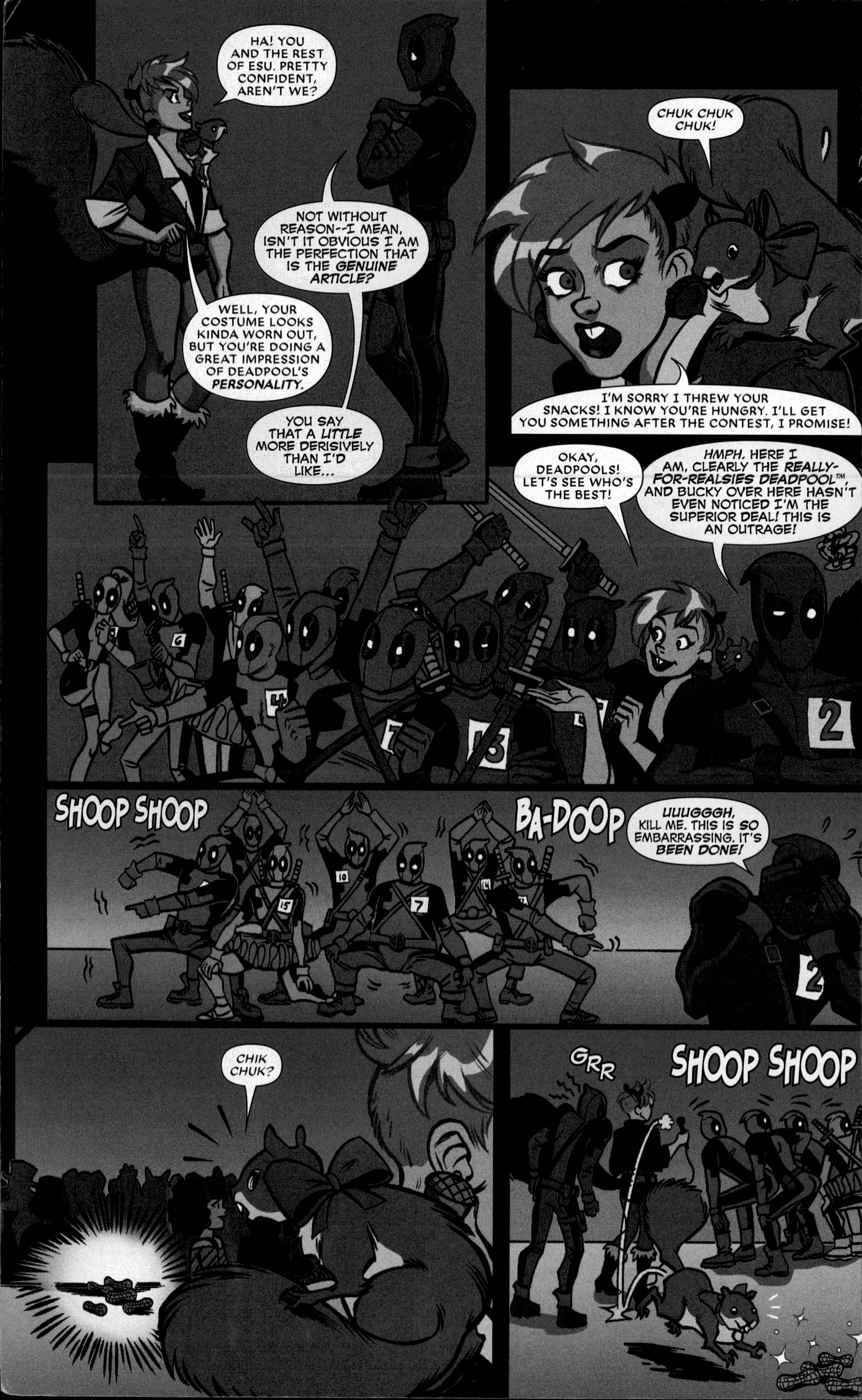
HA! YOU AND THE REST OF ESU. PRETTY CONFIDENT, AREN'T WE?
NOT WITHOUT REASON--I MEAN, ISN'T IT OBVIOUS I AM THE PERFECTION THAT IS THE GENUINE ARTICLE?
WELL, YOUR COSTUME LOOKS KINDA WORN OUT, BUT YOU'RE DOING A GREAT IMPRESSION OF DEADPOOL'S PERSONALITY.
YOU SAY THAT A LITTLE MORE DERISIVELY THAN I'D LIKE...
CHUK CHUK CHUK!
I'M SORRY I THREW YOUR SNACKS! I KNOW YOU'RE HUNGRY. I'LL GET YOU SOMETHING AFTER THE CONTEST, I PROMISE!
OKAY, DEADPOOLS! LET'S SEE WHO'S THE BEST!
HMPH. HERE I AM, CLEARLY THE REALLY-FOR-REALSIES DEADPOOL™, AND BUCKY OVER HERE HASN'T EVEN NOTICED I'M THE SUPERIOR DEAL! THIS IS AN OUTRAGE!
SHOOP SHOOP
BA-DOOP
UUUGGGH, KILL ME. THIS IS SO EMBARRASSING. IT'S BEEN DONE!
CHIK CHUK?
GRR
SHOOP SHOOP

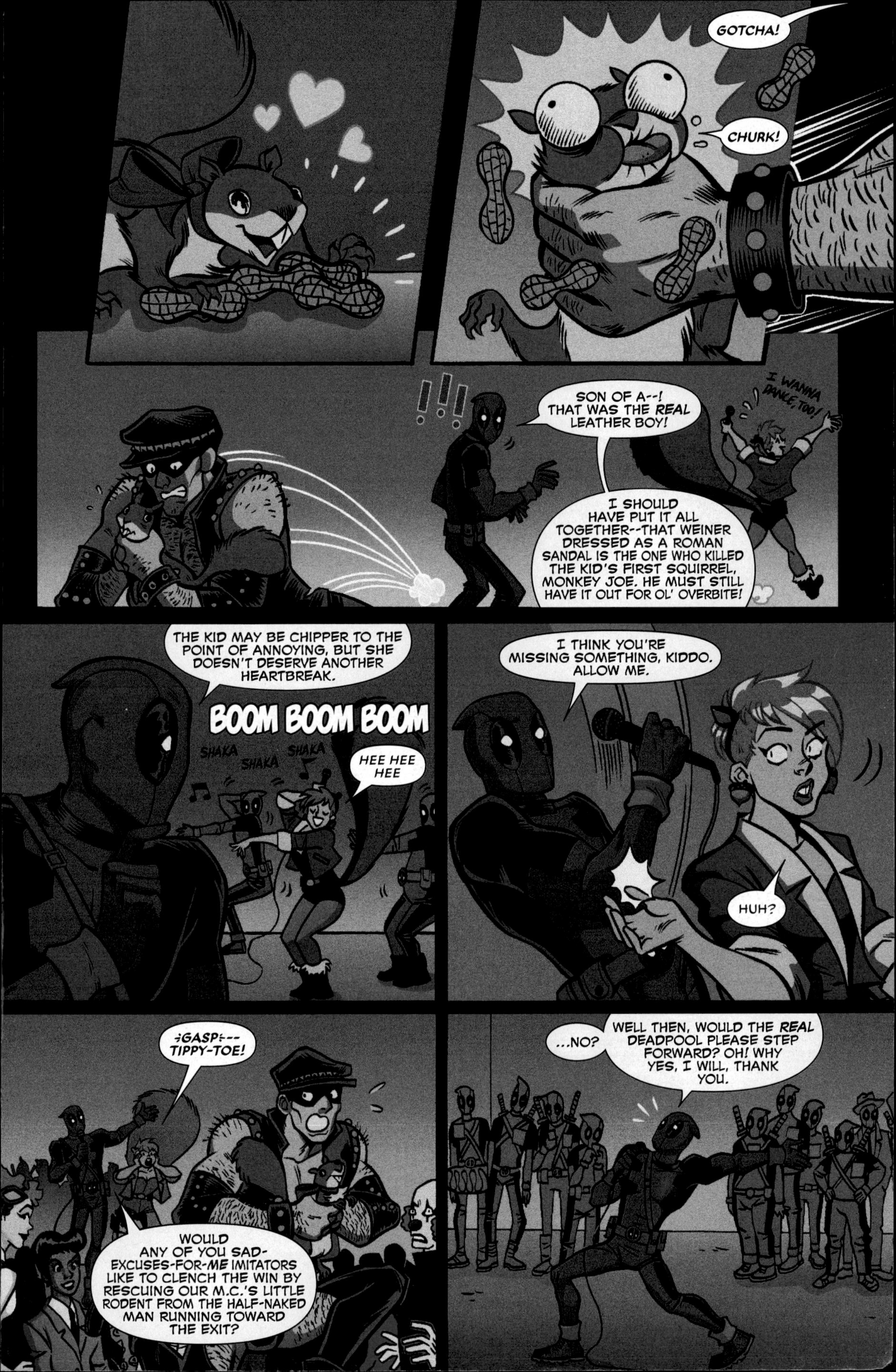
GOTCHA!
CHURK!
SON OF A--! THAT WAS THE REAL LEATHER BOY!
I WANNA DANCE, TOO!
I SHOULD HAVE PUT IT ALL TOGETHER--THAT WEINER DRESSED AS A ROMAN SANDAL IS THE ONE WHO KILLED THE KID'S FIRST SQUIRREL, MONKEY JOE. HE MUST STILL HAVE IT OUT FOR OL' OVERBITE!
THE KID MAY BE CHIPPER TO THE POINT OF ANNOYING, BUT SHE DOESN'T DESERVE ANOTHER HEARTBREAK.
BOOM BOOM BOOM
SHAKA SHAKA SHAKA
HEE HEE HEE
I THINK YOU'RE MISSING SOMETHING, KIDDO. ALLOW ME.
HUH?
GASP--- TIPPY-TOE!
WOULD ANY OF YOU SAD-EXCUSES-FOR-ME IMITATORS LIKE TO CLENCH THE WIN BY RESCUING OUR M.C.'S LITTLE RODENT FROM THE HALF-NAKED MAN RUNNING TOWARD THE EXIT?
...NO?
WELL THEN, WOULD THE REAL DEADPOOL PLEASE STEP FORWARD? OH! WHY YES, I WILL, THANK YOU.

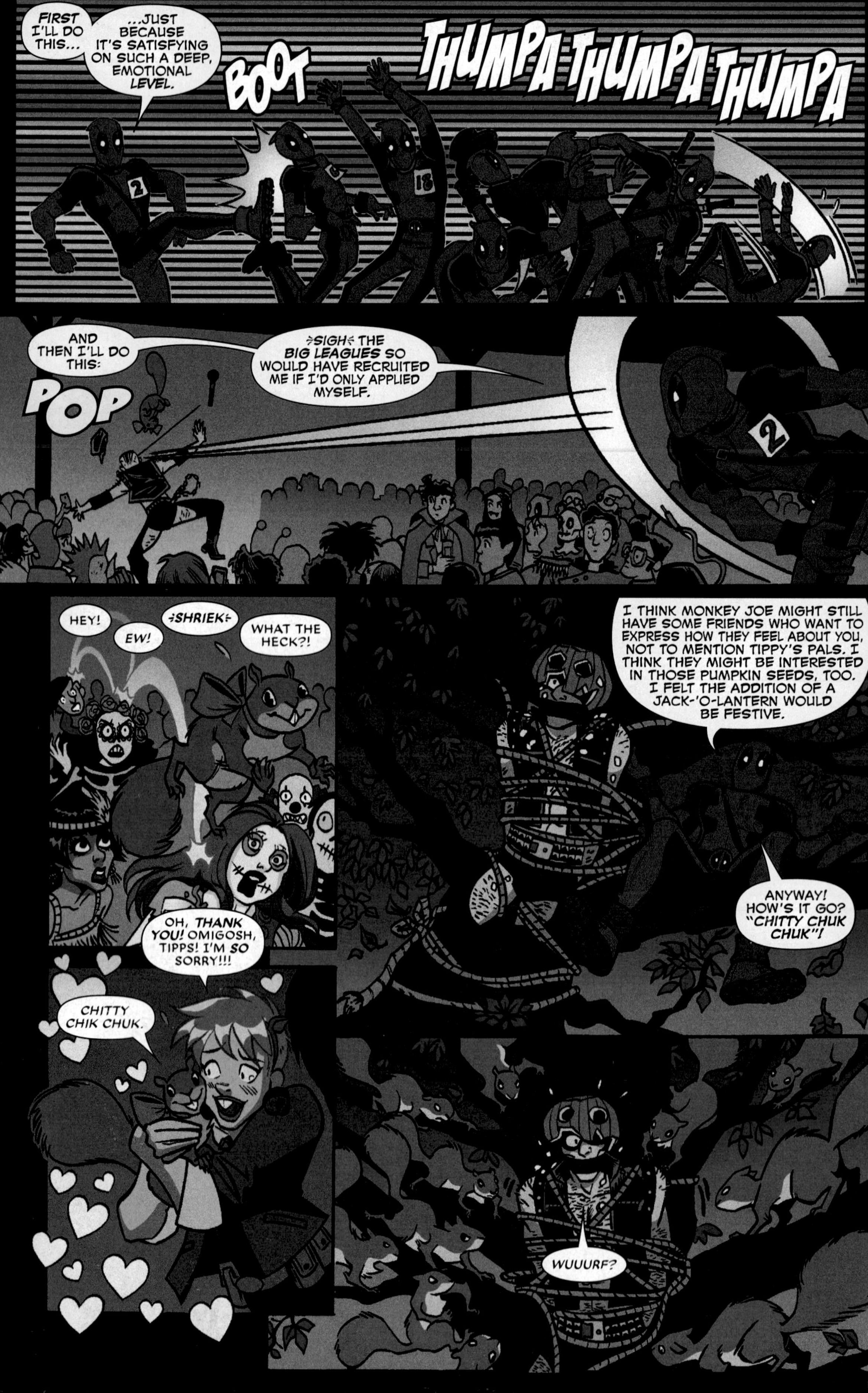
FIRST I'LL DO THIS...
...JUST BECAUSE IT'S SATISFYING ON SUCH A DEEP, EMOTIONAL LEVEL.
BOOT
THUMPA THUMPA THUMPA
AND THEN I'LL DO THIS:
SIGH THE BIG LEAGUES SO WOULD HAVE RECRUITED ME IF I'D ONLY APPLIED MYSELF.
POP
HEY!
EW!
SHRIEK
WHAT THE HECK?!
OH, THANK YOU! OMIGOSH, TIPPS! I'M SO SORRY!!!
CHITTY CHIK CHUK.
I THINK MONKEY JOE MIGHT STILL HAVE SOME FRIENDS WHO WANT TO EXPRESS HOW THEY FEEL ABOUT YOU, NOT TO MENTION TIPPY'S PALS. I THINK THEY MIGHT BE INTERESTED IN THOSE PUMPKIN SEEDS, TOO. I FELT THE ADDITION OF A JACK-'O-LANTERN WOULD BE FESTIVE.
ANYWAY! HOW'S IT GO? "CHITTY CHUK CHUK"!
WUUURF?

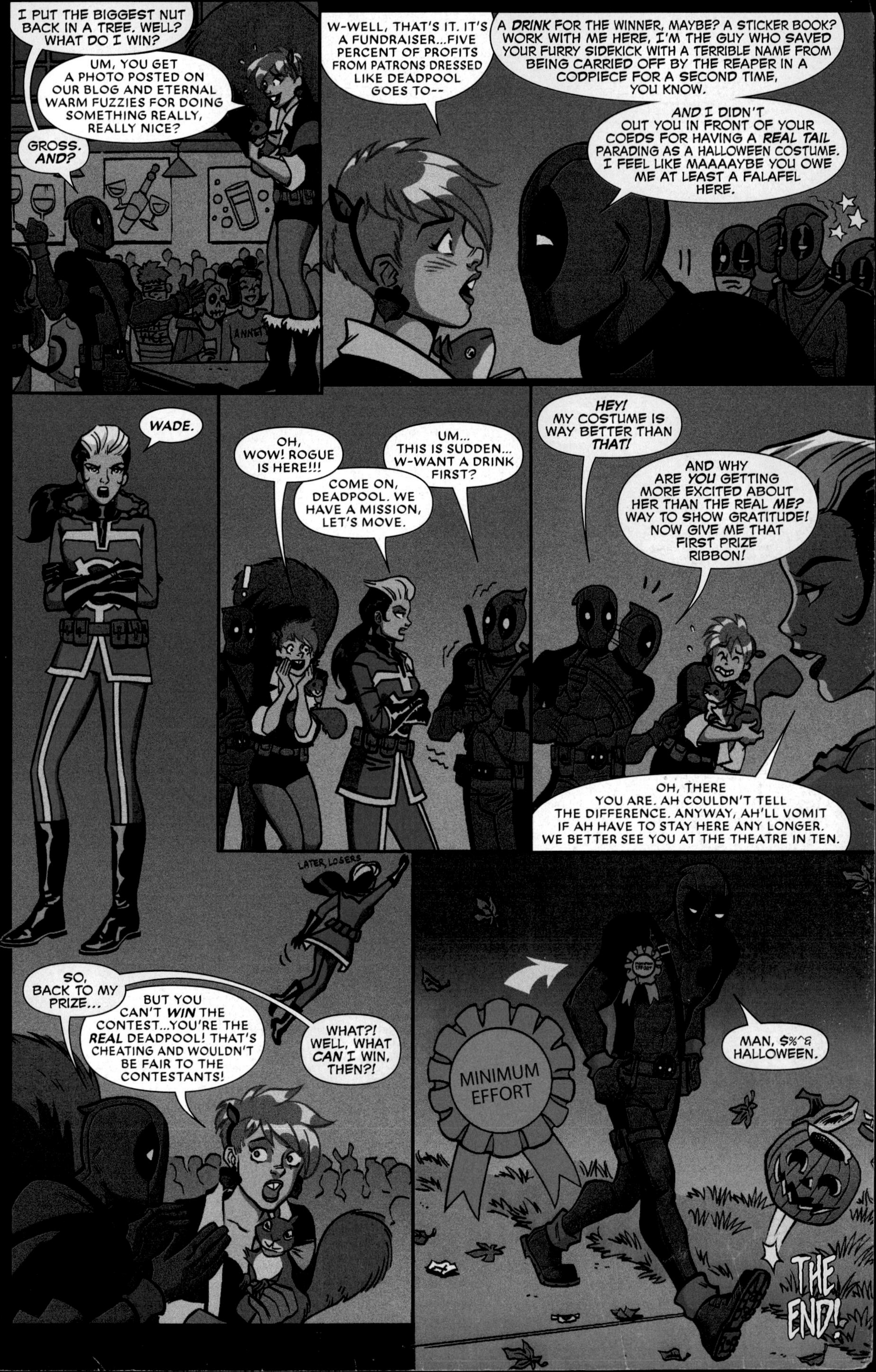
I PUT THE BIGGEST NUT BACK IN A TREE. WELL? WHAT DO I WIN?
UM, YOU GET A PHOTO POSTED ON OUR BLOG AND ETERNAL WARM FUZZIES FOR DOING SOMETHING REALLY, REALLY NICE?
GROSS. AND?
W-WELL, THAT'S IT. IT'S A FUNDRAISER...FIVE PERCENT OF PROFITS FROM PATRONS DRESSED LIKE DEADPOOL GOES TO--
A DRINK FOR THE WINNER, MAYBE? A STICKER BOOK? WORK WITH ME HERE, I'M THE GUY WHO SAVED YOUR FURRY SIDEKICK WITH A TERRIBLE NAME FROM BEING CARRIED OFF BY THE REAPER IN A CODPIECE FOR A SECOND TIME, YOU KNOW.
AND I DIDN'T OUT YOU IN FRONT OF YOUR COEDS FOR HAVING A REAL TAIL PARADING AS A HALLOWEEN COSTUME. I FEEL LIKE MAAAAYBE YOU OWE ME AT LEAST A FALAFEL HERE.
WADE.
OH, WOW! ROGUE IS HERE!!!
COME ON, DEADPOOL. WE HAVE A MISSION, LET'S MOVE.
UM... THIS IS SUDDEN... W-WANT A DRINK FIRST?
HEY! MY COSTUME IS WAY BETTER THAN THAT!
AND WHY ARE YOU GETTING MORE EXCITED ABOUT HER THAN THE REAL ME? WAY TO SHOW GRATITUDE! NOW GIVE ME THAT FIRST PRIZE RIBBON!
OH, THERE YOU ARE. AH COULDN'T TELL THE DIFFERENCE. ANYWAY, AH'LL VOMIT IF AH HAVE TO STAY HERE ANY LONGER. WE BETTER SEE YOU AT THE THEATRE IN TEN.
LATER, LOSERS
SO, BACK TO MY PRIZE...
BUT YOU CAN'T WIN THE CONTEST...YOU'RE THE REAL DEADPOOL! THAT'S CHEATING AND WOULDN'T BE FAIR TO THE CONTESTANTS!
WHAT?! WELL, WHAT CAN I WIN, THEN?!
MINIMUM EFFORT
MAN, $%^& HALLOWEEN.
THE END!

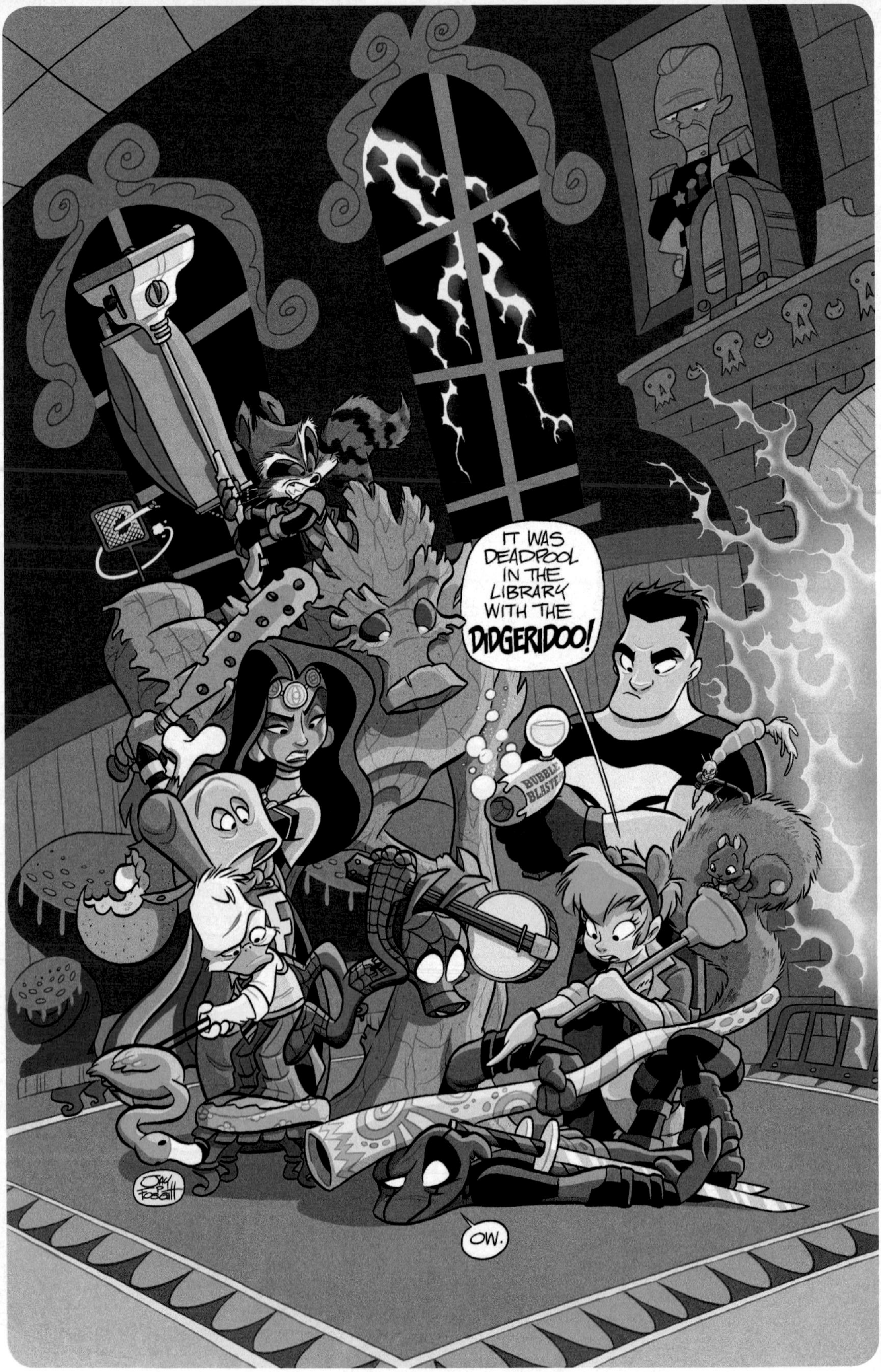
IT WAS DEADPOOL IN THE LIBRARY WITH THE DIDGERIDOO!
BUBBLE BLASTER
OW.

JAY FOSGITT

1 variant

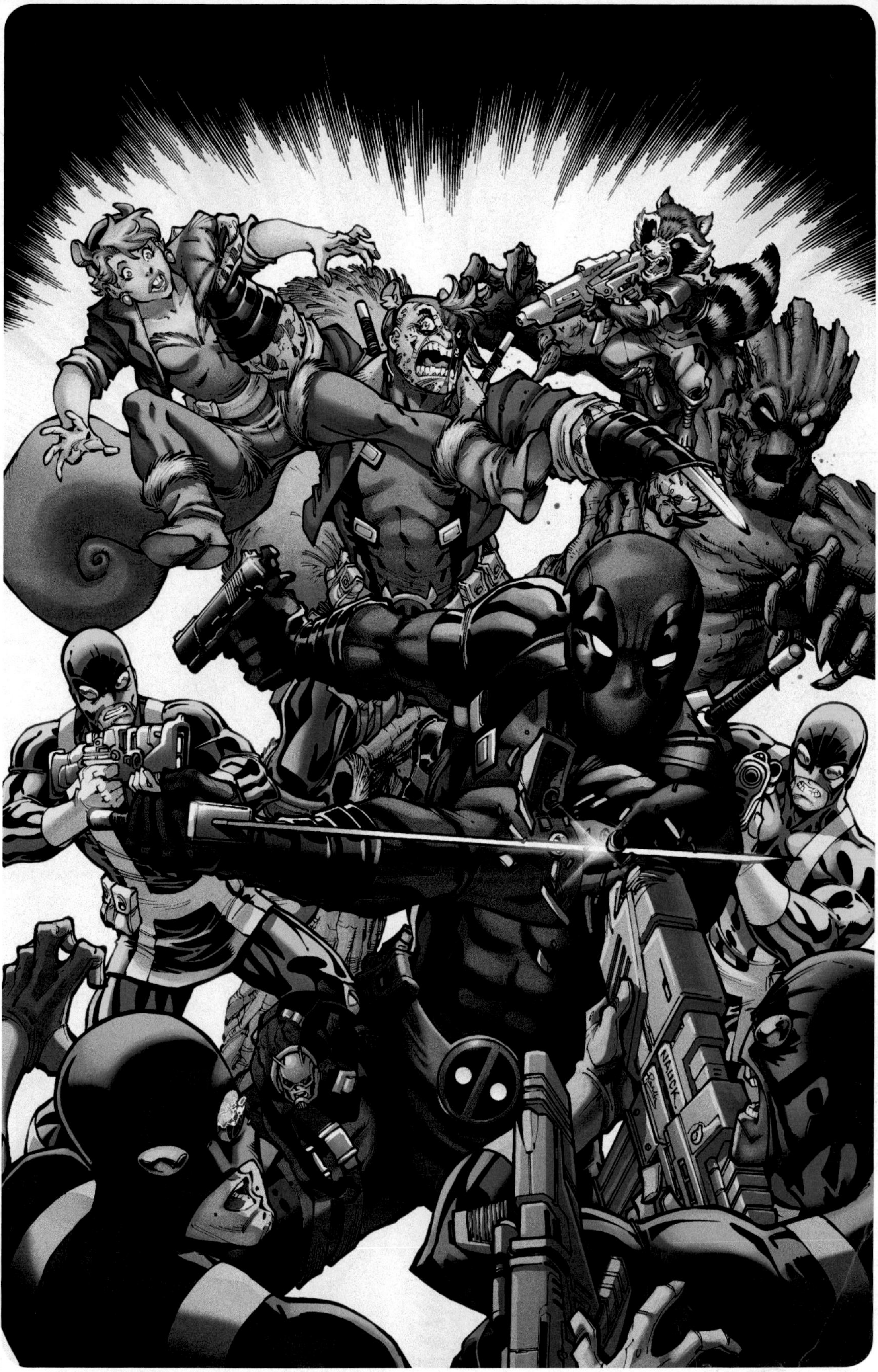

TODD NAUCK & RACHELLE ROSENBERG

2 variant

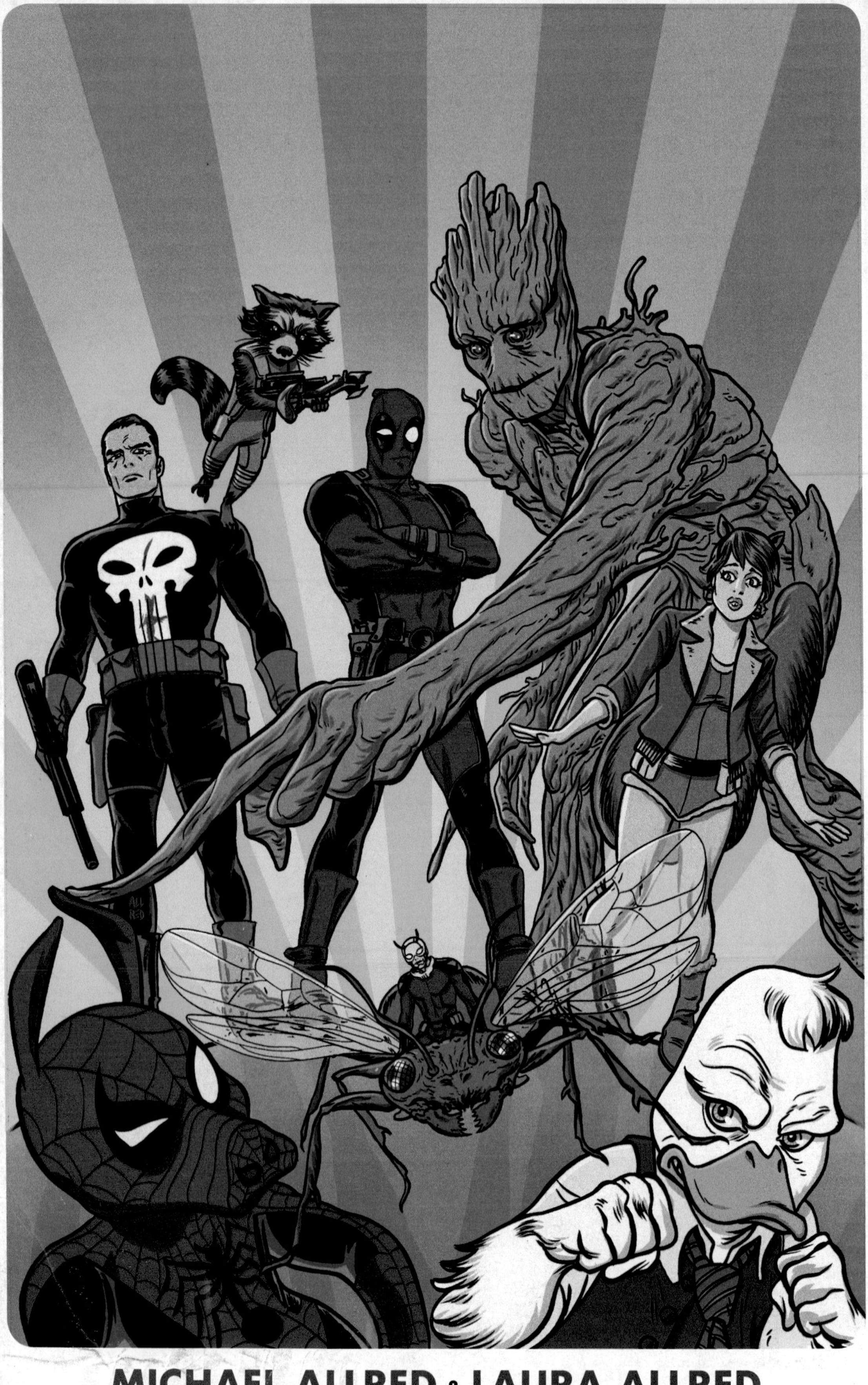
ALL
RED

MICHAEL ALLRED & LAURA ALLRED

3 variant

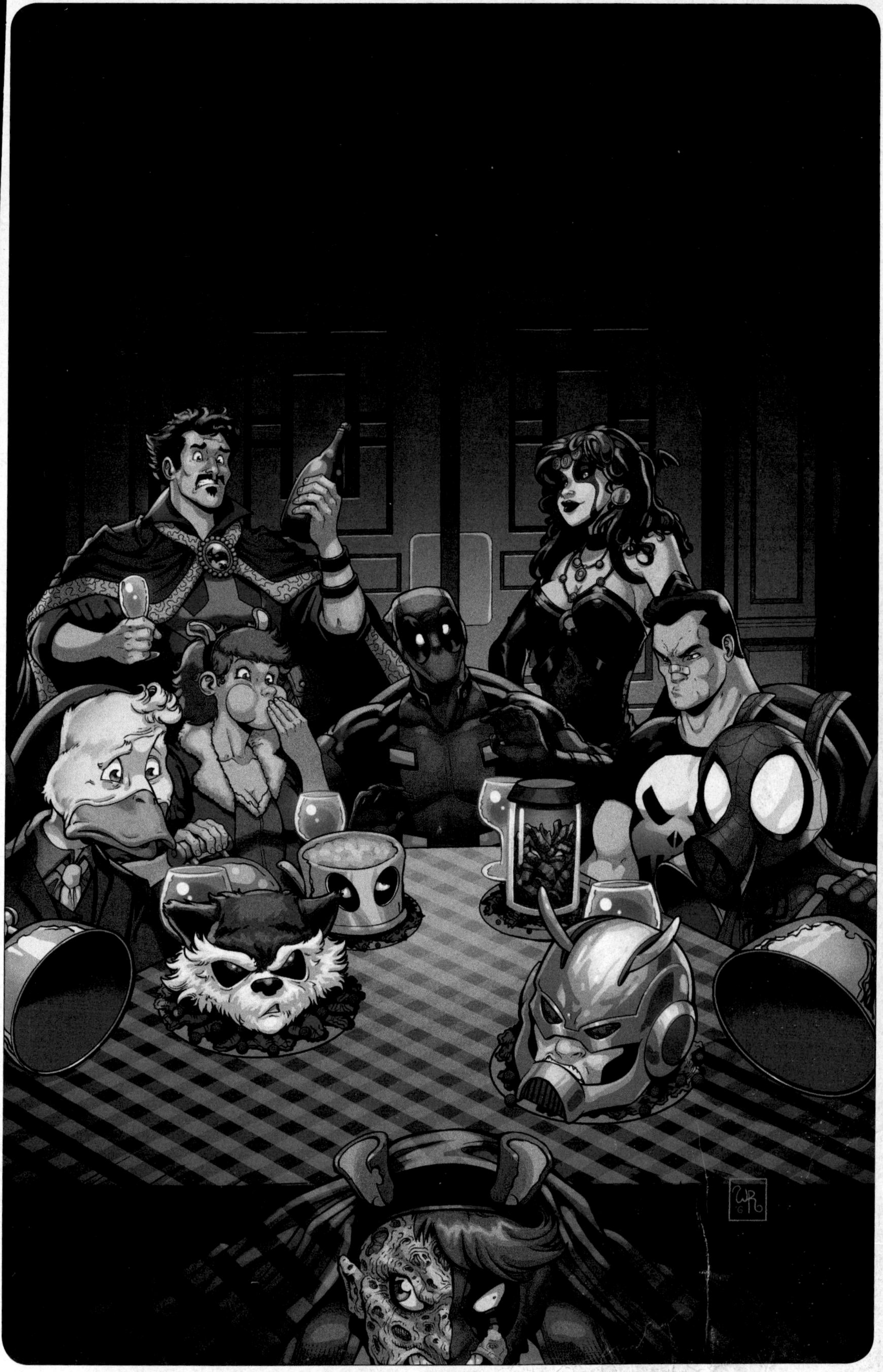

WILL ROBSON & JAVA TARTAGLIA

4 variant